Mechanisms in Bioenergetics

By
E F R A I M   R A C K E R

DEPARTMENT OF BIOCHEMISTRY
THE PUBLIC HEALTH RESEARCH INSTITUTE OF THE
CITY OF NEW YORK, INC.
NEW YORK, NEW YORK

1965

ACADEMIC PRESS
New York and London

ACADEMIC PRESS INC.
111 Fifth Avenue, New York, New York 10 003

United Kingdom Edition published by
ACADEMIC PRESS INC. (LONDON) LTD.
Berkeley Square House, London W.1

Library of Congress Catalog Card Number: 65-18433

First Printing, April, 1965
Second Printing, August, 1965

PRINTED IN THE UNITED STATES OF AMERICA

PREFACE

This book is based on lectures given during the spring semester of 1963 at Cornell University, Ithaca, New York. Although some changes have had to be introduced because of advances made during the past year, the format of the lectures has been retained. A lecture on photophosphorylation was omitted because a more extensive treatment of the subject will appear in this series of publications. The lectures are based mainly on work carried out in my laboratory. Like all research, it is closely linked to and dependent on the work of other investigators. If their names are not quoted frequently enough, it is not because they do not deserve it, but because if I had done so these lectures would no longer be lectures. A young composer once came to Rossini with the score of an opera and asked him to place a cross at each error he could find. When the young man returned several weeks later and saw no crosses on the manuscript, he asked jubilantly, "Then there are no mistakes in my score?" "My dear friend," replied Rossini sadly, "if I had made a cross at each mistake, this would be no opera, it would be a cemetery."

An attempt is made in these lectures to integrate experimental work in two broad areas of bioenergetics; namely, the enzymatic mechanism of ATP formation, and the regulatory mechanisms that control its metabolic utilization. The demarcation line between these two areas is not always sharp, because several important control mechanisms are intimately linked to the mechanisms of ATP production. I am attempting to convey the general trends in our thinking in these two areas, and some of the difficulties in the experimental approach. The lectures are directed primarily to advanced students of biochemistry both at the graduate and professorial levels, and I have assumed that the readers will be familiar with the elementary aspects of the chemistry, biochemistry, and thermodynamics of the metabolic reactions involved in ATP synthesis. I have therefore omitted a historical review in most instances.

It seems appropriate that the dedication of this book should be divided. I want to dedicate Parts I and II to the graduate students who symbolize our potential energy in biochemistry and who will be stimulated, I hope, by the flow of information and ideas in this book. I want to dedicate Part III to my wife Franziska and my daughter Ann, who effectively controlled the rate of this flow. Without them this book would have been published earlier and completely out of date by now. I am also indebted to many friends and collaborators who have contributed greatly by critically reading numerous chapters in this book: M. E. Pullman, A. San Pietro, R. Wu, I. Krimsky, H. S. Penefsky, and J. M. Fessenden; special thanks go to Miss Isabel Davis, my secretary, who has displayed great patience and contributed much with editorial assistance. I should also like to extend my thanks to the young men at Telluride House at Cornell University, who provided the appropriate background of hospitality and music during the preparation of the lectures.

New York   EFRAIM RACKER
January, 1965

CONTENTS

PART I

FORMATION OF ADENOSINE TRIPHOSPHATE IN SOLUBLE SYSTEMS

PART II

FORMATION OF ADENOSINE TRIPHOSPHATE IN PARTICULATE SYSTEMS

Contents

ABBREVIATIONS

ADP	Adenosine diphosphate
AMP	Adenosine 5'-phosphate
ATP	Adenosine triphosphate
BAL	2,3-Dimercaptopropanol
CCP	Carbonyl cyanide m-chlorophenyl hydrazone
CDP	Cytidine diphosphate
CoA	Coenzyme A
CTP	Cytidine triphosphate
DNP	2,4-Dinitrophenol
DPN	Diphosphopyridine nucleotide
DPND	Reduced deutero-DPN
DPNH	Reduced DPN
EDTA	Ethylene diamine tetraacetate
EPR	Electronparamagnetic resonance
FAD	Flavin-adenine dinucleotide
FADH	Reduced FAD
GDP	Guanosine diphosphate
GSH	Reduced glutathione
GTP	Guanosine triphosphate
HDP	Hexose diphosphate
HMP	Hexose monophosphate
IAA	Iodoacetate
IDP	Inosine diphosphate
ITP	Inosine triphosphate
NEM	N-ethylmaleimide
P_i	Inorganic phosphate
PP	Pyrophosphate
PPNR	Photosynthetic pyridine nucleotide reductase
Q_{10}	Ubiquinone-coenzyme Q_{10}
SP	Structural protein
TDP	Tetrose diphosphate
TPN	Triphosphopyridine nucleotide
TPNH	Reduced TPN
TPP	Thiamine pyrophosphate
UDP	Uridine diphosphate
UDPG	Uridine diphosphoglucose
UMP	Uridine monophosphate
UTP	Uridine triphosphate

REFERENCE ABBREVIATIONS

ABB	*Archives of Biochemistry and Biophysics*
BBA	*Biochimica et Biophysica Acta*
BBRC	*Biochemical and Biophysical Research Communications*
BJ	*The Biochemical Journal*
BZ	*Biochemische Zeitschrift*
FP	*Federation Proceedings*
JACS	*The Journal of the American Chemical Society*
JBC	*The Journal of Biological Chemistry*

PART I

Formation of Adenosine Triphosphate in Soluble Systems

LECTURE 1

GENERAL CONSIDERATIONS OF ENERGY PRODUCTION

Common, unending is the sisters' pathway; taught by the gods, alter-
nately they travel;
Fair-formed, of different hues, and yet, one-minded, they clash not,
neither do they tarry.

* * *

Transversely was their severing line extended: what was above it then
and what below it?
There were begetters, there were mighty forces, free action here and
energy up yonder.

—The Hymns of the Rig-Veda

Cells require energy in order to live. Without a supply of energy, cells cease to grow, to move, or to transport ions, and eventually die after exhausting their reserves of metabolically combustible substrates. Chlorophyll-containing cells obtain energy from light, and some microorganisms can oxidize inorganic substrates, but most animals depend on organic matter, synthesized by plants, for their supply of energy. The process of converting these nutrients into forms of useful energy is the essence of energy metabolism.

In this field of activity, one can distinguish between general practitioners of energy production, and specialists. The general practitioners utilize the multi-enzyme systems of (1) glycolysis, (2) oxidative phosphorylation, or (3) photo-phosphorylation. These processes are widely distributed in nature and are not exclusive of each other. Most animal cells utilize glycolysis as well as oxidative phosphorylation, and plant cells also catalyze photophosphorylation. On the other hand, there are microorganisms that utilize only glycolysis or only oxidative phosphorylation for energy production. The acquisition by microorganisms of multiple pathways of energy production probably contributes greatly to their survival under unfavorable conditions.

Then there are the specialists in energy production. These are usually found among microorganisms that have learned to obtain energy from a specific chemical, which may be inorganic or organic. Barker has cultivated, from the mud of California, bacteria with most fascinating biochemical properties.[1] There are bacteria that utilize amino acids, purines, choline, creatine, or rare sugars, both as sources of carbon and as sources of energy.

In contrast to these specialists in energy production, the general practitioners deal primarily with carbohydrates. A plausible explanation for this fact is that the major products of photosynthesis in plants are carbohydrates, which for millions of generations have served as an important nutrient for nonphotosynthetic organisms.

Adenosine triphosphate is generally considered to be the most important mobile carrier of metabolically available energy in cells. It is the end product of the three major pathways of energy metabolism: glycolysis, oxidative phosphorylation, and photophosphorylation. Other "high-energy" triphosphonucleotides, such as UTP, GTP, and CTP, are usually, although not always, produced via ATP.

A representative list of phosphorylated compounds with high-energy group potential is shown in Table 1.I. They fall into three groups: (1) precursors in biosynthetic pathways, (2) energy stores, and (3) precursors of ATP. This type of classification is useful, but as usual, there is considerable overlapping. For example, carbamyl phosphate is primarily an intermediate in the biosynthesis of arginine and pyrimidine, but in bacteria it may serve as a precursor of ATP. Acetyl phosphate can either donate its phosphoryl group to ADP, or its acetyl group to CoA to make acetyl CoA, which is used directly for biosynthesis. In certain anaerobic microorganisms, the latter appears to be the major pathway.[1] Similarly, phosphoenolpyruvate, the classical precursor of ATP in glycolysis, serves as a precursor of oxaloacetate, of

[1] H. A. Barker, "Bacterial Fermentations." Wiley, New York, 1956.

TABLE 1.I

Phosphorylated Compounds with High-Energy Group Potential

Compounds	Mode of formation	Metabolic function
Ribonucleoside di- and triphosphates	Mono- and diphosphate nucleosides + ATP	Precursors of RNA, UDPG, phospholipids, etc.
Deoxyribonucleoside di- and triphosphates	Mono- and diphosphate nucleosides + ATP	Precursors of DNA
Phosphoribosyl pyrophosphate	Ribose 5-phosphate + ATP	Biosynthesis of purines;
Aspartyl phosphate	Aspartate + ATP	of diaminopimelate and threonine;
Mevalonyl pyrophosphate	Mevalonate + ATP	of cholesterol;
Amino acid adenylates	Amino acids + ATP	of proteins
Carbamyl phosphate	$CO_2 + NH_3 + ATP$ *or* Citrulline + P_i	Biosynthesis of arginine and pyrimidines
Creatine phosphate	Creatine + ATP	Energy store in muscle and nerve cells
Arginine phosphate	Arginine + ATP	
Acetyl phosphate	Oxidation of acetaldehyde *or* Acetate + ATP *or* Keto sugar phosphate + P_i	Precursor of ATP and acetyl CoA in bacteria
1,3-Diphosphoglycerate	Oxidation of glyceraldehyde 3-phosphate	Precursor of glycolytic ATP
Phosphoenolpyruvate	Dehydration of 2-phosphoglycerate	Precursor of glycolytic ATP Biosynthesis of oxaloacetate, heptonate, sialate, etc.

TABLE 1.II

THIOL ESTERS IN METABOLISM

Compounds	Mode of formation	Metabolic function
Lactyl glutathione	GSH + methylglyoxal	Detoxification
Acetyl CoA	Oxidation of pyruvate Acetate + ATP + CoA Acetyl phosphate + CoA Breakdown of acetoacetyl CoA	Intermediate in Krebs and glyoxalate cycles; synthesis of fatty acids and cholesterol; detoxification (acetylation)
Malonyl CoA	Acetyl CoA + CO_2 + ATP	
CoA derivatives of saturated and unsaturated fatty acids	Fatty acids + CoA + ATP	Intermediates in fat metabolism
Crotonyl CoA	Oxidation of butyryl CoA	
L-β-Hydroxybutyryl CoA	Hydration of crotonyl CoA	
Acetoacetyl CoA	Oxidation of L-β-hydroxybutyryl CoA	
β-Hydroxy-β-methylglutaryl CoA	Acetoacetyl CoA + acetyl CoA	Synthesis of cholesterol
Succinyl CoA	Oxidation of α-ketoglutarate	Intermediate in Krebs cycle; synthesis of porphyrin
Methylmalonyl CoA	Propionyl CoA + CO_2 + ATP	Intermediate in propionate metabolism; transcarboxylation
Benzoyl CoA	Benzoate + ATP + CoA	Detoxification
Enzyme thiol esters	Oxidation of aldehydes and keto acids	Intermediates in Krebs cycle and glycolysis

2-keto-3-deoxyheptonate, of sialic acid, and of other related compounds.

The thiol esters, compounds that also have a high-energy group potential, have received increasing attention in the past 10 years. As shown in Table 1.II, they exhibit an impressive diversity of function, which ranges from serving as precursors of ATP and as intermediates in the biosynthesis of fat and cholesterol to detoxification processes such as hippurate formation. It so happens that the first two metabolic thiol esters which were discovered, lactyl glutathione and acetyl CoA, are formed by the cells without the intervention of ATP; in anaerobic glycolysis, probably a very primitive process of energy production, a thiol ester serves as a precursor of ATP. Thiol esters may possibly represent the evolutionary ancestors of "high-energy" ATP.

Cells essentially use four types of reactions to generate ATP (Table 1.III). The mechanisms of these reactions show similarities which will be discussed later. The first three types,

TABLE 1.III

TYPES OF REACTIONS CHANNELING INTO ATP FORMATION

A. Substrate level oxidative phosphorylation
B. Cleavage of C—S, C—C, and C—N bonds
C. Dehydration of 2-phosphoglycerate
D. Phosphorylation linked to electron transport
   (oxidative phosphorylation and photophosphorylation)

which are catalyzed by soluble enzymes that can be purified and are readily susceptible to analysis, have served as models for the study of the fourth type of reaction, phosphorylation linked to electron transport, which occurs in complex structures such as mitochondria and chloroplasts.

SUBSTRATE LEVEL OXIDATIVE PHOSPHORYLATION

Let us consider, as an example of substrate level oxidative phosphorylation, the reaction catalyzed by the glycolytic enzyme glyceraldehyde-3-phosphate dehydrogenase; see Scheme 1.1 (E = enzyme; R = $CH_2OPO_3H_2$—CHOH).[1a]

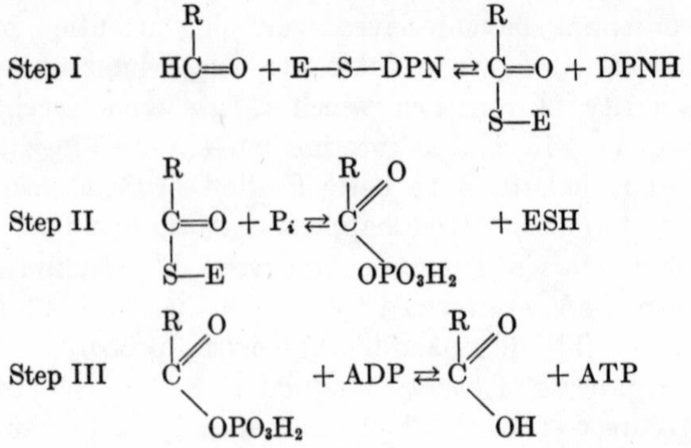

Step I $\overset{\text{R}}{\underset{}{\text{HC}}}$=O + E—S—DPN ⇌ $\overset{\text{R}}{\underset{\text{S—E}}{\text{C}}}$=O + DPNH

Step II $\overset{\text{R}}{\underset{\text{S—E}}{\text{C}}}$=O + P_i ⇌ $\overset{\text{R}}{\underset{\text{OPO}_3\text{H}_2}{\text{C}}}\diagup^{\text{O}}$ + ESH

Step III $\overset{\text{R}}{\text{C}}\diagup^{\text{O}}_{\text{OPO}_3\text{H}_2}$ + ADP ⇌ $\overset{\text{R}}{\text{C}}\diagup^{\text{O}}_{\text{OH}}$ + ATP

Scheme 1.1

Substrate Level Oxidative Phosphorylation

It is now widely accepted that the first step in this reaction is the oxidation of the aldehyde substrate to an enzyme-bound thiol ester.[2] The second step consists of a phosphorolysis of the thiol ester, yielding 1,3-diphosphoglycerate. In the next lecture, the details of these steps will be discussed more fully, but I want to emphasize that the primary step in this reaction sequence is an oxidation, resulting in the formation of a nonphosphorylated high-energy intermediate. Phosphate enters in the second step, to yield an acyl phosphate, which in a third step donates its phosphate to ADP. In 1939, Warburg and Christian postulated another mechanism.[3] They suggested that inorganic phosphate interacts nonenzymatically with glyceraldehyde 3-phosphate to form an addition compound which is directly oxidized by the dehydrogenase

---

[1a] No attempt was made in this or subsequent schemes to present electronically balanced equations. This was done partly for the sake of simplicity and partly because in many instances the electronic configuration of the reactants (e.g., of the DPN-enzyme) is unknown.

[2] E. Racker and I. Krimsky, *JBC* **198,** 731 (1952).

[3] O. Warburg and W. Christian, *BZ* **303,** 40 (1939).

to 1,3-diphosphoglycerate. So powerful is Warburg's persuasiveness that an enterprising New York firm even advertises this hypothetical intermediate for sale. I mention Warburg's formulation, which is not supported by experimental evidence, only because, as will be seen later, it represents an alternative mechanism that may operate in other systems.

There are numerous variants of the theme of substrate oxidation to high-energy intermediates, as shown in Table 1.IV. In the oxidation of α-ketoglutarate, the primary acyl

TABLE 1.IV
VARIANTS OF SUBSTRATE OXIDATIONS TO
HIGH-ENERGY INTERMEDIATES

Substrate	Primary acyl acceptor	Secondary acyl acceptor	Hydrogen acceptor
α-Keto acids	Enzyme-sulfur (lipoate)	CoA	Lipoate
α-Keto acids	CoA	P_i	Ferredoxin
Glyceraldehyde 3-phosphate	Enzyme-sulfur	P_i	DPN
Aspartaldehyde	Enzyme-sulfur (?)	P_i	TPN
Acetaldehyde	CoA	P_i	DPN
Methylglyoxal	GSH	H_2O	Carbon 2 of substrate
Xylulose 5-phosphate } Fructose 6-phosphate }	Enzyme-thiamine pyrophosphate (?)	P_i	Carbon 1 of substrate

acceptor is protein-bound sulfur as with glyceraldehyde-3-phosphate dehydrogenase and probably also with aspartaldehyde dehydrogenase. Acetaldehyde oxidation in bacteria and methylglyoxal dismutation proceed with soluble acyl acceptors such as CoA or glutathione. In the oxidation of the active glycolaldehyde by phosphoketolase, the acyl acceptor is presumably thiamine pyrophosphate. The secondary acyl group acceptor can be either P_i or an SH compound. In the case of methylglyoxal, water serves as secondary acyl acceptor, presumably for the purpose of detoxification of the ketoaldehyde. The hydrogen acceptor is even more variable; it may be DPN, TPN, one sulfur of lipoate, ferredoxin, or a carbon atom of the substrate itself.

PHOSPHOROCLASTIC REACTIONS

Many microorganisms that are specialists in energy production utilize a variant of this group of reactions. They all have in common the cleavage of a C—C, a C—S, or a C—N bond, as shown in Scheme 1.2. These cleavages are, in prin-

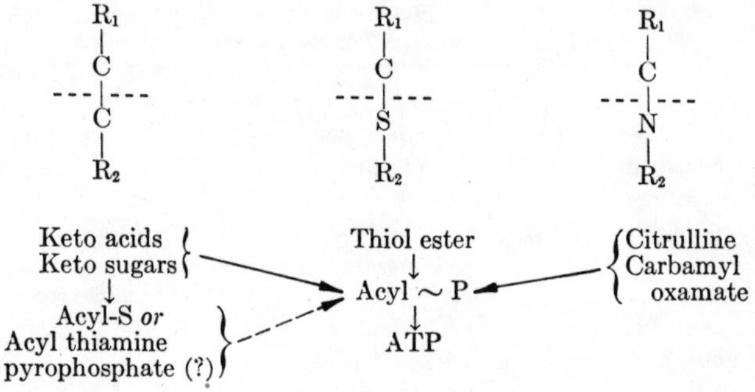

Scheme 1.2

Cleavage of C—C, C—S, and C—N Bonds Leading to
ATP Formation

ciple, quite similar. The breakdown of pyruvate to acetyl phosphate was the first phosphoroclastic reaction discovered.[4]

Bacteria catalyze several variants of this type of reaction. In *Escherichia coli* the carboxyl group of pyruvate appears as formate; in most clostridia, carbon dioxide and molecular hydrogen are evolved. In some microorganisms CoA, flavin, thiamine pyrophosphate, Fe^{++}, or ferredoxin may participate in these reactions. As will be discussed later, the phosphoroclastic reaction with pyruvate plays a curious and apparently

[4] F. Lipmann, *JBC* **134**, 463 (1940).

specific role in nitrogen fixation.[5] One of the difficulties in studying the mechanism of the cleavage of pyruvate has been the instability of the system. Considerably more stable is phosphoketolase, an enzyme which also catalyzes a phosphoroclastic reaction. The enzyme is produced by *Lactobacillus plantarum*[6] grown in a medium containing xylose, or a constitutive enzyme in *Acetobacter xylinum*.[7] These enzymes cleave xylulose 5-phosphate to acetyl phosphate and glyceraldehyde 3-phosphate, as shown in Scheme 1.3. In essence,

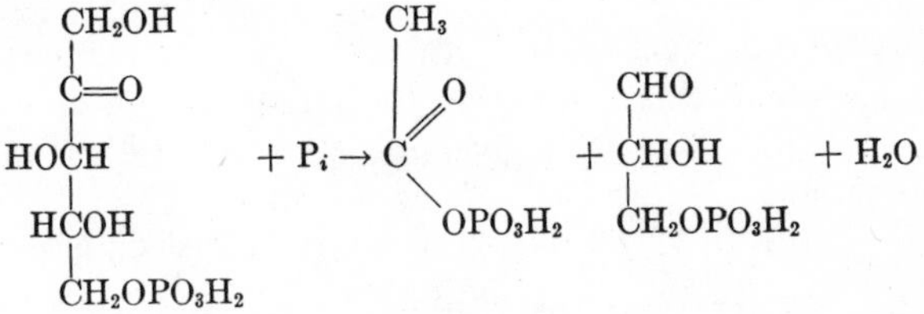

Scheme 1.3

Cleavage of Xylulose 5-Phosphate Catalyzed
by Phosphoketolase

this is another example of substrate level oxidative phosphorylation, with an intramolecular oxidoreduction; one carbon of the substrate becomes more oxidized, another carbon becomes more reduced. The conservation of energy is at the carbon which becomes more oxidized. Included tentatively in this group of phosphoroclastic reactions are also the cleavages of carbon-nitrogen bonds, which will be discussed later in more detail; the cleavage of citrulline or of carbamyl oxamate, both of which yield carbamyl phosphate; the cleavage of glycine in the presence of ADP and P_i in *Clostridia*, which yields acetate, ATP, and ammonia; the cleavage of formyl tetrahydrofolate; and perhaps the bacterial fermentations of choline and creatinine. The cleavage

[5] L. E. Mortenson, R. C. Valentine, and J. E. Carnahan, *JBC* **238**, 794 (1963).
[6] E. C. Heath, J. Hurwitz, B. L. Horecker, and A. Ginsburg, *JBC* **231**, 1009 (1958).
[7] M. Schramm, V. Klybas, and E. Racker, *JBC* **233**, 1283 (1958).

of glutamine, arginino-succinate, and even the biotin-dependent decarboxylation of methylmalonyl CoA to propionyl CoA may be pressed, with a little effort, into this category. However, the major metabolic role of most of these reactions is biosynthesis, which proceeds in the direction of energy expenditure.

DEHYDRATION OF 2-PHOSPHOGLYCERATE CATALYZED BY ENOLASE

This type of reaction is represented by only one enzyme, enolase, which catalyzes the formation of phosphoenolpyruvate from 2-phosphoglycerate (Scheme 1.4). Two as-

$$
\begin{array}{ll}
CH_2OH & CH_2 \quad \dotfill \text{(Reduced)} \\
| & \| \\
CHOPO_3H_2 \rightleftharpoons C{-}OPO_3H_2 \quad \dots\dots \text{(Oxidized)} \\
| & | \\
COOH & COOH
\end{array}
$$

Scheme 1.4

Oxidoreduction Catalyzed by Enolase

pects of this interesting reaction should be emphasized. First, the process is again one of oxidation-reduction. Carbon 2 is being oxidized and carbon 3 is being reduced by removal of oxygen. The conservation of energy is at carbon 2, again at the site of oxidation. Second, the oxidation-reduction process that results in the formation of a "high-energy" $\sim$ P intermediate takes place *after* the introduction of the phosphate group. Phosphoenolpyruvate is the only unambiguous example of a high-energy phosphate intermediate which is produced by the oxidation of a phosphate ester. It represents, in principle, an example of a mechanism originally proposed by Warburg for the oxidation of glyceraldehyde 3-phosphate. There is, however, one important difference. In the case of 2-phosphoglycerate, it is not inorganic phosphate that enters into the reaction, but a phosphate ester originally formed by expenditure of ATP.

OXIDATIVE PHOSPHORYLATION
AND PHOTOPHOSPHORYLATION

In contrast to other types of reactions, oxidative phosphorylation and photophosphorylation have not been successfully demonstrated in completely soluble systems. The mechanism of reactions catalyzed by such complex structures as mitochondria or chloroplasts are difficult to unravel.

The principal reactions underlying these two processes are in all probability similar: namely, electron transport coupled to phosphorylation. In oxidative phosphorylation, the electrons are derived from the substrate that enters the Krebs cycle, either from carbohydrates or fats via acetyl CoA, or from amino acids, e.g., via oxaloacetate or α-ketoglutarate. In photophosphorylation, it is water in the presence of light which furnishes the electrons that reduce the appropriate electron transport carriers.

For many years it has been known, as a result of the work of Ochoa, Lehninger, Lardy, and others, that electron transport between DPNH and oxygen is coupled to the formation of 3 moles of ATP from ADP and P_i. I shall refer to the three sites within the electron transport chain at which the phosphorylation process occurs as Sites 1, 2, and 3; see Scheme 1.5 (F_p = flavoprotein; a, b, c = cytochromes).

How much is known about the intimate mechanism of the actual coupling process at these three phosphorylation sites? How does one approach a complex pathway which contains multiple steps? Biochemical history has taught us that the study of partial reactions has frequently served as a wedge to facilitate the analysis of complex multi-enzyme systems. In the case of oxidative phosphorylation, exchange reactions and studies on the breakdown of ATP have been most fruitful. The incorporation of P_i^{32} into ATP in the absence of substrate first indicated that the process of oxidative phosphorylation is reversible, and permitted what Lehninger has called the back-door approach to the problem. The occurrence of this exchange reaction indicated, furthermore, that an intermediate was formed from ATP which could incorporate

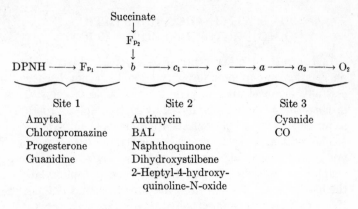

Scheme 1.5

Location of Sites of Phosphorylations and
Inhibitions in the Respiratory Chain

Mechanism A	$ATP^{32} + X \rightleftarrows ADP \sim X + P_i^{32}$
Mechanism B	$ATP^{32} + X \rightleftarrows X \sim P + ADP$
	$X \sim P + Y \rightleftarrows X \sim Y + P_i^{32}$

Scheme 1.6

Intermediates in Oxidative Phosphorylation

P_i^{32}. The simplest formulation of such a process is shown in Scheme 1.6 as Mechanism A. The $ADP \sim X$ intermediate formed from ATP could incorporate P_i^{32} directly into ATP. The bridge oxygen in ATP should be derived from inorganic phosphate. According to Mechanism B, ATP phosphorylates X to $X \sim P$, which is in equilibrium with another intermediate, $X \sim Y$. In this formulation, the bridge oxygen in ATP should be derived from ADP. Experiments with O^{18} by Boyer[8] have shown that the bridge oxygen in ATP is derived from ADP. Consequently, Mechanism B with two unknowns, X and Y, is more likely to operate. But this experi-

[8] P. D. Boyer, *Proc. Intern. Symp. Enzyme Chem., Tokyo and Kyoto, 1957* p. 301. Maruzen, Tokyo, 1958.

ment establishes only the last step in the process $X \sim P$ + ADP $\rightleftarrows$ X + ATP. The formation of $X \sim P$ can occur by either of the processes shown in Scheme 1.7, in which the

Formulation A	Step I	$AH_2 + B + X \rightleftarrows A \sim X + BH_2$
	Step II	$A \sim X + P_i \rightleftarrows A + X \sim P$
	Step III	$X \sim P + ADP \rightleftarrows X + ATP$
Formulation B	Step I	$AH_2 + X + P_i \rightleftarrows A + XH_2—P$
	Step II	$XH_2—P + B \rightleftarrows X \sim P + BH_2$
	Step III	$X \sim P + ADP \rightleftarrows X + ATP$

Scheme 1.7

Mechanism of Oxidative Phosphorylation

unknown, A, is listed instead of Y, to indicate the simplest possibility—that X interacts with a member of the respiratory chain. The major difference between Formulation A and Formulation B is the sequence of oxidation and phosphorylation. Formulation A is an analogy of glyceraldehyde 3-phosphate oxidation, in which phosphorylation follows oxidation. In Formulation B, phosphate enters first and oxidation follows. As you will see, evidence in favor of Formulation A is steadily accumulating. On the other hand, organic chemists have provided us with a rather attractive model system, involving an oxidation of quinol phosphates, which yields ATP in a reaction representative of Formulation B.

In addition to this fundamental question of sequence, there are several other basic questions that need to be answered. For example, is the unknown Y a member of the respiratory chain, as written in Scheme 1.6? Is $X \sim P$ a compound of small molecular weight, such as quinol phosphate, or is it a phosphorylated protein? Are there other phosphorylated and nonphosphorylated intermediates in addition to those listed? How many enzyme-catalyzed steps are there between the primary oxidation product and ATP?

Experience has taught us several general approaches that

are useful in unraveling complex multi-enzyme systems: (1) the use of inhibitors which result in the accumulation of intermediates; (2) the isolation of intermediates; (3) the study of partial reactions; and (4) the resolution of the system into its catalytic components. These approaches have led to important progress in our understanding of phosphorylation linked to electron transport.

LECTURE 2

SUBSTRATE LEVEL OXIDATIVE PHOSPHORYLATION (A)

The tragedy of science: a beautiful hypothesis slain by an ugly little fact.

—Thomas Henry Huxley

However, let us recognize the ugly little facts for what they are—circumstantial evidence at best, sometimes artifacts. Before pronouncing a verdict of murder, let us make sure we have a corpse. A good hypothesis is worth a few ugly little facts and a few hundred negative experiments.

OXIDATION OF GLYCERALDEHYDE 3-PHOSPHATE

Glyceraldehyde-3-phosphate dehydrogenase, the oxidizing enzyme of glycolysis, was the first to be well characterized in the group of enzymes catalyzing substrate level oxidative phosphorylation. It was crystallized from yeast by Warburg and Christian[3] in 1939. With DPN as hydrogen acceptor the enzyme oxidizes glyceraldehyde 3-phosphate very rapidly, but it also oxidizes glyceraldehyde and acetaldehyde (Scheme 2.1) though at a very slow rate. In the presence of arsenate and excess DPN, glyceraldehyde 3-phosphate is completely oxidized to phosphoglycerate; but in the presence of inorganic phosphate an equilibrium is established in which the oxidized product is 1,3-diphosphoglycerate. Warburg's proposal, based on these findings, was that glyceraldehyde 3-phosphate reacts with phosphate to form an adduct which is directly oxidized to 1,3-diphosphoglycerate (Scheme 2.1). This formulation was not challenged until 1947, when Meyerhof and Oesper attempted in vain to obtain kinetic evidence for the formation of the adduct intermediate.[9] An alternative mechanism was

[9] O. Meyerhof and P. Oesper, *JBC* **170**, 1 (1947).

(1)

$$\underset{\substack{| \\ \text{CHOH} \\ |}}{\text{CH}_2\text{OPO}_3\text{H}_2} \quad \overset{\text{O}}{\underset{\text{H}}{\text{C}}} \quad + \text{P}_i + \text{DPN} \rightleftarrows \underset{\substack{| \\ \text{CHOH} \\ |}}{\text{CH}_2\text{OPO}_3\text{H}_2} \quad \overset{\text{O}}{\underset{\text{OPO}_3\text{H}_2}{\text{C}}} \quad + \text{DPNH}$$

(2)

$$\underset{\substack{| \\ \text{CHOH} \\ | \\ \text{HC}=\text{O}}}{\text{CH}_2\text{OH}} + \text{DPN} \rightleftarrows \underset{\substack{| \\ \text{CHOH} \\ | \\ \text{COOH}}}{\text{CH}_2\text{OH}} + \text{DPNH}$$

(3)

$$\underset{\substack{| \\ \text{C} \\ \text{H}}}{\overset{\text{CH}_3}{\overset{\text{O}}{|}}} + \text{P}_i + \text{DPN} \rightleftarrows \underset{\substack{| \\ \text{C} \\ \text{OPO}_3\text{H}_2}}{\overset{\text{CH}_3}{\overset{\text{O}}{|}}} + \text{DPNH}$$

Warburg's Formulation of the Mechanism

$$\underset{\substack{| \\ \text{CHOH} \\ \text{OH} \\ \text{HC} \\ | \\ \text{OPO}_3\text{H}_2}}{\text{CH}_2\text{OP}} + \text{DPN} \rightarrow \underset{\substack{| \\ \text{CHOH} \\ \text{O} \\ \text{C} \\ | \\ \text{OPO}_3\text{H}_2}}{\text{CH}_2\text{OP}} + \text{DPNH}$$

New Formulation of the Mechanism

Step I

$$\underset{\substack{| \\ \text{CHOH} \\ | \\ \text{HCO}}}{\text{CH}_2\text{OP}} + \text{DPN}—\text{E} \rightarrow \underset{\substack{| \\ \text{CHOH} \\ | \\ \text{C}=\text{O} \\ | \\ \text{E}}}{\text{CH}_2\text{OP}} + \text{DPNH}$$

Step I-a

$$\text{Enzyme} + \text{DPN} \rightarrow \text{DPN}—\text{E} \left(\underset{\substack{\diagdown \\ \text{S}}}{\text{E}} \overset{\text{DPN}}{\diagup} \right)$$

Step I-b

$$\underset{\substack{\diagdown \\ \text{S}}}{\text{E}}\overset{\text{DPN}}{\diagup} + \text{RCHO} \rightarrow \text{E}—\text{S}—\underset{\text{O}}{\text{C}}—\text{R} + \text{DPNH}$$

Step II

$$\underset{\substack{| \\ \text{CHOH} \\ | \\ \text{C}=\text{O} \\ | \\ \text{E}}}{\text{CH}_2\text{OP}} + \text{P}_i \rightarrow \underset{\substack{| \\ \text{CHOH} \\ \text{O} \\ \text{C} \\ | \\ \text{OPO}_3\text{H}_2}}{\text{CH}_2\text{OP}}$$

Scheme 2.1

Over-all Reactions Catalyzed by
Glyceraldehyde-3-Phosphate Dehydrogenase

proposed by us a few years later, by analogy with another aldehyde oxidation; namely, the oxidoreduction of methylglyoxal to lactic acid.[10] We had studied this reaction, which is catalyzed by glyoxalase, merely for the purpose of developing a micromethod for the estimation of glutathione, which is an essential cofactor in this reaction. Tired of the nystagmus associated with manometric experiments in the Warburg apparatus, we had become addicted to the more sensitive spectrophotometric methods. Accordingly, we proceeded to measure methylglyoxal and its disappearance by following the absorption of ultraviolet light. Instead of the expected decrease in absorption, on addition of a dilute glyoxalase preparation from yeast a large increase at 240 mμ was observed.[10] On addition of a second enzyme obtained from liver, the absorption disappeared. The compound responsible for the absorption of ultraviolet light at 240 mμ was identified as the thiol ester, lactyl glutathione. As shown in Scheme 2.2, the formation of lactyl glutathione catalyzed by gly-

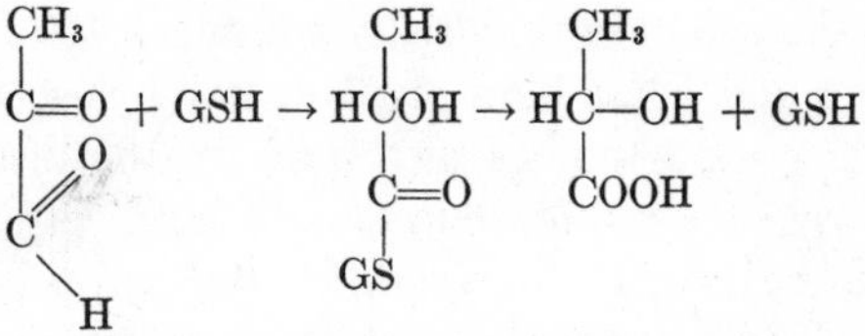

Scheme 2.2

Reactions Catalyzed by Glyoxalase I and II

oxalase I is an intramolecular oxidoreduction accomplished by hydride shift[11] from carbon 1 to carbon 2. The reaction looked similar to that catalyzed by glyceraldehyde-3-phosphate dehydrogenase, except that the hydrogen was transferred to an intramolecular acceptor rather than to an extramolecular acceptor (carbon 4 of DPN). We therefore proposed that glyceraldehyde 3-phosphate oxidation pro-

[10] E. Racker, *JBC* **190**, 685 (1951).
[11] I. A. Rose, *BBA* **25**, 214 (1957).

ceeded via a thiol ester which was cleaved by phosphate. After Lynen *et al.*[12] discovered acetyl CoA as an intermediate of alcohol oxidation in yeast, and further evidence for a primary oxidative step in glyceraldehyde 3-phosphate oxidation was obtained, the thiol ester theory became widely accepted. I shall refrain from an elaboration of the experimental details that were reported from several laboratories[2,13,14] in favor of a mechanism of glyceraldehyde-3-phosphate dehydrogenase involving a thiol ester. Instead, I shall present our most recent scheme of the mechanism and I shall indicate which aspects of the formulation are firmly supported by experimental evidence and which are not.

In Scheme 2.1 the aldehyde is shown to interact with the DPN-enzyme. The enzyme readily combines with DPN (Step I-a). The isolated crystalline enzyme from rabbit muscle contains from 3 to 3.6 moles of DPN per mole of enzyme. The DPN-enzyme exhibits an absorption band around $360 \text{ m}\mu$ (Fig. 2.1) which disappears on removal of DPN with charcoal.[2]

What is the evidence that DPN combines with a sulfur on the enzyme, and what kind of bond is it? Susceptibility of the DPN-enzyme bond, as measured by the disappearance of the absorption band at $360 \text{ m}\mu$, to a large variety of compounds that react with SH groups is the major evidence for the first point. Although p-hydroxymercuribenzoate, iodoacetate, and N-ethylmaleimide can also react with other groups, their common denominator of reactivity is the SH group. Moreover, treatment of the enzyme with H_2O_2, or aging, results in the formation of "oxidized" enzyme, which shows neither activity nor absorption at $360 \text{ m}\mu$. Both activity and absorption are restored by reduction with, e.g., GSH or thioglycerol. More direct evidence that iodoacetate does indeed react with enzyme-sulfur was obtained in experi-

[12] F. Lynen, E. Reichert, and L. Rueff, *Liebigs Ann.* **574,** 1 (1951).

[13] J. Harting and S. F. Velick, *JBC* **207,** 867 (1954).

[14] P. D. Boyer and H. L. Segal, *in* "The Mechanism of Enzyme Action" (W. D. McElroy and B. Glass, eds.), p. 520. Johns Hopkins Press, Baltimore, 1954.

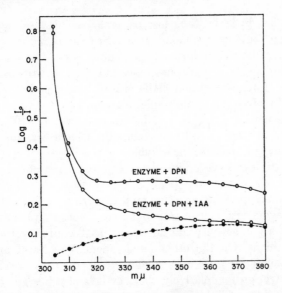

FIG. 2.1. Spectrum of DPN-enzyme. Absorption measurements were carried out in a Beckman quartz spectrophotometer in silica micro cells with a light path of 10 mm and a total volume of 1 ml. In this experiment, 6.4 mg of reduced and charcoal-treated glyceraldehyde-3-phosphate dehydrogenase, 0.18 μmole of DPN, and 0.5 μmole of iodoacetate were used. The broken line represents the calculated values for the absorption due to the interaction between DPN and the enzyme.

ments on tryptic digestion of the enzyme, which will be discussed later. Furthermore, model systems have been described[15] in which an interaction between DPN and mercaptans (e.g., GSH) gives rise to an absorption at about 335 mμ.

What kind of bond is formed between DPN and the enzyme? In view of the well-known aldehydic properties of the pyridine ring of DPN, the interaction is thought of as analogous to the formation of a thiohemiacetal, and the bond is considered as equivalent to a covalent bond. Perhaps, as has been suggested, it is a charge transfer bond. In any case, DPN is very firmly bound to the enzyme, as is apparent from the

[15] J. van Eys and N. O. Kaplan, *JBC* **228,** 305 (1957).

fact that little DPN is lost on prolonged dialysis or after passage through Sephadex. It is also clear that the attachment of the pyridine ring to the sulfur is not the only site, because DPN is still enzyme-bound after treatment with iodoacetate. The second mode of attachment of DPN probably involves the pyrophosphate group.[16]

The nature of the groups adjacent to the reactive SH group on the enzyme is still uncertain. Glutathione was found to be firmly attached to the enzyme and was identified in several laboratories. However, it did not seem to be part of the active center since the free peptide was present only in small amounts (up to 0.5 moles per mole of enzyme), and treatment of enzyme with iodoacetate under conditions that eliminated all catalytic activity did not result in alkylation of the free glutathione. On the other hand, about 2 moles of an SH compound per mole of enzyme were liberated by treatment with trypsin for relatively short periods of time. The emergence of this peptide was assayed by the following test: The mixture was oxidized with H_2O_2, and, after removal of excess H_2O_2 with catalase, it was exposed to TPNH and yeast glutathione reductase. After interaction with alloxan, it was measured spectrophotometrically at 305 mμ.

Although both glutathione reductase and the reaction with alloxan are considered relatively specific for glutathione, the nature of the compound released by trypsin remains uncertain since it has not yet been isolated in pure form. Let us assume, for the time being, that it is a peptide sequence closely related to GSH.[17] How do we know that this peptide released by trypsin is indeed part of the prosthetic group?

[16] L. Astrachan, S. P. Colowick, and N. O. Kaplan, *BBA* **24**, 141 (1957).
[17] Recent findings [I. Harris, B. P. Meriwether, and J. H. Park, *Nature* **198**, 154 (1963)] indicate an amino acid sequence of aspNH$_2$, ala, ser, cys, thr, thr, aspNH$_2$ at the active site. However, H. L. Segal and A. H. Gold [*JBC* **238**, PC2589 (1963)] suggest an amino acid sequence of aspNH$_2$, cys, ala, ser, thr at the active site. In any case, it appears that neither glutamine nor glycine are adjacent to the cysteine at the active site. Thus the conclusion, based on the glutathione reductase assay, that the active site has the amino acid sequence of glutathione, must be erroneous.

Here again we have only indirect evidence. One type of evidence rests on the rather remarkable specific interaction of iodoacetate with DPN-enzyme. As mentioned before, the 360 mμ absorption band disappeared when iodoacetate was added to the enzyme. What was not expected from previous experience with SH compounds and iodoacetate was the rapidity and sensitivity of this process. As shown in Table 2.I, iodoacetate in dilute solutions reacted very sluggishly

TABLE 2.I

INTERACTION OF GLYCERALDEHYDE-3-PHOSPHATE DEHYDROGENASE
WITH SH REAGENTS

| | Percent interaction[a] | | |
Reagent	Iodo-acetate	Iodo-acetamide	N-Ethyl-maleimide
GSH (67 μM)	4	12	100
Enzyme (30 μM)	5	30	97
DPN-enzyme (30 μM)	94	22	26

[a] Inhibitors (110 μM) were incubated for 12 minutes at 25° in 10 mM phosphate (pH 6.5). Interaction with GSH was measured with nitroprusside; interaction with enzyme by activity tests.

with GSH. Only about 4% of GSH disappeared after 12 minutes at room temperature. The enzyme was also nonreactive, whereas the DPN-enzyme was virtually completely inactivated. Iodoacetamide, which was more reactive with free SH and with enzyme alone, did not react rapidly with DPN-enzyme—in fact, DPN seemed to protect. Such protection was particularly apparent with N-ethylmaleimide, which reacted very rapidly with free SH but was ineffective with the DPN-enzyme. The specific and almost instantaneous reaction between iodoacetate and DPN-enzyme permitted accurate titrations, as shown in Table 2.II. The correlation was excellent between loss of activity and absorption at 360 mμ. Moreover, it was shown that considerable excess of GSH in solution did not interfere with this interaction. With C[14]-labeled iodoacetate, the uptake of radioactivity by the

TABLE 2.II

CORRELATION BETWEEN ACTIVITY AND ABSORBANCY AT 360 mμ

Reagent	Absorbancy (%)	Activity (%)
Enzyme (6 mg)	100	100
Enzyme + 9.3 μg iodoacetate	66	69
Enzyme + 18.6 μg iodoacetate	26	28
Enzyme + 27.9 μg iodoacetate	0	0

enzyme showed a rather sharp end-point coinciding with the disappearance of the 360-mμ band.

I have presented these experiments in some detail to illustrate an approach to the mode of action of glyceraldehyde-3-phosphate dehydrogenase, and to emphasize the ambiguity (1) of the concept of an "SH-enzyme," and (2) of the use of inhibitors. Whereas free enzyme is highly susceptible to N-ethylmaleimide and relatively resistant to iodoacetate, the situation is reversed with DPN-enzyme. Iodoacetamide is a poor inhibitor for both forms of the enzyme.

When DPN-enzyme was treated with iodoacetate and then with trypsin, the SH compound released in the absence of iodoacetate could not be detected. In similar experiments with N-ethylmaleimide, the appearance of SH groups following proteolytic digestion was suppressed. When the treatment of enzyme with N-ethylmaleimide was carried out in the presence of a substrate (e.g., acetyl phosphate), both activity and release of "GSH" were partly protected.

These experiments indicated that the peptide released on tryptic digestion is either closely associated with the catalytic site of the enzyme or is part of it.

For the interaction between glyceraldehyde 3-phosphate and the enzyme there are two possibilities. One is formulated as an aldehydolysis of the C—S bond of the DPN-enzyme (Scheme 2.1). This results in the direct formation of an acyl-enzyme and DPNH. The alternative formulation consists of a reaction between substrate and E—SH to form a thio-hemiacetal-enzyme, which is then oxidized to acyl-enzyme.

This was actually our original formulation, but it was subsequently abandoned for the following reasons:

1. The absorption at 360 mμ disappeared not only on addition of SH reagents, but also on addition of substrates such as 1,3-diphosphoglycerate or acetyl phosphate.

2. The rapid interaction with iodoacetate (but not with iodoacetamide) indicated a high reactivity of the DPN-enzyme with negatively charged compounds, which may aid interaction with glyceraldehyde 3-phosphate. The interaction between free SH compounds and aldehydes is relatively slow in dilute solutions.

3. Even with a nonphosphorylated substrate such as acetaldehyde, which must be added in fairly high concentrations, it seemed likely that the active species was DPN-enzyme rather than free enzyme. When the enzyme was freed of DPN by treatment with charcoal, addition of acetaldehyde prior to DPN resulted in a reaction rate of less than 10% of the rate observed with DPN-enzyme.

The proposal of an aldehydolysis mechanism in glyceraldehyde 3-phosphate oxidation stimulated the formulation of a similar mechanism in pyruvate and α-ketoglutarate oxidation.[17a] Aldehydolysis of the S—S group of lipoic acid, rather than of a C—S bond, was visualized as taking place. Although the evidence is equally circumstantial, the aldehydolysis mechanism in α-keto acid oxidations has been generally accepted. The aldehydolysis mechanism may, of course, be operative in α-keto acid oxidation and not in glyceraldehyde 3-phosphate oxidation. Analogies are useful but do not represent evidence. The experimental evidence that has been cited seems to favor the aldehydolysis mechanism rather than a thiohemiacetal formation, which would require dissociation of DPN from the SH group of the enzyme prior to interaction with the substrate.

Briefly, the evidence for the formation of an acyl-enzyme is as follows: In the forward reaction, oxidation of substrate by DPN-enzyme in the absence of P_i can readily be demon-

[17a] P. C. Gunsalus, Personal communication (1951).

strated. Actually, not all of the DPN that is combined with the crystalline enzyme becomes reduced, and the enzyme does not become fully acylated even in the presence of a large excess of glyceraldehyde 3-phosphate. This phenomenon will be discussed later. The most effective method of making acyl-enzyme is by the reverse reaction with either acetyl phosphate or 1,3-diphosphoglycerate as substrate. Since 1,3-diphospho-glycerate is not readily available, a generating system consist-ing of ATP, phosphoglycerate kinase, and phosphoglycerate in the presence of Mg^{++} can be used instead. Acyl-enzyme formation can be measured simply by precipitating the protein with trichloroacetic acid, washing it, and measuring the thiol ester content with hydroxylamine.

But we also wanted to catch the acyl-enzyme intermediate alive, and this proved difficult at first because of its con-siderable instability. When we discovered that the hydrolysis of acyl-enzyme was dependent on DPN, the task became a rather simple one. After acylation of the enzyme, either with 1,3-diphosphoglycerate or with acetyl phosphate, DPN was quickly removed by treatment with charcoal. The acyl-enzyme became stable and was readily crystallized.[18] As an aside, I might mention that whereas it was rather difficult to crystallize the muscle enzyme in the absence of DPN, it was quite easy to crystallize either DPN-enzyme or acyl-enzyme. The isolated acyl-enzyme reacted as would be expected of an intermediate. In the presence of arsenate it was cleaved, yielding phosphoglycerate. Addition of DPNH to acyl-enzyme resulted in an oxidation of DPNH stoichiometric to the acyl groups present (Table 2.III). The product of the reduction was glyceraldehyde 3-phosphate in the case of phosphoglyceryl-enzyme and acetaldehyde in the case of acetyl-enzyme.

The formation of acyl-enzyme in the reverse direction was conveniently measured in a kinetic assay that depended on the arsenolysis reaction. In the presence of a regenerating system for 1,3-diphosphoglycerate, the over-all reaction was a cleavage of ATP to ADP and P_i, as shown in Scheme 2.3.

[18] I. Krimsky and E. Racker, *Science* **122**, 319 (1955).

TABLE 2.III
REDUCTION OF ACYL-ENZYME WITH DPNH

Reagent	Moles of thiol ester per mole of enzyme	Moles of DPNH oxidized per mole of enzyme
Acetyl-enzyme	0.80	0.82
Phosphoglyceryl-enzyme	0.96	1.04

It is apparent that this partial reaction catalyzed by glyceraldehyde-3-phosphate dehydrogenase represents a transphosphorylation step which is independent of a reducing system (DPNH). According to Warburg's formulation, the reverse reaction should consist of a primary reductive step followed by phosphate release. We shall return to this problem in the discussion of ATPase in oxidative phosphorylation.

$$ATP + 3\text{-phosphoglycerate} \rightleftarrows 1,3\text{-diphosphoglycerate} + ADP$$
$$\overset{\text{As}}{1,3\text{-diphosphoglycerate} \rightarrow P_i + 3\text{-phosphoglycerate}}$$
$$ATP \rightarrow ADP + P_i$$

Scheme 2.3

ATPase Activity in the Presence of Glyceraldehyde-3-Phosphate
Dehydrogenase and Phosphoglycerate Kinase

A number of years ago we looked into the substrate specificity of glyceraldehyde-3-phosphate dehydrogenase, and found that many aldehydes, such as erythrose 4-phosphate, methylglyoxal, and glycolaldehyde, were slowly oxidized. However, glycolaldehyde 2-phosphate appeared inactive. Some of us are absent-minded in the laboratory, and it is one of our rules that when nothing happens in an assay system we add a known active substrate, to be sure that we have not forgotten a reagent. But when we added glyceraldehyde 3-phosphate after glycolaldehyde 2-phosphate, no reduction of DPN took place. It was thus apparent that we were dealing with a very powerful inhibitor. We soon exhausted our supply

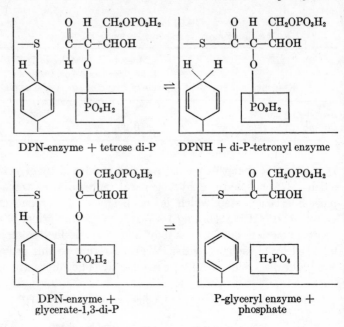

Scheme 2.4

Mechanism of Action of Tetrose Diphosphate

of an old sample of glycolaldehyde 2-phosphate and had to make a new preparation. Although the new preparation analyzed well for glycolaldehyde 2-phosphate, it had less than 10% of the inhibitory capacity of the old preparation, and it became clear that we had been dealing with an impurity. Shortly thereafter, Dr. Ballou reported on a synthetic preparation of glycolaldehyde 2-phosphate and generously supplied us with this compound. We found it completely inactive as an inhibitor, but after storing a solution for several months it acquired considerable inhibitory activity. Analysis of this phenomenon proceeded both in Dr. Ballou's laboratory and our own; the findings, which were similar in both laboratories, were published simultaneously.[19,20] The inhibitor was formed

[19] E. Racker, V. Klybas, and M. Schramm, *JBC* **234,** 2510 (1959).
[20] A. L. Fluharty and C. E. Ballou, *JBC* **234,** 2517 (1959).

by an aldol condensation of two glycolaldehyde 2-phosphate molecules to give rise to a tetrose 2,4-diphosphate. This, as well as a synthetic preparation of D-threose 2,4-diphosphate (TDP) prepared by Fluharty and Ballou,[20] was oxidized by the enzyme to form a stable threonyl-diphosphate enzyme which was resistant to attack by either P_i or As and was only slowly hydrolyzed by water. In the presence of excess DPN, up to 3.6 acyl groups were formed per enzyme molecule, and in view of their low order of reactivity, this resulted in an effective immobilization of the enzyme. Whereas glyceraldehyde 3-phosphate did not displace these acyl groups on the enzyme, 1,3-diphosphoglycerate acted as a competitive inhibitor. This property led to the rather rare situation of an inhibitor being very potent in one direction of enzyme catalysis and much less so in the reverse reaction. The mode of action of this inhibitor is visualized as shown in Scheme 2.4. The threose diphosphate is oxidized to the threonyl-phosphate enzyme, with the second phosphate group of threonyl diphosphate attached to the "P_i site" of the enzyme. This mode of attachment anchors the acyl group firmly to the enzyme and prevents phosphate or arsenate from reacting with the enzyme in the usual manner. This concept requires the effectiveness of this inhibitor to be dependent on the intactness of the phosphate transfer site. In the next lecture we shall see that this is the case.

LECTURE 3

SUBSTRATE LEVEL OXIDATIVE PHOSPHORYLATION (B)

A scientist living at Staines
Is searching with infinite pains
For a new type of sound
Which he hopes, when it's found,
Will travel much faster than planes.

—*Punch*, August 13, 1952

OXIDATION OF GLYCERALDEHYDE 3-PHOSPHATE

It became apparent during the last lecture that we could spend many hours discussing the fascinating properties of glyceraldehyde-3-phosphate dehydrogenase. However, the discussion will be restricted to six properties that have a specific bearing on the problem of oxidative phosphorylation.

1. The protein is a double-headed enzyme with an oxido-reduction "head" and a transfer "head." During the process of glyceraldehyde 3-phosphate oxidation in the presence of P_i, these two catalytic sites act sequentially. However, by setting up artificial conditions, the two steps can be investigated separately. For example, the oxidation of glyceraldehyde 3-phosphate can be measured in the absence of P_i, but with thioglycerol or thioglycolate at very high concentration (0.1 to 0.5 M) as acceptor of the acyl group. This procedure has been of particular value in studies of a derivative enzyme in which the transfer head was destroyed.[21] The transfer reaction can be studied independently of the oxidation step by measuring arsenolysis of 1,3-diphosphoglycerate or, more conveniently, by measuring the hydrolysis of ATP in the presence of arsenate in the coupled system with phosphoglycerate kinase.

[21] I. Krimsky and E. Racker, *Biochemistry* **2**, 512 (1963).

The arsenolysis of ATP requires DPN, although the reaction does not include an oxidoreduction step. This requirement suggests that DPN has an effect on the configuration of the enzyme. A pronounced change in the tertiary structure is also indicated by experiments with proteolytic enzymes. As shown in Table 3.I, the DPN-enzyme is very resistant

TABLE 3.I

EFFECT OF PROTEOLYTIC ENZYMES ON
GLYCERALDEHYDE-3-PHOSPHATE DEHYDROGENASE

	Digestion after 30 minutes	
Enzyme	Enzyme + DPN (%)	Enzyme (%)
Chymotrypsin (60 μg)	<5	51
Trypsin (60 μg)	<5	31
Papain (600 μg)	<5	84

to the action of trypsin, chymotrypsin, or papain, whereas without DPN rapid proteolysis takes place.[22] Reduced DPN did not substitute for DPN as a protecting agent. Evidence for the DPN requirement in the phosphate transfer reaction was presented in the elegant experiments of Hilvers and Weenen.[23] The reduction of acetyl phosphate in the presence of DPNH and glyceraldehyde-3-phosphate dehydrogenase was shown to require DPN; DPNase effectively inhibited the reaction, DPN restored it.

2. The reaction catalyzed by glyceraldehyde-3-phosphate dehydrogenase is "tightly coupled." Without P_i the oxidation of glyceraldehyde 3-phosphate does not proceed beyond the stoichiometric amounts of enzyme available as acyl acceptor. Under physiologic conditions, catalytic amounts of both P_i and ADP are required to permit the reaction to proceed in the glycolytic pathway.

You may wonder why the acyl-enzyme is not hydrolyzed in the absence of phosphate, in view of my previous remarks

[22] E. Racker and I. Krimsky, *FP* **17,** 1135 (1958).
[23] A. G. Hilvers and J. H. M. Weenen, *BBA* **58,** 380 (1962).

that the acyl-enzyme is very unstable in the presence of
DPN. Since this apparent discrepancy illustrates a rather
important principle, which one should be aware of in dealing
with enzymes as reactants rather than as catalysts, I should
like to elaborate on this phenomenon. As shown in Table
3.II, the turnover number of glyceraldehyde-3-phosphate

TABLE 3.II

THE ENZYME AS CATALYST AND AS REACTANT

Reaction	Enzyme action	Turnover number
Oxidation of glyceraldehyde 3-phosphate	Catalyst	15,000
Hydrolysis of acyl-enzyme	Reactant	<0.1

dehydrogenase with glyceraldehyde 3-phosphate is very large
compared to the hydrolysis of the acyl-enzyme. In the catalytic reaction, the acyl-enzyme is therefore virtually stable.
While the enzyme is going at 15,000 turnovers per minute, a
hydrolysis of acyl-enzyme at 0.1 turnover per minute is
negligible. But when one attempts to isolate the acyl-enzyme,
a turnover of 0.1 means that after 10 minutes there is no
acyl-enzyme left. You can see that what is good enough for
General Motors is not good enough for the country.

3. Oxidation can be uncoupled from phosphorylation at
three different stages: (a) at the acyl-enzyme stage; this
occurs either by hydrolysis or by transfer of the acyl group
to an SH compound or to arsenate; (b) at the 1,3-diphospho-
glycerate stage; hydrolysis occurs slowly and spontaneously
and is accelerated by an acylase which is present in tissues;
(c) at the ATP stage in the coupled system; this process,
which is actually not true uncoupling, is accomplished by
ATPase. However, as in other uncoupled systems, oxidation
occurs without net phosphate esterification. The first type of
uncoupling takes place before the entrance of P_i and is in
competition with it; the second type is in competition with
ADP. The third type is in competition with biosynthesis. It

will be discussed in detail under control mechanisms of energy metabolism.

4. The enzyme catalyzes the hydrolysis of acetyl phosphate. Like phosphate transfer, this reaction is also dependent on DPN. It is relatively slow with native enzyme, but much more rapid in aged preparations that have become "oxidized," as was first shown by Harting.[24] Treatment of the enzyme with oxidizing agents such as H_2O_2 accelerates its hydrolytic activity. Glutathione, KCN, and many other compounds which react readily with aldehydes, inhibit the hydrolytic reaction (Table 3.III) without affecting phosphate transfer

TABLE 3.III
STABILIZATION OF PHOSPHOGLYCERYL-ENZYME

Additions	Hydrolysis of acyl-enzyme after 12 minutes at 25° (%)
None	53
Potassium cyanide (1 mM)	0
Glutathione (1 mM)	0
Semicarbazide (30 mM)	6
Phenyl hydrazine (30 mM)	22

or arsenolysis. Although we do not understand the mechanism of the differential action of these agents, it is apparent that in their presence a complete functional separation of hydrolysis and phosphate transfer can be achieved.[22] For example, in the presence of glutathione, hydrolysis of acetyl phosphate is suppressed, whereas arsenolysis may even be accelerated.

5. The formation of acyl-enzyme in the forward reaction is strongly inhibited by DPNH. This phenomenon, of which we have only recently become fully aware,[19] explains some of the previously mentioned difficulties in acylating the enzyme in the forward direction. It also explains the curious discrepancies in the K_m values for DPN recorded in the litera-

[24] J. Harting, *in* "The Mechanism of Enzyme Action" (W. D. McElroy and B. Glass, eds.), p. 536. Johns Hopkins Press, Baltimore, 1954.

ture. As shown in Fig. 3.1, the rate of DPN reduction falls off very rapidly at 0.38 mM DPN, but is zero order at very high concentrations (5.7 mM). If DPNH is removed by pyruvate and lactate dehydrogenase, the oxidation of glyceraldehyde 3-phosphate is rapid and zero order even at the low DPN concentrations.

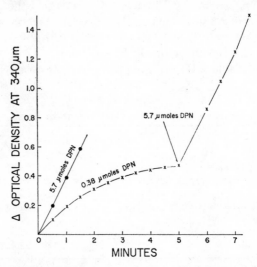

Fig. 3.1. Effect of DPN concentration on oxidation rate of glyceraldehyde 3-phosphate by glyceraldehyde-3-phosphate dehydrogenase. In a final volume of 1 ml, the following reagents were added: 30 μmoles of sodium pyrophosphate buffer (pH 8.6); 15 μmoles of potassium phosphate (pH 8.5); 2.6 μg of glyceraldehyde-3-phosphate dehydrogenase; 50 μg of aldolase; 5 μmoles of fructose diphosphate; and the amounts of DPN indicated in the figure.

The high concentration of DPN required to overcome the inhibition by DPNH contrasts with the relatively high affinity of the enzyme to DPN in the absence of substrate. As mentioned earlier, DPN is not removed by repeated recrystallization or by dialysis of the enzyme. Moreover, in the absence of substrate, considerable excess of DPNH is required to displace DPN in competition experiments.[25] The

[25] S. F. Velick, *JBC* **233**, 1455 (1958).

observations on the inhibition of glyceraldehyde 3-phosphate oxidation by relatively low concentrations of DPNH therefore pointed to an altered affinity of the acyl-enzyme in regard to reduced and oxidized pyridine nucleotides. This was demonstrated directly by the following experiment.[21] Phosphoglyceryl-enzyme was prepared in the presence of a regenerating system for 1,3-diphosphoglycerate and was passed through a Sephadex column. The emerging protein was analyzed and found to have lost more than 75% of its DPN content. Control experiments with untreated enzyme, or with enzyme treated with the same mixture of reagents except for ATP, which was omitted, revealed no loss of DPN. A lowered affinity to DPN after acylation of the enzyme is also apparent from the requirement for high DPN concentration for optimal rates of arsenolysis of 1,3-diphosphoglycerate. Recent measurements have shown that in this reaction 1.6 mM DPN is required for saturation of the enzyme, which was used in catalytic amounts (10 μg protein per milliliter). These experiments show that during catalysis there is a profound change in the relative affinity of the enzyme to DPN and DPNH. The relatively higher affinity of DPNH for the acyl-enzyme helps to explain the inhibition of glyceraldehyde 3-phosphate oxidation at low DPN concentration. We shall return to this problem when we discuss the properties of the partially digested enzyme.

6. The last property of glyceraldehyde-3-phosphate dehydrogenase brings us to some recent experiments in our laboratory on the proteolytic digestion of this enzyme.[21] Exposure of the DPN-less enzyme for a short period of time to chymotrypsin results in the loss of its phosphorolytic ability, but its oxidative capacity is maintained. As shown in Fig. 3.2, native enzyme oxidizes glyceraldehyde in the absence of phosphate, but not as rapidly as in its presence. The digested enzyme is not affected by phosphate, however, and the rate of glyceraldehyde oxidation without P_i is actually faster with digested than with native enzyme. Of particular interest are the findings with tetrose diphosphate. Whereas the native enzyme is almost completely inhibited by this

compound, the digested enzyme shows little or no impair-
ment of oxidation. It appears from these experiments that
the site of phosphate entrance had been either destroyed or
removed from the active site. We felt that it was desirable,
however, to repeat these experiments with the physiological

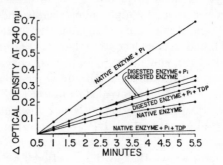

FIG. 3.2. Rate of glyceraldehyde oxidation. The measurements were
made in a Beckman model DU spectrophotometer in solutions of 0.04 M
Tris-HCl buffer (pH 7.9); 0.005 M EDTA (pH 7.9); 0.0012 M DPN;
0.011 M DL-glyceraldehyde; 0.006 M thioglycerol; 1.25 mg per milliliter
of native or digested glyceraldehyde-3-phosphate dehydrogenase; also,
where indicated, 0.001 M potassium phosphate (pH 7.9); 0.000053 M
threose diphosphate. (Temperature, 16°.)

substrate, glyceraldehyde 3-phosphate. But these experiments
are more complicated, because of the rapidity of the reaction
and because (as mentioned earlier) in the absence of P_i or
arsenate, the reaction with native enzyme virtually comes to
a standstill after a fraction of the enzyme has been acylated.
It was therefore necessary to devise new methods of measuring the reactions. Two procedures were used: (*a*) transfer of
the acyl group to a thiol, a chemical reaction which is known
to occur at a slow rate; and (*b*) use of stoichiometric amounts
of enzyme as acyl acceptor in a more sensitive test system.

(*a*) Various thiols were tested, including ethyl mercaptan,
glutathione, and cysteine. The most suitable were thioglycolate (0.05 M) and α-monothioglycerol (0.5 M) since, in
their presence, the rate of reduction of DPN was proportional
to the amount of enzyme over a fairly broad range. Although

the rate with thioglycerol was only 10% of the rate with thioglycolate and only 0.6% of the rate with arsenate, it was the preferred acceptor, because the rate with thioglycolate was affected by treatment of the enzyme with chymotrypsin. It appears that the site on the enzyme which permits the more efficient utilization of the charged thioglycolate is affected by proteolytic digestion in about the same way as the site that interacts with phosphate.

Following digestion of glyceraldehyde-3-phosphate dehydrogenase with chymotrypsin, about 60% of the oxidative activity, when measured in the presence of thioglycerol, was retained, but only about 2.5% when measured with arsenate as acyl acceptor. In view of the rather sluggish transfer of the acyl group to the thiol, it was desirable to compare the forward and reverse reactions with the same thiol acceptor. Whereas with native enzyme the rates of the forward and reverse reactions were about the same, with digested enzyme the forward reaction was about 5 times as rapid as the reverse reaction (Table 3.IV).

TABLE 3.IV

RATE OF PHOSPHOGLYCERYL THIOGLYCEROL FORMATION
IN FORWARD AND REVERSE DIRECTIONS

Enzyme	Substrate	μmoles of phosphoglyceryl thioglycerol formed per minute per milligram
Native	Glyceraldehyde 3-phosphate	0.43
	1,3-Diphosphoglycerate	0.38
Digested	Glyceraldehyde 3-phosphate	0.24
	1,3-Diphosphoglycerate	0.05

The oxidation of glyceraldehyde 3-phosphate by native enzyme was inhibited by 50% at $2 \times 10^{-7} M$ threose 2,4-diphosphate, and was almost completely inhibited at $10^{-6} M$. Digested enzyme preparations varied, showing between 0 and 40% inhibition at $10^{-6} M$ threose diphosphate. The uninhibited portion of digested enzyme was not affected even when the threose diphosphate concentration was raised to 10^{-5} M. This finding was the first indication that the enzyme after digestion was not homogenous, but a mixture of derivatives of the native protein.

The experiments with glyceraldehyde or with thiols as acyl acceptors, although strongly suggesting a greater loss of phosphorylative than of oxidative activity after chymotrypsin digestion, had the defect that the measurement included a second step (hydrolysis or transfer of the acyl group) which complicated the evaluation of the data. Direct measurements of the rate of acyl-enzyme formation were therefore carried out.

(*b*) Initial rates of oxidation with large amounts of enzymes were too rapid, even with digested enzyme, to permit meas-

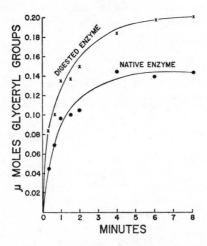

Fig. 3.3. Rate of glyceryl-enzyme formation. Incubation mixtures, 1 ml volume, were deproteinized at the times indicated. The mixtures contained 0.08 M triethanolamine-HCl buffer (pH 7.28); 0.006 M DL-glyceraldehyde; 0.048 M potassium pyruvate; 150 μg of lactate dehydrogenase; and as last addition, 11 mg of native or digested glyceraldehyde-3-phosphate dehydrogenase (including 4.3 moles of DPN per mole of enzyme). (Temperature, 0°.) To this was added 7 ml of cold 6% trichloroacetic acid; the protein was sedimented, washed 3 times with 8.5 ml of 5% trichloroacetic acid, and assayed for glyceryl-enzyme.

urements under standard conditions. With the collaboration of Dr. B. Chance, initial rate measurements of DPN reduction were carried out at low substrate concentrations with native and digested enzyme. Although the rates were accordingly slow, DPNH formation was actually more rapid and extensive in the case of the digested enzyme.

With glyceraldehyde as substrate, the rate at 0° was slow enough to be measured by determination of protein-bound acyl groups at short intervals. As can be seen from Fig. 3.3, the digested enzyme was acylated more rapidly and to a greater extent. This difference in the apparent equilibrium position between native and digested enzyme was investigated further. As shown in Table 3.V, the amount of acyl

TABLE 3.V

ACYL-ENZYME FORMATION FROM GLYCERALDEHYDE 3-PHOSPHATE
AND FROM GLYCERALDEHYDE

Experiment	Enzyme	Lactate dehydrogenase and pyruvate	Moles of acyl groups formed per mole of glyceraldehyde-3-phosphate dehydrogenase	
			d-Glyceraldehyde 3-phosphate	d-Glyceraldehyde
1	Native	Absent	0.99	0.44
		Present	2.16	1.50
	Digested	Absent	1.86	1.99
		Present	2.27	2.32
2	Native	Absent	1.3	—
		Present	3.1	—
	Digested	Absent	3.2	—
		Present	3.2	—

groups that can be formed per mole of enzyme, with either glyceraldehyde or glyceraldehyde 3-phosphate as substrate, is considerably larger with digested than with native enzyme. Since experiments discussed earlier have implicated DPNH as a potent inhibitor of the forward reaction, acyl-enzyme formation was also measured in the presence of lactate dehydrogenase and pyruvate. A pronounced stimulation of

acyl-enzyme formation was observed and the difference between native and digested enzyme was virtually obliterated,
particularly at higher concentrations of glyceraldehyde
3-phosphate and DPN (Experiment 2). During the 6-minute
incubation period used in these experiments, the amount of
acyl groups formed per mole of enzyme reached a constant
level.

These experiments clearly show that the differences in
acylation between native and digested enzyme are mainly
due to an inhibitory effect of DPNH, which is largely lost
after proteolytic digestion. It is quite conceivable that the
evolution of the double-headed enzyme not only led to an
increased efficiency of the phosphorylation process, but also
resulted in the additional feature of a control mechanism:
Glyceraldehyde 3-phosphate oxidation is controlled by the
rate of removal of DPNH. Since pyruvate, the hydrogen
acceptor for DPNH, is formed only when ADP is available,
it is apparent that multiple safety devices exist that restrain
the glycolytic process.

An examination of the digested enzyme in the analytical
ultracentrifuge revealed inhomogeneity. The major component had a sedimentation coefficient $S_{20,w}$ of 4.83 compared
to 7.19 for the native enzyme. As shown in Table 3.VI, samples from a run in a separation cell also revealed differences
in susceptibility to threose diphosphate; the sample removed
from the top compartment exhibited considerably greater
resistance to the inhibitor. Sedimentation in a sucrose gradi-
ent also showed that digested enzyme sedimented more
slowly, and consisted of a family of proteins with increasing
resistance to tetrose diphosphate correlated with decreasing
molecular weights.

Also apparent from Table 3.VI is the variability of different
fractions in their capacity to use arsenate as acyl acceptor.
Since in all cases there was some residual arsenolytic activity
(although only 0.2 to 2% of the activity with native enzyme),
the question arose whether proteolytic digestion splits off
from the double-headed enzyme a phosphorylating head
which persists as a contaminant of the oxidizing enzyme. An

alternative possibility was that proteolysis results in a damaged enzyme molecule, which can catalyze the complete process but at a greatly reduced rate. Examples of such "crippled" enzymes have been described, for example, when phosphoglucomutase and chymotrypsin have been exposed to photo-oxidation.[26]

TABLE 3.VI

PROPERTIES OF DIGESTED ENZYME SEDIMENTED
IN ANALYTICAL ULTRACENTRIFUGE

| Enzyme | Micromoles of DPNH formed per minute per milligram of protein | | Inhibition by threose diphosphate $(1 \times 10^{-5} M)$ |
| | Acceptor | | |
	Arsenate	Thioglycerol	
Native (dialyzed)	103.8	0.43	100
Digested (dialyzed)	4.6	0.35	44
Digested centrifuged			
Top compartment	0.06	0.10	4
Bottom compartment	1.44	0.35	49

In order to obtain an answer to this question, we embarked on what might be called a rational procedure of purification of the digested enzyme. Surprisingly enough, it even worked.[21] 3-Phosphoglycerate is an inhibitor of glyceraldehyde 3-phosphate oxidation and has been shown to protect the enzyme against iodoacetate.[22] We took advantage of this interaction to achieve separation of the digested enzyme. Native enzyme adsorbed on a P-cellulose column was readily eluted with 3-phosphoglycerate $(0.01 M)$, whereas the digested enzyme was not. High salt concentrations $(0.5 M \text{ KCl})$ were required to elute the digested enzyme. As shown in Table 3.VII, after fractionation of the digested enzyme on the column, the activity with arsenate decreased from about 2 to 0.12%, whereas

[26] W. J. Ray, Jr., and D. E. Koshland, Jr., *Brookhaven Symp. Biol.* **13**, p. 135.

TABLE 3.VII

FRACTIONATION OF DIGESTED ENZYME ON
PHOSPHATE CELLULOSE COLUMN

		Micromoles of DPNH formed per minute per milligram of protein	
		Acceptor	
		Thioglycerol	
Enzyme	Arsenate	− TDP[a]	+ TDP[a]
Native	81.1	0.47	<0.02
Native, dialyzed[b]	85.0	0.62	<0.02
Native, after column	80.0	0.57	<0.02
Digested	1.55	0.25	0.23
Digested, dialyzed[b]	2.54	0.27	0.15
Digested, after column	0.10	0.20	0.20

[a] TDP = D-threose-2,4-diphosphate $(1 \times 10^{-5} \ M)$.

[b] Enzyme was dialyzed against 1000 volumes of 0.005 M EDTA (pH 7.5) for 2 hours; the EDTA solution was changed at the end of the first hour.

there was only a minor decrease in specific activity with thioglycerol as acceptor; these preparations reacted, in fact, more rapidly with thioglycerol than with arsenate, whereas native enzyme reacted more than 100 times as rapidly with arsenate. The digested enzyme eluted from the column was completely resistant to threose diphosphate.

These findings seem to favor the proposition of a separable "head" for phosphate transfer. In favor of a "crippled" enzyme is the failure, even in these experiments, to remove the last traces of arsenolytic activity, and attempts to demonstrate a separable phosphorylating head have thus far yielded only suggestive results.

A summary of the comparative properties of digested and native enzyme is presented in Table 3.VIII.

Before leaving the subject of glyceraldehyde-3-phosphate dehydrogenase, mention should be made of some of the reactions it catalyzes in conjunction with other catalysts of the glycolytic multi-enzyme community.

1. Since the enzyme has acyl phosphatase activity,[24] it catalyzes, in conjunction with phosphoglycerate kinase and in the presence of catalytic amounts of phosphoglycerate, a slow hydrolysis of ATP. The reaction is greatly stimulated by

TABLE 3.VIII
PROPERTIES OF NATIVE AND DIGESTED ENZYME

Native enzyme	Digested enzyme
1. Oxidation of glyceraldehyde is stimulated by P_i	Oxidation of glyceraldehyde is faster, but not stimulated by P_i
2. Oxidation of glyceraldehyde 3-phosphate is "controlled" by DPNH inhibition	Complete acylation by glyceraldehyde 3-phosphate. Little or no inhibition by DPNH
3. Oxidation of glyceraldehyde 3-phosphate is tightly coupled to phosphorylation	No phosphorylation
4. Inhibition by threose diphosphate	No inhibition by threose diphosphate

addition of arsenate. Diphosphopyridine nucleotide is required in the oxidized rather than in the reduced form. It should be noted that mitochondria catalyze an ATP hydrolysis which also operates optimally when the hydrogen carriers are in the oxidized state.[27]

2. In conjunction with phosphoglycerate kinase, the dehydrogenase catalyzes a P_i^{32}-ATP exchange which requires the presence of DPN. In mitochondria, the P_i^{32}-ATP also operates optimally when the hydrogen carriers are in the oxidized state.[27]

3. The oxidation of glyceraldehyde 3-phosphate to 1,3-diphosphoglycerate requires a phosphate transfer step which is dependent on DPN and on the removal of inhibitory DPNH. Thus, pyruvate and lactate dehydrogenase enter

[27] C. L. Wadkins and A. L. Lehninger, *JBC* **234**, 681 (1959).

the reaction sequence in a compulsory manner, as expressed by the formulation of the sequence of events in Scheme 3.1.

Step I   Glyceraldehyde 3-phosphate + DPN-enzyme ⇌ Acyl-enzyme + DPNH

Step II   DPNH + pyruvate ⇌ DPN + lactate

Step III   Acyl-enzyme—DPN + P_i ⇌ 1,3-diphosphoglycerate + DPN-enzyme

Scheme 3.1

Compulsory Oxidation of DPNH in
Glyceraldehyde 3-Phosphate Oxidation

The multiple similarities with phenomena observed in phosphorylation linked to electron transport are apparent. And now, in leaving glyceraldehyde-3-phosphate dehydrogenase, I make a promise: "I shall return . . . . "

LECTURE 4

SUBSTRATE LEVEL OXIDATIVE PHOSPHORYLATION (C)

According to the concept of the unity of biochemistry, all enzymes with the same function are created equal. However, some enzymes are created more equal than others.

—after George Orwell

OXIDATION OF ACETALDEHYDE IN BACTERIA

The oxidation of acetaldehyde in *Clostridium kluyveri*[28] and in *Escherichia coli*[29] is not catalyzed by a single double-headed dehydrogenase but by two readily separable catalysts, as shown in Scheme 4.1. The first step is catalyzed by a

Step I   Acetaldehyde + DPN + CoA $\underset{}{\overset{\text{dehydrogenase}}{\rightleftharpoons}}$ acetyl CoA + DPNH

Step II   Acetyl CoA + P$_i$ $\underset{}{\overset{\text{phosphotransacetylase}}{\rightleftharpoons}}$ acetyl phosphate + CoA

Step III Acetyl phosphate + ADP $\underset{}{\overset{\text{acetokinase}}{\rightleftharpoons}}$ acetate + ATP

Scheme 4.1

Oxidation of Acetaldehyde

dehydrogenase which transfers the hydrogen to DPN and the acyl group to CoA. In the second step, the acyl group is transferred to phosphate, by a second enzyme called phosphotransacetylase, to yield acetyl phosphate and regenerate the

[28] R. M. Burton and E. R. Stadtman, *JBC* **202**, 873 (1953).
[29] G. B. Pinchot and E. Racker, *in* "Phosphorus Metabolism" (W. D. McElroy and B. Glass, eds.), Vol. I, p. 366. Johns Hopkins Press, Baltimore, 1951.

CoA. The third step is the transfer of the phosphate group from acetyl phosphate to ADP by a third enzyme, called acetokinase, producing ATP and acetate. The over-all reaction is the oxidation of acetaldehyde to acetate with DPN as hydrogen acceptor and CoA as coenzyme. The important difference from the reaction catalyzed by glyceraldehyde-3-phosphate dehydrogenase is that CoA, the acyl acceptor, is a dissociable coenzyme. The numerous other variants on the theme of aldehyde oxidation have been mentioned previously (Table 1.IV). You may wonder why nature has selected so many different modes of catalysis. About 12 years ago, at a meeting of biochemists in Atlantic City, a number of aldehyde dehydrogenases were described, some operating with CoA and some without it. Sometimes several different enzymes catalyzing the same over-all reaction were reported found in a single microorganism. Dr. S. Ochoa raised the significant question of why these microorganisms possess so many different mechanisms of aldehyde oxidation. I answered by challenging Dr. Ochoa to explain why animal tissues contain both malic dehydrogenase and malic enzyme, which he had just discovered. He laughed, and the discussion ended. Rather dissatisfied with my answer to his question, I gave the problem some further thought that night, and the next day I proposed that these enzymes have different physiological functions. As a rule, we find double- and multi-headed enzymes where high efficiency is needed and where the intermediates are metabolically unimportant or even undesirable; for example, in channeling the energy of oxidation of glyceraldehyde 3-phosphate into ATP, or in the synthesis of malate from CO_2, pyruvate, and TPNH, catalyzed by malic enzyme. In the case of the CoA-linked acetaldehyde dehydrogenase, the significance of the separation of enzymes and coenzymes can be readily understood since we now know that the major function of these reactions is not energy generation but production of acetyl CoA, an important biosynthetic intermediate in these microorganisms.[1]

A second feature of interest is that, according to the investigations of Burton and Stadtman,[28] the first step is most probably an interaction of acetaldehyde with CoA, presumably nonenzymatically, to form the thiohemiacetal, which is oxidized by the enzyme to acetyl CoA. This difference in mechanism between the double-headed enzyme and the bacterial two-enzyme system can perhaps also be ascribed to the need for dissociable intermediates in the metabolism of the 2-carbon substrate, whereas with glyceraldehyde 3-phosphate, oxidation is used primarily for energy production. It may be mentioned here, in passing, that acetokinase, which catalyzes Step III, has been a very useful analytical tool for acetate determinations, as well as a reagent for the regeneration of ATP from acetyl phosphate and for the measurement of a number of reactions which utilize ATP. Since acetyl phosphate can be simply measured as the hydroxamate, the determination of the disappearance of this compound by any ATP-utilizing system linked to the acetokinase system is a convenient procedure.

ASPARTIC SEMIALDEHYDE DEHYDROGENASE

The oxidative phosphorylation of aspartaldehyde to aspartyl phosphate so much resembles glyceraldehyde 3-phosphate oxidation that it does not need to be discussed in detail.[30] However, it should be mentioned that TPN is the coenzyme, and that the reaction is much less sensitive to iodoacetate. The enzyme also catalyzes the cleavage of aspartyl phosphate in the presence of arsenate, but does not appear to require the addition of a pyridine nucleotide for this reaction. It is quite likely that the major significance of this TPN-linked system resides in the reverse direction, namely, the reduction of the aspartyl phosphate to aspartic semialdehyde, which is an intermediate in the biosynthesis of lysine, threonine, and diaminopimelate.

OXIDATION OF α-KETOGLUTARATE AND PYRUVATE

The complete oxidation of pyruvate to CO_2 and water in mitochondria includes, in addition to phosphorylation linked

[30] S. Black and N. G. Wright, *JBC* **213**, 27, 39 (1955).

to electron transport, one step of phosphorylation at the substrate level, namely, the oxidation of α-ketoglutarate. In contrast to the respiratory chain phosphorylations, this ATP-yielding reaction is insensitive to dinitrophenol. The multi-enzyme system that catalyzes this substrate level phosphorylation has been studied extensively by Ochoa, Kaufman, Gunsalus, Hunter, Sanadi, Massey, and Reed, and considerable progress has been made in our understanding of the reaction sequence and its regulation. The over-all reaction is written in six steps, as shown in Scheme 4.2 [E_1 = car-

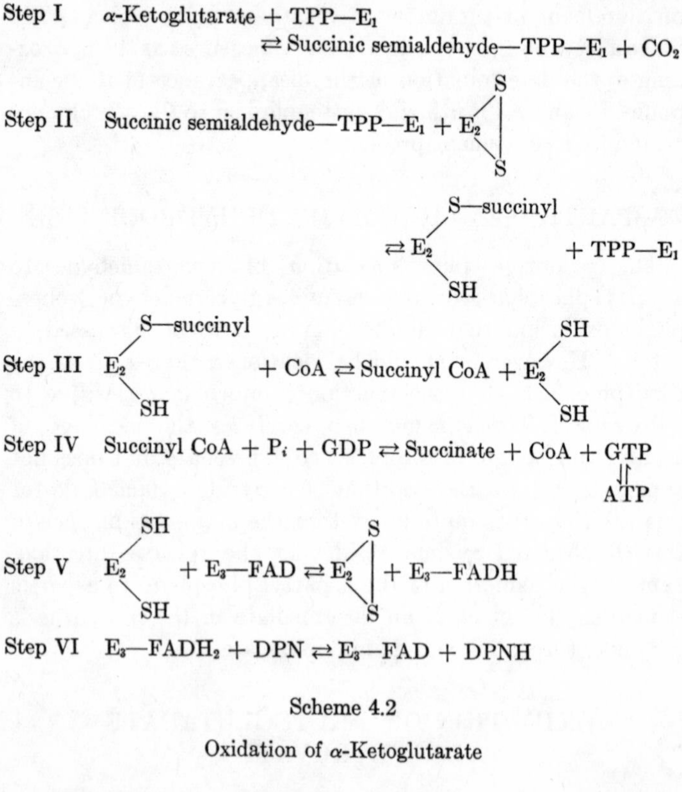

Step I α-Ketoglutarate + TPP—E_1
$$\rightleftharpoons \text{Succinic semialdehyde—TPP—}E_1 + CO_2$$

Step II   Succinic semialdehyde—TPP—E_1 + $E_2\!\!\begin{array}{c}S\\[2pt]\diagdown\\[2pt]S\end{array}$

$$\rightleftharpoons E_2\!\!\begin{array}{c}\text{S—succinyl}\\[4pt]\diagup\\[4pt]\text{SH}\end{array} + \text{TPP—}E_1$$

Step III $E_2\!\!\begin{array}{c}\text{S—succinyl}\\[4pt]\diagup\\[4pt]\text{SH}\end{array} + \text{CoA} \rightleftharpoons \text{Succinyl CoA} + E_2\!\!\begin{array}{c}\text{SH}\\[4pt]\diagup\\[4pt]\text{SH}\end{array}$

Step IV   Succinyl CoA + P_i + GDP $\rightleftharpoons$ Succinate + CoA + GTP
$$\Updownarrow$$
$$\text{ATP}$$

Step V $E_2\!\!\begin{array}{c}\text{SH}\\[4pt]\diagup\\[4pt]\text{SH}\end{array} + E_3\text{—FAD} \rightleftharpoons E_2\!\!\begin{array}{c}S\\[2pt]\diagdown\\[2pt]S\end{array} + E_3\text{—FADH}$

Step VI $E_3\text{—FADH}_2 + \text{DPN} \rightleftharpoons E_3\text{—FAD} + \text{DPNH}$

Scheme 4.2

Oxidation of α-Ketoglutarate

boxylase; E_2 = [aldehyde] dehydrogenase (lipoate reductase); E_3-dihydrolipoate dehydrogenase].

The first step consists of a decarboxylation of α-ketoglutarate to an active succinic semialdehyde, which is thought to be linked to thiamine pyrophosphate and is analogous to the "active aldehyde" produced by pyruvate carboxylase or transketolase. Carbon dioxide is liberated in the first step.

The second step consists of an oxidation of the succinic semialdehyde thiamine pyrophosphate intermediate by enzyme-bound lipoate, resulting in the formation of succinyl lipoate. Thiamine pyrophosphate becomes available again for another cycle of decarboxylation. As mentioned previously, the mechanism of this oxidation has been visualized as similar to the mechanism of glyceraldehyde 3-phosphate oxidation, except that the hydrogen acceptor is a sulfur of lipoate rather than carbon 4 of DPN. On the other hand, it is conceivable that there is an intermediate step, e.g., forming acyl thiamine. No direct evidence on this point is available. The succinicaldehyde dehydrogenase needs further characterization, and even the evidence for succinyl lipoate formation is rather indirect. Sanadi and his collaborators[31] added α-ketoglutarate labeled with C^{14} at carbon 5, together with hydroxylamine, to the oxidizing enzyme in the absence of CoA. The formation of C^{14}-labeled succinyl hydroxamate indicated that an acyl compound was formed prior to CoA acylation. Experiments with arsenite, which reacts with dithiol groups, have further implicated bound lipoate as succinyl acceptor. Experiments by Gunsalus[32] have shown that in some bacterial systems free lipoate can serve as acceptor of the acyl group. Bound lipoate was shown by Reed[33] and his collaborators to be attached by peptide linkage to a lysine group of the enzyme.

In the third step, the succinyl enzyme is cleaved by CoA, resulting in the formation of succinyl CoA and the enzyme-

[31] D. R. Sanadi, M. Langley, and F. White, *JBC* **234**, 183 (1959).
[32] I. C. Gunsalus, *in* "The Mechanism of Enzyme Action" (W. D. McElroy and B. Glass, eds.), p. 545. Johns Hopkins Press, Baltimore, 1954.
[33] L. J. Reed, *in* "The Enzymes," 2nd ed. (P. D. Boyer *et al.*, eds.), Vol. 3, p. 195. Academic Press, New York, 1960.

bound dihydrolipoate. In the fourth step, succinyl CoA is cleaved in the presence of inorganic phosphate and GDP to yield succinate, CoA, and GTP. The terminal phosphate of the latter is transferred to ADP by a nucleoside diphosphate kinase. In the fifth step, the dithiol enzyme is oxidized by a flavoprotein to yield oxidized lipoate enzyme and reduced flavoprotein. The flavoprotein transfers its hydrogen to yield oxidized flavoprotein and reduced DPN. The sum of the overall reaction is the oxidation of α-ketoglutarate with DPN as the hydrogen acceptor, yielding one ATP. This scheme differs from the earlier versions of Gunsalus in only two details. One is the inclusion of enzyme-bound lipoate, the second is recognition of a flavoprotein as a hydrogen carrier between reduced lipoate and DPN. This flavoprotein has been recently identified as Straub's classical diaphorase,[34,35] which for many years had puzzled biochemists in regard to its possible function. The reduction of DPN by a sulfhydryl compound was unexpected, particularly since it was mediated via a flavin-linked enzyme. The potential of most SH compounds and of most flavoproteins is more positive than that of the DPN system. This example is therefore a particularly good illustration of the changes in potentials that may take place when a prosthetic group such as FAD is linked to proteins. Moreover, dihydrolipoate, the hydrogen donor in this reaction, has, in contrast to monothiols, a potential considerably more negative than that of DPN.

Some progress has been made in the resolution of this complex multi-enzyme system, e.g., in the separation of dihydrolipoate dehydrogenase from the α-ketoglutarate dehydrogenase.[34,35]

More extensive resolution has been accomplished in the case of the pyruvate dehydrogenase, which operates through a rather similar sequence of steps. Three components have been separated[36,37] from a bacterial complex of a large mole-

[34] V. Massey, *BBA* **38**, 447 (1960).

[35] R. L. Searles and D. R. Sanadi, *JBC* **235**, 2485 (1960).

[36] A. D. Gounaris and L. P. Hager, *JBC* **236**, 1013 (1961).

[37] M. Koike, L. J. Reed, and W. R. Carrol, *JBC* **238**, 30 (1963).

cular weight. In one system,[36] advantage was taken of an acetate-requiring mutant of *E. coli* which had lost the ability to produce acetate from pyruvate but still contained lipoate transacetylase and dihydrolipoate dehydrogenase. These two enzymes, together with pyruvate carboxylase from wild-type *E. coli*, yielded a system of pyruvate oxidation which showed a dependency on the addition of the three enzymes, as well as on CoA, DPN, and thiamine pyrophosphate. In the presence of lactate dehydrogenase and phosphotransacetylase (added as contaminants of lipoate transacetylase), the complete system converted 2 moles of pyruvate to acetyl phosphate and lactate. If acetokinase was added, ATP and acetate were formed from acetyl phosphate; see Scheme 4.3 [E_1 = carboxylase; E_2 = [aldehyde] dehydrogenase (lypoate reductase); E_3 = dihydrolipoate dehydrogenase]. Separation was also achieved by physical methods.[37] At pH 9.5 pyruvate carboxylase was removed from a yellow fraction, which, following treatment with 4.0 M urea, was separated by chromatography with Ca–P gel-cellulose into a lipoate transacetylase and dihydrolipoate dehydrogenase. A separation of the aldehyde dehydrogenase from the lipoate transacetylase had not been achieved by either of the two approaches. Koike *et al.*,[37] therefore, referred to their preparation of transacetylase as lipoate reductase-transacetylase. This complex is still large (molecular weight about 1.6×10^6) and combines with about 12 to 14 units of the pyruvate carboxylase (molecular weight 1.8×10^5) and 6 to 8 units of the dihydrolipoate dehydrogenase (molecular weight 1.1×10^5, with 2 FAD per mole).

The reconstituted complex had properties and catalytic activities quite similar to the original particles from which the components were derived. It contained approximately 12 mμmoles of lipoate and 3 mμmoles of flavin per milligram of protein.

The substrate level oxidative phosphorylation associated with pyruvate or α-ketoglutarate oxidation represents a much more complex system than the reactions catalyzed by glyceraldehyde-3-phosphate dehydrogenase. Since the hydrogen is

Step I   Pyruvate + thiamine pyrophosphate—E_1
               $\rightleftarrows$ acetaldehyde thiamine pyrophosphate—E_1 + CO_2

Step II   Acetaldehyde—thiamine pyrophosphate + $E_2 \begin{array}{c} S \\ | \\ S \end{array}$

$$\rightleftarrows E_2 \begin{array}{c} \text{S-acetyl} \\ \\ SH \end{array} + \text{TPP}$$

Step III $E_2 \begin{array}{c} \text{S-acetyl} \\ \\ SH \end{array} + \text{CoA} \rightleftarrows \text{acetyl CoA} + E_2 \begin{array}{c} SH \\ \\ SH \end{array}$

Step IV   (Bacteria)

                          phosphotransacetylase
      Acetyl CoA + P_i $\rightleftarrows$ acetyl phosphate + CoA

                           acetokinase
Step V   Acetyl phosphate + ADP $\rightleftarrows$ acetate + ATP

Step VI $E_2 \begin{array}{c} SH \\ \\ SH \end{array} + E_3\text{—FAD} \rightleftarrows E_2 \begin{array}{c} S \\ | \\ S \end{array} + E_3\text{—FADH}$

Step VII E_3—FADH + DPN $\rightleftarrows E_3$—FAD + DPNH

                        lactate dehydrogenase
Step VIII DPNH + pyruvate $\rightleftarrows$ DPN + lactate

$$\overline{}$$

2 pyruvate + P_i + ADP $\rightarrow$ lactate + acetate + ATP
                                        + CO_2

Scheme 4.3

Pyruvate Oxidation

not accepted by a dissociable nucleotide but by protein-bound lipoate, it is mandatory that the hydrogen transfer to the flavoprotein occur by protein-protein interaction. To make this process efficient, considerable accuracy in the alignment of the catalytic components is required. It is, therefore, most remarkable and encouraging that after resolution by treatment with urea, and at pH 9.5, the components appear to find their home-base without difficulty.

The dismutation of 2 moles of α-ketoglutarate and 1 mole of ammonia in the presence of mitochondria and fluoride yields 1 mole of succinate, 1 mole of glutamate, and 1 mole of ATP.[38] Several curious aspects of this reaction have recently been noted by Danielson and Ernster.[39] In the absence of fluoride, the dismutation proceeded more rapidly than in its presence, but the energy yield was low (P:2e$^-$ ratio about 0.3 to 0.5). Addition of fluoride caused an inhibition of the rate of the dismutation without depressing the rate of phosphorylation, thus allowing the P:2e$^-$ ratio to approach unity. The authors proposed that the reduction of α-ketoglutarate to glutamate is driven by energy provided by oxidative phosphorylation. Fluoride is visualized as acting by preventing drainage of ATP via a hydrolytic side reaction. The key to this phenomenon of glutamate formation is the energy-driven reduction of TPN by DPNH, which will be discussed later.

OTHER VARIANTS

There are several other examples of substrate level oxidative phosphorylation, but because of insufficient available information they will not be discussed in great detail. However, it should be mentioned that some of these are very fascinating reactions and look quite promising as possible models for oxidative phosphorylation. Stadtman and her collaborators have described a partially purified enzyme preparation from *Clostridium sticklandii* which catalyzed an oxidation-reduction that resulted in ATP formation.[40] Glycine was the hydrogen acceptor and a dithiol (e.g., 1,3-dimercaptopropanol) served as a hydrogen donor. The balance analysis of the over-all reaction revealed that for each mole of inorganic phosphate which was transferred to ADP, two SH groups were oxidized, 1 mole of glycine disappeared, and 1 mole of acetate and 1 mole of ammonia appeared. The reac-

[38] F. E. Hunter, Jr., and W. S. Hixon, *JBC* **181**, 67 (1949).

[39] L. Danielson and L. Ernster, *BBRC* **10**, 85 (1963).

[40] T. C. Stadtman, P. Elliott, and L. Tiemann, *JBC* **231**, 961 (1958).

tion is shown in Scheme 4.4. Attempts to detect an intermediate such as acetyl phosphate or phosphoramidate have
thus far been unsuccessful—indeed, these two compounds
seem to have been ruled out as possible intermediates. One
particular observation is of interest, namely, the stimulation

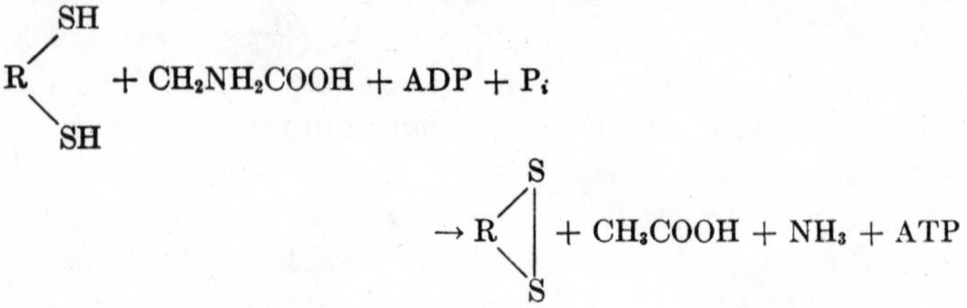

$$R\diagdown\!\!\!\!\begin{matrix} SH \\ \\ SH \end{matrix} + CH_2NH_2COOH + ADP + P_i$$

$$\rightarrow R\diagdown\!\!\!\!\begin{matrix} S \\ | \\ S \end{matrix} + CH_3COOH + NH_3 + ATP$$

Scheme 4.4

Phosphorylation in *Clostridium Sticklandii*

of the conversion of glycine to acetate by imidazole. Since
imidazole is known to serve as an acyl transfer agent in a
nonenzymic reaction, as well as in some enzyme-catalyzed
reactions in bacteria, this finding may represent an important
clue to the mechanism of the reaction.

LECTURE 5

PHOSPHOROCLASTIC REACTIONS:
PHOSPHOKETOLASE

Rather I prize the doubt
Low kinds exist without,
Finished and finite clods, untroubled by a spark.
                    —Robert Browning, "Rabbi ben Ezra"

The reactions of the second group, which lead to ATP formation via a phosphoroclastic cleavage of a carbon-carbon, a carbon-nitrogen, or a carbon-sulfur bond, are found primarily among microorganisms. These reactions have in common the intermediate formation of an acyl phosphate which can donate its phosphate group to ADP. Although the phosphoroclastic reaction with pyruvate was historically the first representative of this group, because of its complexity. I shall discuss it later.

PHOSPHOKETOLASE

The reaction catalyzed by phosphoketolase[6,7] is the simplest in this group, and the enzyme has been obtained in crystalline form.[41] I should like to tell you how we became involved with this enzyme, since the story illustrates how fruitful it sometimes is to allow the experiments to guide the research. Several years ago we became interested in the possibility that some microorganisms may use TPNH formed in the pentose phosphate cycle as a source of energy. Studies on the biosynthesis of cellulose from glucose in *Acetobacter xylinum*[42] revealed that neither iodoacetate, which inhibits

---

[41] M. L. Goldberg and E. Racker, *JBC* **237,** PC3841 (1962).
[42] M. Schramm, Z. Gromet, and S. Hestrin, *BJ* **67,** 669 (1957).

glycolysis, nor fluoroacetate, which inhibits the Krebs cycle, were very effective inhibitors of cellulose biosynthesis. Moreover, a role for the very active pentose phosphate cycle in cellulose synthesis was clearly indicated by isotope studies. It seemed logical to us, therefore, to search in this microorganism for energy production due to oxidation of TPNH. When Dr. Schramm came to work in our laboratory we started to test this idea. The very first experiments showed that phosphate was esterified by crude extracts of *A. xylinum* in the presence of glucose 6-phosphate and TPN at iodoacetate concentrations that blocked glycolysis. It soon became apparent, however, that the observed phenomenon had nothing to do either with the pentose phosphate cycle or with the oxidation of TPNH, since neither TPN nor oxygen were required. Further analysis revealed that the substrate in the reaction was fructose 6-phosphate and the products were acetyl phosphate and erythrose 4-phosphate. The reaction looked similar to that discovered by Heath *et al.* in *Lactobacillus plantarum.*[6] When these microorganisms were grown in the presence of xylose, they contained an enzyme which cleaved xylulose 5-phosphate phosphorolytically to glyceraldehyde 3-phosphate and acetyl phosphate. The action of this enzyme, phosphoketolase, is dependent on thiamine pyrophosphate and Mg^{++}, and is stimulated by SH compounds. Since acetyl phosphate is the product, the reaction resembles the phosphoroclastic reaction with pyruvate; since xylulose 5-phosphate is the substrate and glyceraldehyde 3-phosphate is a product, it resembles the reaction catalyzed by transketolase. We have recently conducted studies on the mechanism of action of crystalline phosphoketolase from *Leuconostoc mesenteroides.*[41] I shall therefore report mainly on this enzyme, but it is apparent from the work of Holzer and Schröter[43] that phosphoketolase from *L. plantarum* operates by the same mechanism. With fructose 6-phosphate or xylulose 5-phosphate as substrate, the enzyme catalyzed the reduction of ferricyanide to ferrocyanide. This reaction was carried out with C^{14}-labeled fructose 6-phosphate as

[43] H. Holzer and W. Schröter, *BBA* **65,** 271 (1962).

substrate, and the product was isolated and identified as glycolic acid. This pointed to the formation of an active glycolaldehyde-enzyme intermediate. In support of this conclusion was the discovery that glycolaldehyde itself served as substrate for the enzyme. In the presence of ferricyanide as electron acceptor, oxidation of glycolaldehyde to glycolic acid took place. In the presence of P_i, glycolaldehyde yielded acetyl phosphate. As shown in Table 5.I, the enzyme reacted

TABLE 5.I
GLYCOLALDEHYDE UTILIZATION BY PHOSPHOKETOLASE

Reagent	Millimicromoles of acetyl phosphate produced from		Millimicromoles of ferrocyanide produced from	
	Xylulose 5-phos-phate	Glycol-aldehyde	Xylulose 5-phos-phate	Glycol-aldehyde
Unresolved enzyme	5600	120	1430	40
Resolved enzyme	35	0	8	0
Resolved enzyme + Mg^{++} (1 mM)	51	0	12	0.3
Resolved enzyme + thiamine pyrophosphate (0.15 mM)	100	0	12	0.75
Resolved enzyme + Mg^{++} + thiamine pyrophosphate	750	16	190	3.5

about 3 times as rapidly with phosphate as with ferricyanide when either xylulose 5-phosphate or glycolaldehyde was used as substrate. The rate of reaction with glycolaldehyde was only a small fraction of the rate with xylulose 5-phosphate. Resolution of the enzyme by extensive dialysis against ethylenediaminetetraacetate resulted in considerable loss in activity, which was only partially restored by addition of thiamine pyrophosphate and Mg^{++}. It is apparent, nevertheless, from the experiments shown in Table 5.I, that restoration of activity on addition of cofactors is parallel with glycolaldehyde and xylulose 5-phosphate as substrates, and that phosphorolysis and ferricyanide reduction both require thiamine pyrophosphate. The formation of a glycolaldehyde-thiamine pyrophosphate-enzyme appeared to be the first step, and isolation of this intermediate was therefore attempted. Highly radioactive C^{14}-labeled fructose 6-phosphate was allowed to interact with phosphoketolase and the mixture was passed through a very long column of Sephadex G-75. The first radioactive peak that appeared contained the enzyme, then an eluate low in radioactivity followed, and finally, radioactive fructose 6-phosphate was eluted. An analysis of the radioactive enzyme after protein denaturation yielded the data shown in Table 5.II. The major small-

TABLE 5.II

RADIOACTIVE COMPONENTS IN SUBSTRATE-ENZYME INTERMEDIATE

Component	Amounts ($m\mu$moles)
Enzyme from Sephadex column	4.4
Fructose 6-phosphate	0.3
Glycolaldehyde	0.3
Erythrose 4-phosphate	0.03

molecular components were glycolaldehyde and fructose 6-phosphate, together with traces of erythrose 4-phosphate. A control experiment with C^{14}-labeled fructose 6-phosphate without enzyme revealed no radioactivity in the early eluates. It was apparent, therefore, that a glycolaldehyde-enzyme could be formed in the absence of an acceptor. The presence of some fructose 6-phosphate was probably due to an effective competition of the enzyme with Sephadex, and may be a reflection of the dissociation constant of the substrate-enzyme complex. We have made similar observations on the retention of substrate with transketolase and transaldolase.

Since the over-all phosphorolytic activity of phosphoketolase was markedly stimulated by SH compounds, it was of interest to analyze whether the reduction of ferricyanide

was similarly affected. In order to avoid the use of SH inhibitors such as *p*-mercuribenzoate, which in addition to
interacting with SH groups may interact with other groups
in the protein (e.g., histidine), or because of its large size
may sterically hinder the reaction, we compared an aged
preparation of phosphoketolase with a relatively fresh preparation. We reasoned that an aged preparation, which had
lost most of its phosphorolytic activity, in the absence of
SH compounds might still have been able to catalyze a rapid
reduction of ferricyanide. However, as can be seen from
Table 5.III, this was not the case. The rate of reduction of

TABLE 5.III
EFFECT OF AGING ON PHOSPHOKETOLASE

Reagent	Acetyl phosphate (mμmoles)	Ferrocyanide (mμmoles)
Enzyme I (2 months old)	900	280
Enzyme I + thioglycerol	2700	—
Enzyme II (13 days old)	2900	1100
Enzyme II + thioglycerol	4600	—

ferricyanide was low in the aged preparation, and the activity ratios of phosphorolysis to reduction were fairly constant with this and with several other preparations that were
tested. The phosphorolytic activity was restored in the aged
enzyme by addition of an SH compound, but ferricyanide
reduction could not be tested because of the nonenzymic
reduction of ferricyanide by SH compounds.

The reactions catalyzed by phosphoketolase are illustrated
schematically in Scheme 5.1. The first step is the formation
of a 2-(α,β-dihydroxyethyl) thiamine-pyrophosphate-Mg^{++}-
enzyme intermediate. Holzer and Schröter [43] have identified
the active aldehyde as dihydroxyethylthiamine pyrophosphate, which they obtained after denaturation of phosphoketolase that had reacted with substrate. The second step
is shown as an interaction between the active glycolaldehyde
enzyme and arsenate that yields acetate, with phosphate that

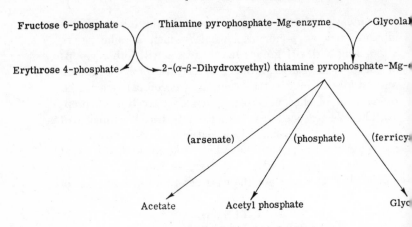

Scheme 5.1

Reactions of Phosphoketolase

yields acetyl phosphate, or with ferricyanide that yields glycolic acid. By what mechanisms do these reactions proceed? The first possibility that occurred to us, by analogy with glyceraldehyde-3-phosphate dehydrogenase, was an oxidation of the aldehyde to an enzyme thiol ester which is phosphorolytically cleaved to yield acetyl phosphate. However, attempts to trap such an acetyl-enzyme intermediate were uniformly unsuccessful. For example, experiments were carried out in which hydroxylamine was added to the enzyme in the presence of substrate, with and without phosphate. At 50 mM hydroxylamine, no hydroxamate was formed without phosphate, and considerable amounts were formed with phosphate. These negative findings persuaded us to think in terms of another possibility. We considered that the active glycolaldehyde was transferred on the enzyme from thiamine pyrophosphate to P_i to form a phosphate aldehyde adduct from which water is eliminated (Scheme 5.2). This formulation can readily be recognized as a variant of the Warburg theory of glyceraldehyde 3-phosphate oxidation, and may well prove equally wrong. A third attractive theory, proposed by Breslow,[44] envisaged an intramolecular oxidation-reduc-

[44] R. Breslow, *J. Cell. Comp. Physiol.* **54,** Suppl. 1, 100 (1959).

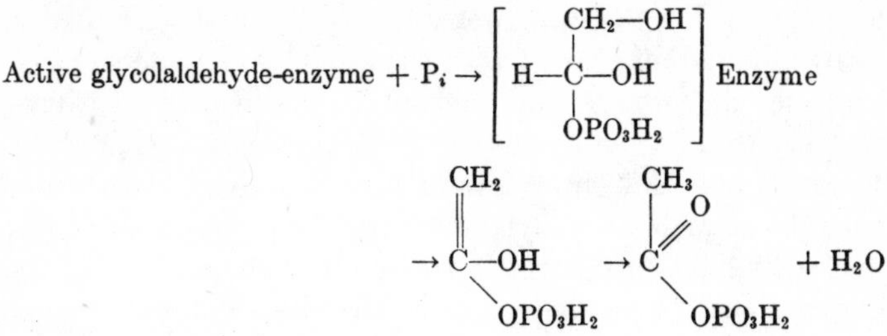

Active glycolaldehyde-enzyme $+ \; P_i \rightarrow \left[\begin{array}{c} CH_2\!-\!OH \\ | \\ H\!-\!C\!-\!OH \\ | \\ OPO_3H_2 \end{array} \right]$ Enzyme

$$\rightarrow \begin{array}{c} CH_2 \\ \| \\ C\!-\!OH \\ | \\ OPO_3H_2 \end{array} \qquad \rightarrow \begin{array}{c} CH_3 \\ | \\ C\!=\!O \\ | \\ OPO_3H_2 \end{array} + H_2O$$

Scheme 5.2

Early Formulation of Mechanism of Action of Phosphoketolase

tion of the dihydroxyethyl thiamine pyrophosphate to yield acetyl thiamine pyrophosphate, which is attacked by phosphate to yield acetyl phosphate (Scheme 5.3). Breslow's

Step I   Fructose 6-phosphate $+ \; E \rightarrow$ Active glycolaldehyde—E $+$ erythrose 4-phosphate

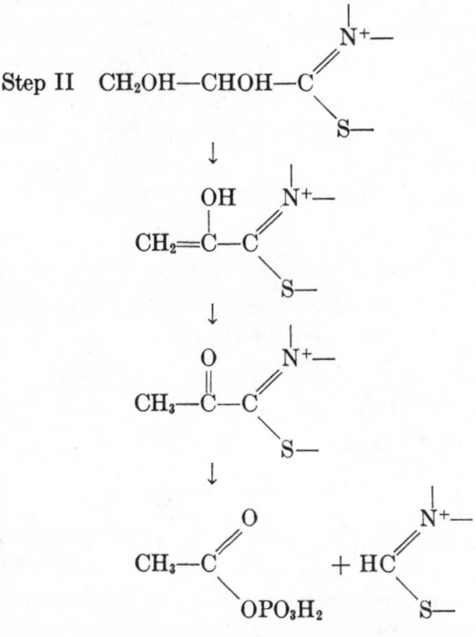

Step II $CH_2OH\!-\!CHOH\!-\!C \overset{\displaystyle N^{+}\!-}{\underset{\displaystyle S\!-}{\big|}}$

$$\downarrow$$

$$CH_2\!=\!\underset{}{\overset{OH}{C}}\!-\!C\overset{\displaystyle N^{+}\!-}{\underset{\displaystyle S\!-}{\big|}}$$

$$\downarrow$$

$$CH_3\!-\!\underset{}{\overset{O}{C}}\!-\!C\overset{\displaystyle N^{+}\!-}{\underset{\displaystyle S\!-}{\big|}}$$

$$\downarrow$$

$$CH_3\!-\!C\overset{\displaystyle O}{\underset{\displaystyle OPO_3H_2}{\big\langle}} \quad + \; HC\overset{\displaystyle N^{+}\!-}{\underset{\displaystyle S\!-}{\big\langle}}$$

Scheme 5.3

Mechanism of Action of Phosphoketolase According to Breslow

formulation has the same weakness as the thiol ester theory, being in apparent conflict with the negative experiments that were designed to trap an acyl intermediate with hydroxylamine. Model compounds of acyl thiazoles prepared by Breslow and McNelis[45] showed high reactivity with water as well as with hydroxylamine. On the other hand, enzymologists have in the past retreated into the crevices of the enzyme surface to defend their theories, and the organic chemists are rapidly learning the game. Indeed, the exclusion of water from the active sites of enzymes is a rather important ingredient of the efficient catalysis of specific transfer reactions, as will become apparent in our discussions of mitochondrial ATPase. There is no reason why a similar exclusion could not apply to hydroxylamine.

There is another possible explanation for the negative experiments with hydroxylamine. It is conceivable that phosphate is not only required for the final cleavage of the acyl group but is also essential for the maintenance of the proper enzyme configuration necessary for the formation of an acyl enzyme. The requirement for DPN in the arsenolysis of 1,3-diphosphoglycerate by glyceraldehyde-3-phosphate dehydrogenase is only one example among many where a component of the over-all reaction is needed for a partial reaction in which it actually does not participate.[45a]

Apart from these speculations, one of the practical approaches to the study of the mechanism of action of phosphoketolase is the use of isotope exchange reactions. We have initiated such experiments with tritiated water, measuring incorporation of tritium into acetate. According to Breslow's formulation, we expected that acetate obtained from the phosphoketolase reaction should contain more than one

---

[45] R. Breslow and E. McNelis, *JACS* **82**, 2394 (1960).

[45a] In recent unpublished experiments by Dr. J. Fessenden (1964) it was shown that glutathione can serve as acyl acceptor instead of phosphate. Therefore, in the reaction catalyzed by phosphoketolase, as with glyceraldehyde-3-phosphate dehydrogenase, oxidation precedes the entrance of phosphate. Moreover, the presence of phosphate does not appear to be required for the formation of the acyl group.

tritium per mole of acetate, since some exchange would be expected at the oxidation step. Experimentally, only one tritium per acetate was formed. Negative experiments of this type are not decisive, since we are faced with many unknowns in the kinetics of the formation of the various substrate-enzyme intermediates.[45b] To reassure you that we are not readily shaken by negative results, I might mention here that attempts in Dr. Horecker's laboratory, as well as in our own, to demonstrate an exchange reaction between C^{14}-labeled glyceraldehyde 3-phosphate and xylulose 5-phosphate catalyzed by phosphoketolase have been consistently unsuccessful. Yet the presence of such an exchange might be expected if an active glycolaldehyde-enzyme is an intermediate. But we too sought refuge in the hilly enzyme surfaces, and postulated a configuration of the protein that allowed the release of glyceraldehyde 3-phosphate from the enzyme but did not favor its return. In any case we proceeded, as you have heard, to look for the glycolaldehyde-enzyme intermediate by other methods, and found it. A good hypothesis is worth many negative experiments. Failure to detect an arsenolysis of acetyl phosphate in the presence of phosphoketolase may be treated with similar misgivings. Yet the irreversibility of the last step may be an important clue to its mechanism.

Finally, a few words regarding the use of the term "phosphoroclastic reaction." It is apparent from the isolation of the glycolaldehyde-enzyme that the carbon-carbon cleavage of the keto sugar phosphate is not "phosphoroclastic." We might call it "thiaminoclastic," but we shall not. The experiments with glycolaldehyde as substrate demonstrate that the carbon-carbon cleavage of the sugar is not even an essential step in the reaction. Yet we are probably still dealing with a phosphoroclastic reaction, breaking the carbon-carbon bond of an acetyl thiamine or the carbon-sulfur bond of a thiol ester. It will be seen that we are plagued by a similar problem

---

[45b] Dr. Fessenden has recently found about 2 moles of tritium per mole of acetate indicating the occurrence of an exchange reaction. These experiments differed from the previous ones: arsenate was added at the end rather than at the beginning of the incubation period.

TABLE 5.IV

PHOSPHOKETOLASE SHUNT

Reactions	Enzymes
1. Fructose 6-phosphate + P_i → acetyl phosphate + erythrose 4-phosphate	Phosphoketolase
2. Erythrose 4-phosphate + fructose 6-phosphate → sedoheptulose 7-phosphate + glyceraldehyde 3-phosphate	Transaldolase
3. Sedoheptulose 7-phosphate + glyceraldehyde 3-phosphate → ribose 5-phosphate + xylulose 5-phosphate	Transketolase
4 and 5. Ribose 5-phosphate → ribulose 5-phosphate → xylulose 5-phosphate	Isomerase and epimerase
6. 2 Xylulose 5-phosphate + 2 P_i → 2 acetyl phosphate + 2 glyceraldehyde 3-phosphate	Phosphoketolase
7 and 8. 2 Glyceraldehyde 3-phosphate → fructose 1,6-diphosphate	Isomerase and aldolase
9. Fructose 1,6-diphosphate → fructose 6-phosphate + P_i	Fructose diphosphatase
Fructose 6-phosphate + 2 P_i → 3 acetyl phosphate	

of terminology in the case of the classical phosphoroclastic reaction with pyruvate.

Before leaving the subject of phosphoketolase, I should like to say a few words regarding its possible role within the communities of enzyme systems where it is found. In *L. plantarum*, the enzyme is induced when the organisms are grown in the presence of xylose. The enzyme apparently participates in the dissimilation of the pentose. The fermentation pattern is in accord with this interpretation. In the case of *A. xylinum*, where the enzyme is constitutive, the function is somewhat less apparent. However, one can formulate a cyclic process, as shown in Table 5.IV. The presence of all the listed enzymes has been demonstrated in crude extracts of *A. xylinum*. The over-all process is the formation of 3 moles of acetylphosphate from each mole of fructose 6-phosphate, and includes the esterification of 2 moles of inorganic phosphate. The acetyl group can be transferred to CoA and enter the Krebs cycle, which has been shown to function in these microorganisms. Alternatively, the phosphoryl group can be transferred to ADP by acetokinase, and ATP is produced. The formulation of this cycle represents a short-circuit pathway for the production of acetate in *A. xylinum*. It may have a very specific function in this microorganism, which appears to be lacking in the glycolytic enzyme phosphofructokinase. The energy yield of this short-circuit pathway in terms of ATP is 3 moles per mole of fructose 6-phosphate, or 2 moles of ATP per mole of glucose, a yield identical with that of glycolysis; and actually, the system is considerably simpler. The energy yield is low, however, compared to that obtained by oxidation of acetate in the Krebs cycle. The phosphoketolase shunt, therefore, probably functions as a short-circuit to acetate, rather than as an important contributor to the energy budget of this microorganism.

LECTURE 6

OTHER PHOSPHOROCLASTIC
REACTIONS

Nature, my dear sir, is only a hypothesis.

—Raoul Dufy

REACTIONS WITH PYRUVATE

Several variants of the cleavage of pyruvate to acetyl phosphate are found in different microorganisms. They all have in common thiamine pyrophosphate participation in the first step, and phosphate as the final acyl acceptor. What differs is the fate of the hydrogens, of carbon 1 of pyruvate, and of the intermediate acyl acceptors (Table 6.I).

In essence, these variants fall into two major groups of reactions. In Reaction I (representing the first major group) the hydrogen acceptor is external; in Reaction II (representing the second major group) there is an intramolecular oxidation-reduction similar to that catalyzed by phosphoketolase.

Reaction I. $CH_3COCOOH + P_i \rightarrow CH_3C\begin{smallmatrix}O\\\\OPO_3H_2\end{smallmatrix} + CO_2 + H_2$ (or H_2O)

Reaction II. $CH_3COCOOH + P_i \rightarrow CH_3C\begin{smallmatrix}O\\\\OPO_3H_2\end{smallmatrix} + HCOOH$

The term "phosphoroclastic reaction" still seems acceptable, although the bond which is cleaved by phosphate may not be the same in each case and certainly is not the bond between carbons 1 and 2 of pyruvate.

66

TABLE 6.I

PHOSPHOROCLASTIC REACTIONS WITH PYRUVATE

Microorganism	Acyl acceptor			H-acceptor	
	I	II	III	I	II
Lactobacillus delbrückii	Thiamine	P_i	—	Flavin	—
Escherichia coli	Thiamine	CoA	P_i	Carbon 1 or pyruvate	—
Clostridium butyricum	Thiamine	CoA	P_i	Fe (?)	H^+
Clostridium pasteurianum	Thiamine	CoA	P_i	Ferredoxin	H^+
Micrococcus lactilyticus	Thiamine	CoA	P_i	Ferredoxin or carbon 1 of pyruvate	—
Peptostreptococcus elsendii	Thiamine	CoA	P_i	Ferredoxin	H^+
Other clostridia	Thiamine	CoA	P_i	Ferredoxin	H^+

In *L. delbrückii*, the end products of pyruvate oxidation are acetyl phosphate, CO_2, and H_2O (Reaction I). The intermediate electron acceptor is a flavoprotein and neither CoA nor lipoate seem to participate.[46] There is no evidence for an intermediate acyl compound and no SH group is involved. This system may therefore be the best in which to study a mechanism involving the phosphorolysis of an acetyl thiamine intermediate. Actually, in all other variants of the phosphoroclastic reaction of pyruvate there is evidence for CoA participation.

In *E. coli*, acetyl phosphate and formate are the end products of the reaction.[47-49] It remains to be determined whether an intermediate hydrogen carrier participates in the reaction, or whether the cleavage is best represented by a "thiaminolysis" of pyruvate, with the carbon of the carboxyl group accepting the hydrogen of thiamine. The secondary acyl acceptor is probably CoA, and P_i the final one.

In *M. lactilyticus*, the cleavage of pyruvate to formate and acetyl phosphate takes place at an alkaline pH, whereas at an acid pH Reaction I predominates.[50] Isotope exchange reactions follow the same pattern: C^{14}-formate incorporation into pyruvate is catalyzed at an alkaline pH and $C^{14}O_2$ into pyruvate at an acid pH.

Cl. butyricum catalyzes Reaction I, which is stimulated by Fe^{++}.[51] The relationship of Fe^{++} to ferredoxin, which acts as hydrogen acceptor in several other clostridia, remains to be elucidated. A reversal of the cleavage of pyruvate in *C. butyricum* was demonstrated[52] in the presence of hydrosulfite, CO_2, and acetyl phosphate. With acetyl phosphate labeled at carbon 1 or with radioactive bicarbonate, the formation of pyruvate was shown by isolation of the radio-

[46] L. P. Hager, D. M. Geller, and F. Lipmann, *FP* **13**, 734 (1954).

[47] M. F. Utter and C. H. Werkman, *ABB* **2**, 491 (1943).

[48] H. Chantrenne and F. Lipmann, *JBC* **187**, 757 (1950).

[49] H. J. Strecker, *JBC* **189**, 815 (1951).

[50] N. G. McCormick, E. J. Ordal, and H. R. Whiteley, *J. Bacteriol.* **83**, 887 (1962).

[51] D. J. O'Kane, *FP* **13**, 739 (1954).

[52] R. P. Mortlock and R. S. Wolfe, *JBC* **234**, 1657 (1959).

active dinitrophenyl hydrazone derivative. The requirement for hydrosulfite for the synthesis of pyruvate is of particular interest in view of the recent observation that hydrosulfite reduces ferredoxin. The reversal of the phosphoroclastic reaction in the presence of hydrosulfite may prove of considerable value in future studies on the mechanism of this reaction.

Another significant observation is that pyruvate utilization was lost when preparations were fractionated with 2-propanol, and that activity could be restored by addition of methyl viologen.[53]

The most important recent development has emerged from a study of nitrogen fixation in *Cl. pasteurianum*, in which the phosphoroclastic reaction was implicated.[5,54,55] Nitrogen fixation in this organism required the oxidation of pyruvate, which served as hydrogen and energy donor. At least four proteins and two cofactors participate in the formation of acetyl phosphate, H_2, and CO_2 from pyruvate in this microorganism. The cofactors are thiamine pyrophosphate and CoA; the proteins are pyruvate dehydrogenase, ferredoxin, phosphotransacetylase, and hydrogenase. Various SH compounds can serve as acyl acceptor instead of phosphate, but catalytic amounts of CoA are still required.

Ferredoxin acts as an electron carrier in pyruvate oxidation not only in several clostridia but also in *M. lactilyticus, P. elsendii, Butyribacterium rettgeri*, and others.[56]

Ferredoxin is a new electron carrier which contains neither heme nor flavin, but contains about 0.8 μmole of Fe per milligram of protein. Its absorption maxima in the oxidized state are at 280, 310, and 388 mμ. It is reduced by either sodium hydrosulfite or by H_2 in the presence of hydrogenase; reduction gives rise to reversible bleaching of the color.

[53] R. P. Mortlock, R. C. Valentine, and R. S. Wolfe, *JBC* **234,** 1653 (1959).

[54] J. E. Carnahan and J. E. Castle, *Ann. Rev. Plant Physiol.* **14,** 125 (1963).

[55] L. E. Mortenson, R. C. Valentine, and J. E. Carnahan, *BBRC* **7,** 448 (1962).

[56] R. C. Valentine, R. L. Jackson, and R. S. Wolfe, *BBRC* **7,** 453 (1962).

The potential of crystalline ferredoxin[57] has been determined and $E_{o'} = -417$, mv at pH 7.55, very close to the hydrogen electrode. The molecular weight has been tentatively given the value of 12,000; thus 1 mole of ferredoxin contains about 10 atoms of iron.

Since phosphotransacetylase is readily demonstrable in extracts of *Cl. pasteurianum*,[57] the over-all reaction of pyruvate cleavage in the phosphoroclastic reaction can be written as shown in Scheme 6.1. The first step is analogous to that

Step   I $CH_3COCOOH$ + E—thiamine pyrophosphate $\rightarrow$ Active
           acetaldehyde thiamine pyrophosphate—E + CO_2

Step II   Active acetaldehyde thiamine pyrophosphate—E +
           ferredoxin$_{ox}$ + CoA $\rightarrow$ Acetyl—CoA + ferredoxin$_{red}$

$$\text{Step III} \quad \text{Ferredoxin}_{red} + 2H^+ \xrightarrow{\text{hydrogenase}} \text{Ferredoxin}_{ox} + H_2$$

$$\text{Step IV} \quad \text{Acetyl CoA} + P_i \xrightarrow{\text{phosphotransacetylase}} \text{Acetyl phosphate} + \text{CoA}$$

Scheme 6.1

Phosphoroclastic Reaction of Pyruvate

catalyzed by pyruvate dehydrogenase, which was discussed in Lecture 4. Direct evidence for the formation of enzyme-bound α-hydroxyethyl thiamine pyrophosphate in this system is not available, however. In the second step, ferredoxin accepts the electrons and CoA accepts the acyl group. It is not yet clear whether the dehydrogenase and carboxylase are separable entities or are linked by peptide bonds in a double-headed enzyme. Since the reduction of ferredoxin is CoA-dependent, it is conceivable that an interaction between CoA and ferredoxin takes place prior to transfer of hydrogen to ferredoxin and the acyl group to CoA. Alternatively, an acetyl thiamine pyrophosphate intermediate may be formed in a primary step of electron transfer to ferredoxin. This reaction cannot proceed further until a suitable acyl acceptor,

[57] K. Tagawa and D. I. Arnon, *Nature* **195,** 537 (1962).

such as CoA, is provided. The last two steps in the phosphoroclastic reaction are catalyzed by ferredoxin and hydrogenase and can be reproduced in simpler systems with hydrosulfite as reductant.

Valentine *et al.*[56] have shown that ferredoxin serves as an electron acceptor in *M. lactilyticus* in the oxidation of hypoxanthine as well as of pyruvate and α-ketoglutarate. Ferredoxin also catalyzes the reduction of hydroxylamine and nitrate to ammonia, and it has been reported[58] to act as electron carrier in the following reductions: 2,4-dinitrophenol to 2-amino,4-nitrophenol; sulfite to dithionite; selenite to selenium; tellurite to tellurium; vanadate to vanadyl; arsenate to arsenite; and Mo^{6+} to Mo^{5+}.

A close relationship has been observed[57,59] between ferredoxin and photosynthetic pyridine nucleotide reductase (PPNR), the electron carrier in chloroplasts. It is apparent, however, that these two catalysts are not identical or completely interchangeable; e.g., in the reduction of TPN by hydrogen or in the reduction of nitrite of hydroxylamine, ferredoxin appears 10 times as active as PPNR, on a molar basis.

PHOSPHOROLYSIS OF A C—N BOND

Like the phosphoroclastic reactions of C—C and C—S bonds, the phosphorolysis of a C—N bond results in the formation of an acyl phosphate, which donates the phosphate to ADP to form ATP.[60] The phosphorolysis of citrulline is an example; see Scheme 6.2(*a*). In the first step, carbamyl phosphate and ornithine are formed by phosphorolysis of citrulline. In the second step, the phosphate group is transferred from carbamyl phosphate to ADP, resulting in the formation of ammonia, CO_2, and ATP. Some streptococci contain large amounts of the enzyme which catalyzes the

[58] H. R. Whiteley and C. A. Woolfolk, *BBRC* **9**, 517 (1962).
[59] R. C. Valentine, W. J. Brill, R. S. Wolfe, and A. San Pietro, *BBRC* **10**, 73 (1963).
[60] E. Racker, *Advan. Enzymol.* **23**, 323 (1961).

phosphorolysis of citrulline, and can utilize this reaction for purposes of ATP production. However, in animals, the major function of this enzyme is in the favored reverse reaction, hence the name ornithine transcarbamylase. In *E. coli* also,

(a)   Step I (ornithine transcarbamylase)

$$
\begin{array}{c}
NH_2 \\
| \\
C{=}O \\
| \\
NH \\
| \\
(CH_2)_3 \\
| \\
CHNH_2 \\
| \\
COOH
\end{array}
\;+\; P_i \;\rightleftarrows\;
\begin{array}{c}
NH_2 \\
\diagup \\
C{=}O \\
\diagdown \\
OPO_3H_2
\end{array}
\;+\;
\begin{array}{c}
NH_2 \\
| \\
(CH_2)_3 \\
| \\
CHNH_2 \\
| \\
COOH
\end{array}
$$

Step II (acetokinase)

$$
\begin{array}{c}
NH_2 \\
\diagup \\
C{=}O \\
\diagdown \\
OPO_3H_2
\end{array}
\;+\; ADP \;\rightleftarrows\; NH_3 + CO_2 + ATP
$$

(b)

$$
\begin{array}{c}
NH_2 \\
| \\
C{=}O \\
| \\
NH \\
| \\
C{=}O \\
| \\
COOH
\end{array}
\;+\; P_i \;\rightleftarrows\;
\begin{array}{c}
NH_2 \\
\diagup \\
C{=}O \\
\diagdown \\
OPO_3H_2
\end{array}
\;+\;
\begin{array}{c}
NH_2 \\
| \\
C{=}O \\
| \\
COOH
\end{array}
$$

Scheme 6.2 ·

Phosphorolysis of Citrulline and Carbamyl Oxamate

the role of transcarbamylase is likely to be biosynthetic, as suggested by the repression of its formation when this organism is grown in the presence of arginine.[61]

Highly active preparations of ornithine transcarbamylase

[61] L. Gorini and W. K. Maas, *in* "The Chemical Basis of Development" (W. D. McElroy and B. Glass, eds.), p. 469. Johns Hopkins Press, Baltimore, 1958.

have been made from microorganisms[62] as well as from mammalian liver,[63,64] but little is known about its mode of action. Reichard could not detect a P_i-carbamyl phosphate exchange or an ornithine-C^{14}-citrulline exchange in the absence of the co-substrate. When arsenate was used instead of P_i, citrulline was completely hydrolyzed to ornithine, CO_2, and NH_3.

The second step is catalyzed by carbamate kinase. The reaction in the direction of ATP synthesis goes presumably via ammonium carbamate, which decomposes to ammonia and CO_2. Recent evidence suggests that carbamate kinase and acetokinase are identical.[65]

Valentine and Wolfe[66] have described the phosphorolysis of carbamyl oxamate to oxamate and carbamyl phosphate [Scheme 6.2(b)] as a step in the fermentation of allantoin in *Streptococcus allantoicus*. The enzyme has been partially purified and appears to require Mg^{++}.

The reaction catalyzed by tetrahydrofolate formylase[67] is used by some anaerobic microorganisms for energy production (Scheme 6.3). The reaction might be visualized as

$$10\text{—formyl tetrahydrofolate} + \text{ADP} + P_i \rightleftharpoons \text{formate} + \text{ATP} + \text{tetrahydrofolate}$$

Scheme 6.3

Reaction Catalyzed by Tetrahydrofolate Formylase

proceeding via a phosphorolysis of the C—N bond of the H—C—N group of formyl tetrahydrofolate to yield an enzyme-bound formyl phosphate, but no evidence of such a mechanism is available. Moreover, failure to demonstrate appreciable ADP formation from ATP in the presence of

[62] J. M. Ravel, M. L. Grona, J. S. Humphreys, and W. Shive, *JBC* **234,** 1452 (1959).
[63] P. Reichard, *Acta Chem. Scand.* **11,** 523 (1957).
[64] G. H. Burnett and P. P. Cohen, *JBC* **229,** 337 (1957).
[65] W. B. Novoa and S. Grisolia, *JBC* **237,** PC2710 (1962).
[66] R. C. Valentine and R. S. Wolfe, *BBRC* **2,** 384 (1960).
[67] R. H. Himes and J. C. Rabinowitz, *JBC* **237,** 2903, 2915 (1962).

either formate or tetrahydrofolate, as well as the absence
of a formate or tetrahydrofolate-dependent ADP-ATP exchange reaction, led Himes and Rabinowitz to postulate a
mechanism of a concerted reaction between enzyme-bound
ATP with formate and tetrahydrofolate. Unfortunately, at
present there are no approaches to the study of enzyme-
catalyzed concerted reactions. I propose that it is therefore
preferable to reject the formulation of such a mechanism,
although it may well be the correct one. It seems more fruitful to make a wrong hypothesis that possibly leads to good
experiments than a correct hypothesis that leads to none.
Evidence based primarily on exchange reactions is particularly vulnerable in view of experiments with, for example,
glyceraldehyde-3-phosphate dehydrogenase, which show that
DPN is required for the arsenolysis of 1,3-diphosphoglycerate
or even for the hydrolysis of acetyl phosphate. There is a
rapidly increasing literature on the effect of substrates, cofactors, and feedback inhibitors on the configuration of
proteins and alteration of their catalytic activity. These
effects should be explored before a concerted mechanism can
be accepted.

In this connection it may be appropriate to discuss briefly
two reactions that can be looked upon as cleavage of a C—N
bond by phosphate or pyrophosphate. The first one is cata-

(a)   Glutamate + ATP + NH$_3$ $\rightleftarrows$ glutamine + ADP + P$_i$

(b)   Citrulline + ATP + aspartate $\rightleftarrows$ argininosuccinate + AMP +
      pyrophosphate

Scheme 6.4

Reactions Catalyzed by Glutamine Synthetase
and by Argininosuccinate Synthetase

lyzed by glutamine synthetase, the second by argininosuccinate synthetase (Scheme 6.4). Meister[68] and his collaborators found that when glutamine synthetase (5 mg) was

[68] A. Meister, *in* "The Enzymes," 2nd ed. (P. D. Boyer *et al.*, eds.),
     Vol. 6, p. 443. Academic Press, New York, 1962.

incubated for 1 minute with C^{14}-L-glutamate, ATP, and Mg^{++}, and the mixture was heated for 1 minute at $55°$, pyrrolidone carboxylate was formed (Table 6.II). The appro-

TABLE 6.II

FORMATION OF PYRROLIDONE CARBOXYLATE
BY GLUTAMINE SYNTHETASE

	Pyrrolidone carboxylate formed ($m\mu$moles) with	
Reaction mixture	L-Glutamate	D-Glutamate
Glutamate, ATP, Mg^{++}, and enzyme	16.8	17.2
Glutamate, ATP, Mg^{++}, and boiled enzyme	0.7	0.5
Glutamate, Mg^{++}, and enzyme	0.5	0.2
Glutamate, ATP, and enzyme	0.7	0.5
Glutamate, ATP, and Mg^{++}	0.7	0.5
Glutamate, ATP, Mg^{++}, enzyme, and NH_4^+	0.6	4.3

priate controls were negative. These data represent evidence for a highly reactive enzyme-bound γ-glutamyl derivative that undergoes very rapid cyclization. The reaction was also observed with D-glutamate, but in the presence of ammonia only the L-glutamate was rapidly utilized for glutamine synthesis, indicating specificity at the second step (transfer to ammonia). Ultracentrifugation experiments indicated that ATP and Mg^{++} were required for binding of glutamate to the enzyme, and that binding and activation of glutamate were associated with cleavage of ATP to ADP and P_i. For the binding of glutamine to the enzyme, as well as for arsenolysis of glutamine, ADP and Mg^{++} were required. These findings are most readily interpreted in terms of an effect of the adenine nucleotide on the configuration of the enzyme, a conclusion supported by the relatively specific protection of the enzyme by ATP and Mg^{++} against heat denaturation.

The second example is the argininosuccinate synthetase, which also lacks significant PP-ATP or AMP-ATP exchange

reactions unless all the reactants of the system are present.[69]
The persevering search for partial reactions has recently been
successful[70] and this may help to eliminate another example
of C—N bond synthesis and cleavage by a concerted reaction.

There are several other reactions which may be classified
in this group: e.g., the cleavage of glycinamide ribotide.[71]
According to Lynen,[72] the reversible and ATP-linked carboxylation of biotin takes place at one of the ring nitrogens.
Thus the biotin and ATP-dependent carboxylation of
β-methyl crotonyl CoA and of propionyl CoA should be
included here. The decarboxylation of methyl malonyl CoA
has actually been shown to generate ATP, which was used
by hexokinase to phosphorylate glucose.[73] It should be reemphasized that although most of the previously mentioned
reactions proceed primarily in the biosynthetic direction,
they can be used for energy production under some circumstances in spite of an unfavorable equilibrium, as illustrated
by the example of ornithine transcarbamylase.

PHOSPHOROLYSIS OF THIOL ESTERS

The group of phosphoroclastic reactions (see Scheme 1.2)
includes the phosphorolysis of thiol esters, which has already
been discussed in connection with substrate level oxidative
phosphorylation. However, I should like to draw your attention to the ubiquitous distribution of glutathione and of
glyoxylase, which form thiol esters in the presence of naturally occurring ketoaldehydes. This might have tempted
nature to exploit and develop energy-yielding processes which
utilize thiol esters of glutathione. A search for enzymes of the
transacetylase type which utilize thiol esters of gluthione
rather than of CoA may therefore be rewarding. Weaver and

[69] O. Rochovansky and S. Ratner, *JBC* **236**, 2254 (1961).

[70] O. Rochovansky and S. Ratner, *FP*. In press (1965).

[71] J. M. Buchanan, *Harvey Lectures* **54**, 104 (1960).

[72] F. Lynen, *J. Cell. Comp. Physiol.* **54**, Suppl. 1, p. 33 (1959).

[73] A. Tietz and S. Ochoa, *JBC* **234**, 1394 (1959).

Lardy[74] have synthesized hydroxypyruvic aldehyde-3-phosphate and have found it to be readily converted, in the presence of GSH and glyoxalase I, to phosphoglycerylglutathione. However, all attempts to show that this thiol ester is utilized for ATP production have thus far been unsuccessful. We had made similar unsuccessful attempts to demonstrate phosphorolysis of lactyl glutathione, but as we all know, negative experiments do not mean too much, particularly when very active side reactions—e.g., those due to thiol esterases—are present.

DEHYDRATION OF 2-PHOSPHOGLY-
CERATE CATALYZED BY ENOLASE

Enolase catalyzes, in conjunction with pyruvate kinase, ATP formation from 2-phosphoglycerate, as illustrated in Scheme 6.5. Of particular significance is the fact, mentioned

$$\text{Step I} \quad \text{2-phosphoglycerate} \quad \overset{\text{enolase}}{\rightleftharpoons} \quad \text{phosphoenolpyruvate} + H_2O$$

$$\text{Step II} \quad \text{phosphoenolpyruvate} + \text{ADP} \quad \overset{\text{pyruvate kinase}}{\rightleftharpoons} \quad \text{pyruvate} + \text{ATP}$$

Scheme 6.5

ATP Synthesis by Enolase and Pyruvate Kinase

previously, that this is the only known reaction in which attachment of the transferable phosphate group takes place before the oxidation-reduction step.

Enolase has been subjected to very extensive analysis.[75] The protein consists of a single peptide chain with alanine as the NH_2-terminal amino acid. It contains no cystine or cysteine; all eight sulfur atoms are accounted for by the

[74] R. H. Weaver and H. A. Lardy, *JBC* **236**, 313 (1961).
[75] B. G. Malmström, J. R. Kimmel, and E. L. Smith, *JBC* **234**, 1108 (1959).

presence of methionine. This finding explains the complete resistance of this enzyme to inhibitors known to react with SH groups. The crystalline enzyme contains no phosphorus and no hexosamine. The molecular weight is 67,000, in agreement with the complete amino acid analysis, leaving little room for any additional cofactor. A thorough kinetic analysis of the interaction of substrate and metal ions with enolase has been carried out by Wold and Ballou.[76] Some of the properties of the enzyme, as well as the response to photo-oxidation studied by Brake and Wold,[77] suggest that histidine may be associated with the active site. However, structural changes of the protein that may accompany destruction of histidine considerably complicate interpretation of such data.

I should like to close the subject of soluble enzymes that catalyze the formation of ATP with a brief discussion of a phenomenon that was observed at the time of the discovery of enolase.[78] It was found that enolase was inhibited by low concentrations of sodium fluoride, provided that inorganic phosphate was present. Warburg and Christian crystallized the enzyme from yeast, and in classical studies elucidated the fluoride inhibition.[79] It appears that magnesium, fluoride, and phosphate interact together on the enzyme surface to form an inhibited enzyme complex. The fluoride inhibition of enolase in the presence of phosphate is so characteristic that this inhibitor can be used as a relatively specific tool for the interruption of glycolysis at the enolase site, in spite of the fact that other enzymes requiring Mg^{++} are susceptible, even within the glycolytic chain, to fluoride at high concentrations. We encountered a similar situation earlier, in the high susceptibility of DPN-glyceraldehyde-3-phosphate dehydrogenase to iodoacetate (but not to iodoacetamide). From intensive studies of enzymes as catalysts and as reactants, each one of them emerges as an individual protein with characteristic features, with preferences and idiosyncrasies

[76] F. Wold and C. E. Ballou, *JBC* **227**, 313 (1957).
[77] J. M. Brake and F. Wold, *BBA* **40**, 171 (1960).
[78] K. Lohmann and O. Meyerhof, *BZ* **273**, 60 (1934).
[79] O. Warburg and W. Christian, *BZ* **310**, 384 (1941).

for substrates and inhibitors respectively. As a result of this knowledge, there has been a slow but steady increase in the availability of relatively specific inhibitors. With the more selective and cautious use of inhibitors, they have become increasingly useful tools for studies of the active site of enzymes. When we discuss rate-limiting steps in intact cells, we shall again discover the need and usefulness of specific metabolic inhibitors, and we shall return to glyceraldehyde-3-phosphate dehydrogenase and enolase.

PART II

Formation of Adenosine Triphosphate in Particulate Systems

LECTURE 7

OXIDATIVE PHOSPHORYLATION IN MITOCHONDRIA

Seek simplicity and then distrust it.

—A. N. Whitehead

Phosphorylation linked to electron transport processes in the Krebs cycle is commonly referred to as oxidative phosphorylation. I shall follow this custom, but not without emphasizing once more that in substrate level phosphorylation and photophosphorylation also, the energy of oxidative processes is used to generate ATP.

STAGES OF DISCOVERY

I should like to give you a brief outline of the history of discoveries in the area of oxidative phosphorylation, which will serve as a gentle introduction to this complex problem. Four stages of development can be distinguished (Scheme 7.1), each of which lasted approximately 10 years. We are

Stage 1.	Recognition of the phenomenon
Stage 2.	Quantitative evaluations
Stage 3.	Localization of sites
Stage 4.	Resolution and reconstitution

Scheme 7.1

History of the Study of Oxidative Phosphorylation

now in the fourth stage, and if we continue to follow this pattern in the future, the major problems in oxidative phosphorylation should be solved by 1969.

The first stage—recognition of the existence of the phenomenon—started in 1930 with the studies of Engelhardt,[80] who recognized with remarkable insight the relationship between the processes of oxidation and phosphorylation. The next breakthrough came with the discovery by Kalckar, in 1937 and 1939, of respiration-dependent formation of ATP in cell-free preparations.[81]

The second stage, that of quantative evaluations, began with the studies by Belitzer and Tsibakova[82] with minced muscle, and by Ochoa[83] with cell-free brain and heart preparations. These investigators observed that close to 2 moles of phosphate were esterfied per atom of oxygen consumed. In classical studies, Ochoa evaluated the quantitative relationship between oxidation and phosphorylation. He recognized that the presence of ATPase interfered with accurate determination of a P:O ratio. He therefore used the ingenious device of generating ATP with glycolytic enzymes in the

TABLE 7.I

QUANTITATIVE EVALUATION OF OXIDATIVE PHOSPHORYLATION

	P:O Ratio	
Reaction	Observed	Corrected
Pyruvate $+ 2\ H_2O + 2.5\ O_2 \rightarrow$ $3\ CO_2 + 4\ H_2O$	1.9	3.1
Glyceraldehyde 3-phosphate $+$ pyruvate $\rightarrow$ phosphoglycerate $+$ lactate	0.62	1.0

presence of fluoride and pyruvate as internal standard for the stability of ATP. The theoretical P:2H (P:lactate) ratio for this system is 1. The average value of 3 for the P:O ratio for the complete oxidation of pyruvate to CO_2 and water was thus calculated, as shown in Table 7.I. This quantitative evaluation of oxidative phosphorylation had four important

[80] W. A. Engelhardt, *BZ* **227**, 16 (1930); **251**, 343 (1932).

[81] H. Kalckar, *Enzymologia* **2**, 47 (1937); *BJ* **33**, 631 (1939).

[82] V. A. Belitzer and E. T. Tsibakova, *Biokhimiya* **4**, 516 (1939).

[83] S. Ochoa, *JBC* **138**, 751 (1941); **151**, 493 (1943).

consequences: (*a*) it permitted a clear differentiation between oxidative phosphorylation and the substrate level oxidative phosphorylation of glycolysis, which has a maximum P:2H ratio of 1; (*b*) it posed problems of thermodynamics and stimulated reevaluation of the free energy of ATP hydrolysis; (*c*) it indicated that phosphorylation was coupled to electron transport between DPNH and oxygen; and (*d*) it stimulated attempts to localize the individual sites of phosphorylation.

The next important event was the identification in Lehninger's laboratory of mitochondria as the subcellular structures in which oxidative phosphorylation took place. Intensive investigations on quantitative aspects with isolated mitochondria, carried out in the laboratories of Lardy, Lehninger, Hunter, Green, and Kielley, established that the oxidation of pyruvate to acetyl CoA, of isocitrate to α-ketoglutarate, and of malate to oxaloacetate, all have a P:O ratio of 3; that the oxidation of succinate to fumarate has a P:O ratio of 2; and that the oxidation of α-ketoglutarate to succinate has a ratio of 4. The last reaction includes the step of substrate level oxidative phosphorylation which we have discussed previously and which, in contrast to phosphorylation linked to electron transport, is not inhibited by dinitrophenol.

The third stage in the study of oxidative phosphorylation, the localization of sites, was initiated by Friedkin and Lehninger,[84] who demonstrated that phosphorylation is linked to electron transport from DPNH to oxygen in the absence of intermediates of the Krebs cycle. The success of these experiments was largely due to a very sensitive assay procedure with P_i^{32} and the use of highly purified preparations of DPNH. Very low P:O ratios were obtained, until it was discovered that mitochondria were not very permeable to DPNH. After they had been treated with hypotonic salt solution, DPNH entered readily and P:O ratios as high as 2.6 were obtained.[85,86]

[84] M. Friedkin and A. L. Lehninger, *JBC* **178**, 611 (1949); A. L. Lehninger, *ibid.* p. 625.

[85] A. L. Lehninger, *Harvey Lectures* **49**, 176 (1955).

[86] E. E. Jacobs and D. R. Sanadi, *JBC* **235**, 531 (1960).

The next step in site localization was to analyze the individual sites of phosphorylation in the chain of respiratory catalysts. Again it was Friedkin and Lehninger who began the analysis;[84] they showed that with P_i^{32}, the oxidation of ascorbate via cytochrome c in liver mitochondria leads to the formation of radioactive ATP. A few years later, Judah confirmed these findings, using unlabeled phosphate, and calculated a P:O ratio approaching unity.[87] He also eliminated the possibility that the oxidation of ascorbate itself beyond dehydroascorbate might have contributed to the phosphorylation process. Maley and Lardy found that adrenalin, as well as 3,4-dihydroxyphenylalanine, replaced ascorbate as the reductant in this reaction.[88] Finally, it was shown that the oxidation of chemically reduced cytochrome c added to the mitochondria was coupled to phosphorylation. This was demonstrated by Lehninger[85] and also by Slater.[89] The phosphorylation linked to this reaction was dinitrophenol-sensitive, and P:O ratios between 0.5 and 0.8 were obtained with liver mitochondria and somewhat lower ones with heart sarcosomes. As in the case of DPNH, the utilization of the external reduced cytochrome c required pretreatment of the mitochrondria with hypotonic solutions. These studies firmly established a site of oxidative phosphorylation between cytochrome c and oxygen, which we refer to as phosphorylating Site 3 (see Scheme 1.5).

Site 1 was explored experimentally by Copenhaver and Lardy,[90] who demonstrated that phosphorylation occurred between DPNH as hydrogen donor and ferricyanide as acceptor. These experiments were carried out in the presence of antimycin A, which blocked the oxidation via the cytochrome system. Site 2 was established in experiments conducted by Slater,[91] in which cytochrome c was used as a hydrogen acceptor. With succinate as substrate, one phos-

[87] J. D. Judah, *BJ* **49**, 271 (1951).

[88] G. F. Maley and H. A. Lardy, *JBC* **210**, 903 (1954).

[89] E. C. Slater, *Proc. 3rd Intern. Congr. Biochem., Brussels, 1955* p. 264. Academic Press, New York, 1956.

[90] J. H. Copenhaver, Jr., and H. A. Lardy, *JBC* **195**, 225 (1952).

[91] E. C. Slater, *BJ* **59**, 392 (1955).

phorylation was coupled to this reaction. With substrates linked to DPN, such as β-hydroxybutyrate, P:O ratios as high as 1.8 were obtained.

Between 1955 and 1960, some physical separation of the sites was obtained by various methods of disintegrating mitochondria. Later, a more detailed description will be given of the way in which treatment with chemicals (digitonin and ethanol) and with physical methods (sonic oscillation and mechanical breakage with glass beads) yielded submitochondrial particles which were partially defective in one or two of the phosphorylation sites.

The fourth and latest stage of discovery, involving the resolution and reconstitution of oxidative phosphorylation, started with the separation of soluble proteins which were required for the phosphorylation process in submitochondrial particles. These experiments had been foreshadowed by the pioneering work of Pinchot with bacterial systems, which yielded the first partial resolution of oxidative phosphorylation. During the past few years, there has been a steady flow of reports [60,92-97] on various soluble factors and intermediates, all said to be related to oxidative phosphorylation, and "confusion now hath made his masterpiece."[98] Fortunately, however, the fog that had settled down upon us, with all the preliminary and too-preliminary communications, now seems to be slowly lifting.

MITOCHONDRIAL ENZYMES

Mitochondria are generally considered to be the residence of the enzymes of the Krebs cycle and of oxidative phos-

[92] M. E. Pullman, H. S. Penefsky, A. Datta, and E. Racker, *JBC* **235,** 3322 (1960).

[93] H. S. Penefsky, M. E. Pullman, A. Datta, and E. Racker, *JBC* **235,** 3330 (1960).

[94] A. W. Linnane and E. B. Titchener, *BBA* **39,** 469 (1960).

[95] A. L. Lehninger, *FP* **19,** 952 (1960).

[96] G. B. Pinchot, *JBC* **205,** 65 (1953); **229,** 1 and 25 (1957).

[97] A. L. Lehninger and C. L. Wadkins, *Ann. Rev. Biochem.* **31,** 47 (1962).

[98] W. Shakespeare, *"Macbeth,"* Act II, iii, 72.

phorylation. This view requires two qualifications: first, oxidative ATP formation has been reported to occur in other organized structures, such as the nuclei;[99] and second, some of the enzymes of the Krebs cycle are abundant outside of the mitochondria. Regarding the first point, it should be recognized that nuclear ATP formation is, from a quantitative point of view, a minor process.[99] It may be of the utmost importance for biosynthetic processes in the nuclei, but it cannot be considered a major contributor to the energy pool of the cell. Moreover, the process is not well enough characterized to warrant discussion of the mechanism, and is still referred to as "oxygen-dependent ATP synthesis" in preference to "oxidative phosphorylation." The process shows some striking similarities to oxidative phosphorylation; for example, its susceptibility to uncoupling agents such as dinitrophenol, sodium azide, dicoumarol, and others; but there are also some important differences, such as its resistance to other uncoupling agents—Ca^{++}, for instance, methylene blue, and histones.[100] These distinctions are rather important in view of the well-recognized problem of the contamination of nuclei by mitochondria and mitochondrial fragments. Perhaps it would be appropriate to suggest that future studies should include comparisons not only with intact mitochondria but with mitochondrial fragments, since curious differences in susceptibility of various submitochondrial particles have been observed, e.g., in response to Ca^{++} or thyroxine. On the other hand, the permeability properties of nuclei with regard to external adenine nucleotides seems to set them clearly apart from mitochondrial fragments.

Two other aspects of nuclear ATP formation are of considerable interest. One is the stimulation of phosphorylation by polymeric anions;[99] the other is the observation that nuclear ATP production is restricted to tissues that are radiosensitive, such as the thymus, spleen, and intestine.[101] More-

[99] V. G. Allfrey and A. E. Mirsky, *Proc. Natl. Acad. Sci. U. S.* **43,** 589 (1957); **44,** 981 (1958).

[100] B. S. McEwen, V. G. Allfrey, and A. E. Mirsky, *JBC* **238,** 758 (1963).

[101] W. A. Creasey and L. A. Stocken, *BJ* **72,** 519 (1959).

over, the phosphorylation process itself is reported to be highly sensitive to relatively low doses of X-radiation. Confirmation and further elucidation of these important findings are needed.

The presence of enzymes of the Krebs cycle outside the mitochondria constitutes a puzzling problem. For example, over 80% of the aconitase activity is found in the soluble fraction.[102] When an investigator makes such an observation he is plagued by the question of its meaning. Are there two enzymes, one inside and one outside the mitochondria, or is there only one mitochondrial enzyme, which has leaked out in the course of preparing the particles? This problem of enzyme localization is a very broad and difficult one. We encounter it with chloroplasts, microsomes, and all other intracellular structures of the cell. Are the isolated structures intact? Are they pure? Or are they mixtures of particles compounded with absorbed impurities of so-called soluble enzymes? Are the soluble enzymes themselves only readily released components of fragile compartments of intracellular structures? In other words, is our method of fractionation like the clumsy undertaking of a car mechanic who attempts to use his crude tools to analyze a watch? I believe that it is almost as bad as that. Nevertheless, we have no alternative and must hope that our tools will become refined as we proceed in the analysis. Meanwhile we have to look out for the signs that guide us in the right direction; we must try to correlate the experimental findings obtained with cell-free systems with the complex physiology of the cell; we must keep in view the metabolic "Gestalt" of the cell; and finally, we must "seek simplicity and then distrust it."

With these generalities in mind, let us return to the specific example of extramitochondrial aconitase. We cannot decide at present whether it is an artifact of preparation or not. But we can ask some pertinent questions that may be answered by properly designed experiments. Is there enough aconitase left in the mitochondria after our isolation procedure to account for the oxidative processes of the intact cell? If so,

[102] S. R. Dickman and J. F. Speyer, *JBC* **206**, 67 (1954).

could we detect, in the pattern of oxidative behavior of the
isolated particles, an alteration indicating a partial depletion
of aconitase? Can we conceive of mechanisms by which the
extramitochondrial enzyme participates in intramitochondrial events, and can we explore this possibility experimentally? What are the arguments for or against leakage of
aconitase from mitochondria? In a review, Schneider pointed
out[103] that since small molecules such as nucleotides and
citrate are kept within mitochondria during isolation, it
seems unlikely that large molecules such as aconitase should
leak out. This argument, although persuasive, is not decisive,
in view of the well-known specificity of cellular membranes
with respect to permeability, even for small ions such as
sodium and potassium. On the other hand, the fact that
citrate rather than any other Krebs cycle intermediate is
found in mitochondria might be interpreted in favor of a low
aconitase in mitochondria. But can we be certain that this
accumulation of citrate is not an artifact that was created
during isolation, just because aconitase leaks out preferentially? Endogenous substrate is known to be present in
mitochondria, and even in the cold it may be metabolized and
accumulate as citrate if aconitase is limiting.

An argument in favor of the existence of extramitochondrial enzymes of the Krebs cycle is based on the fact that
properties of the soluble enzymes differ from those of the
mitochondrial enzymes. This argument may be very valid if
it is properly documented, as in the case of the malate dehydrogenases,[104-106] but it happens to be indecisive with
respect to aconitase. The soluble extramitochondrial enzyme
exhibits a single optimum at pH 7.3, whereas mitochondrial
aconitase exhibits an additional optimum at pH 5.8. However, when the mitochondrial enzyme is solubilized it also
exhibits only the pH 7.3 optimum. There are several examples
of altered properties of enzymes after separation from the

[103] W. C. Schneider, *Advan. Enzymol.* **21**, 1 (1959).
[104] A. Delbrück, E. Zebe, and T. Bücher, *BZ* **331**, 273 (1959).
[105] T. Wieland, G. Pfleiderer, I. Haupt, and W. Wörner, *BZ* **332**, 1
(1959).
[106] L. Siegel and S. Englard, *BBA* **64**, 101 (1962).

cellular structure in which they normally reside. For example, ATPase in mitochondria is very sensitive to oligomycin, whereas the soluble ATPase obtained from the mitochondria is completely resistant to oligomycin; a factor is present in mitochondria which confers oligomycin sensitivity on soluble ATPase.[107] Another example is cytochrome *b*, which exhibits a much lower potential within mitochondria than after isolation. However, when cytochrome *b* is added to a structural protein isolated from mitochondria, the adsorbed pigment exhibits a potential similar to that observed in intact mitochondria.[108] Another example of the modification of the activity of an enzyme due to combination with a structural protein is myosin. The ATPase activity of myosin A is inhibited by Mg^{++}, whereas in combination with actin the enzyme is stimulated by Mg^{++}.[109] Cytochrome *c* is protected against interaction with ascorbate as long as the protein is attached to mitochondria.[110] These examples illustrate the fact that association with structure may not only influence the kinetic properties of an enzyme, but may alter its response to a cofactor or an inhibitor, sometimes imparting resistance as in the case of cyanide, sometimes imparting sensitivity as in the case of oligomycin. Although the possibility that aconitase may have leaked out of mitochondria during the preparative procedure has been left entirely open, a case can be made for a functional role of a naturally occurring extramitochondrial aconitase. It may act in conjunction with extramitochondrial isocitrate dehydrogenase, in a shuttle of tricarboxylic and dicarboxylic acids to and from mitochondria, to regulate the rate of oxidation. This type of mechanism would be similar to the shuttle of adenine nucleotide and phosphate ions that has been proposed for the regulation of glucose utilization; this mechanism will be discussed later. At the same time, these two enzymes may function, in cells that

[107] E. Racker, *BBRC* **10**, 435 (1963).
[108] R. S. Criddle, R. M. Bock, D. E. Green, and H. Tisdale, *Biochemistry* **1**, 827 (1962).
[109] W. W. Kielley, *in* "The Enzymes," 2nd ed. (P. D. Boyer *et al.*, eds.), Vol. 5, p. 159. Academic Press, New York, 1961.
[110] E. E. Jacobs and D. R. Sanadi, *BBA* **38**, 12 (1960).

do not have an adequate pentose phosphate cycle, as a reducing system for the extramitochondrial TPN which is required for several biosynthetic processes.

The existence of mitochondrial and extramitochondrial enzymes with different properties and amino acid composition has been well documented in the case of malate dehydrogenase.[104–106] On the basis of differences in inhibition due to the presence of excess substrates (malate or oxaloacetate) it has been suggested that the mitochondrial dehydrogenase is directed toward oxidation of malate, whereas the soluble enzyme is more effective in reducing oxaloacetate.[111] The purpose of the double location of these enzymes that catalyze identical reactions may be to operate yet another shuttle system, involving a hydrogen transport into mitochondria, which will be dealt with in the next lecture.

The organization of the material in the following lectures is guided by the experimental approach used in our laboratory, which aims at the resolution and characterization of the components of the oxidative and phosphorylating mechanism in the hope of an eventual reconstruction. This approach, which has been successful in studying glycolysis, the pentose phosphate cycle, and several other soluble multi-enzyme systems, has progressed at a snail's pace in studying oxidative phosphorylation. The respiratory and phosphorylating enzymes of mitochondria have been refractory to resolution because of their intimate relationship to each other in a complex lipoprotein structure which may be the very secret of the remarkably high efficiency and control of mitochondrial energy production. I shall not give a conventional description of the mitochondrial morphology just now; the discussion will start with the properties of the individual components and partial reactions that have been characterized. I do not wish to minimize the importance of morphological studies, but I feel that discussion of the relationship between structure and function is more appropriate in a lecture devoted to theories and speculations.

[111] N. O. Kaplan, *in* "Mechanism of Action of Steroid Hormones" (C. A. Villee and L. L. Engel, eds.), p. 247. Macmillan (Pergamon), New York, 1961.

LECTURE 8

THE RESPIRATORY CHAIN

When the dust passes thou wilt see whether thou ridest a horse or an ass.
—Oriental proverb

The respiratory chain in mitochondria will be discussed first without specific consideration of the phosphorylation process. The donors that feed hydrogen atoms into the respiratory chain are nutrients that are degraded by the cell to pyruvate, fatty acids, or amino acids. These compounds are converted to acetyl CoA, oxaloacetate, or α-ketoglutarate, and channeled into a pathway where they are subjected to the well-known intramolecular acrobatics of the Krebs cycle. These complex structural rearrangements of carbon atoms have one purpose: the efficient withdrawal of electron pairs so that they enter the respiratory chain and proceed stepwise through multiple carriers to oxygen, the terminal electron sink. This is a rigidly controlled process and permits the efficient conservation of metabolically utilizable energy which is produced during oxidation. The respiratory chain consists of proteins with firmly bound prosthetic groups, such as the iron porphyrins and flavin nucleotides. In addition, mitochondria contain cofactors, such as pyridine nucleotides and quinones, that can be reversibly removed from the particles. The absorption spectra of the protein-bound prosthetic groups and cofactors change on reduction and are sufficiently different from each other to permit individual measurements even in intact cells. Differences are particularly apparent at liquid nitrogen temperature, which gives rise to a sharpening of the absorption bands. In discussing the respiratory catalysts, historical details and characterization that may be found in textbooks and reviews will be avoided. The discussion will be restricted to properties that seem relevant to the function of these catalysts in oxidative phosphorylation.

CYTOCHROMES a AND a_3

There is considerable controversy regarding the existence of two cytochrome a pigments and the role of copper. The evidence that cytochromes a and a_3 exist as separate entities rests mainly on spectroscopic (reactivity with cyanide and carbon monoxide) and kinetic differentiation. Recent evidence [112,113] leaves little doubt regarding two distinct spectrophotometric entities, but a physical separation of the two components has not been achieved. Highly purified oxidase was found to be a pentamer of subunits with a molecular weight of 72,000 containing 1 heme a, 1 copper, and 1 iron per mole.[114,115] However, the monomer, which was obtained by treatment of the oxidase with thioglycolate and dodecyl sulfate, was inactive. If attempts at the physical separation of cytochrome a and cytochrome a_3 remain fruitless, it might be suggested that polymerization of the inactive monomers containing hemin a gives rise to the active polymer of cytochrome oxidase. This type of polymerization may be responsible for the formation of the site a_3. That a new active center with an altered reactivity to substrate can be formed due to polymerization of subunits is well known from studies on phosphorylase and glutamate dehydrogenase.

Evidence for one tightly-bound copper per mole of heme a is being consolidated.[116,117] Copper was shown to be reduced by cytochrome c and oxidized by air and gave characteristic EPR signals.

Phospholipids are present in cytochrome oxidase prepara-

---

[112] T. Yonetani, *JBC* **235**, 845 (1960); **236**, 1680 (1961).

[113] S. Horie and M. Morrison, *JBC* **238**, 1855 (1963).

[114] K. S. Ambe and A. Venkataraman, *BBRC* **1**, 133 (1959).

[115] R. S. Criddle and R. M. Bock, *BBRC* **1**, 138 (1959).

[116] H. Beinert, D. E. Griffiths, D. C. Wharton, and R. H. Sands, *JBC* **237**, 2337 (1962).

[117] M. Morrison, S. Horie, and H. S. Mason, *JBC* **238**, 2220 (1963).

tions and influence the catalytic activity. The role of phospholipids will be discussed later.

CYTOCHROME *c*

Cytochrome *c* is the best characterized of the cytochromes and has been crystallized from several sources by Okunuki and his co-workers. It has a molecular weight of 13,000 and it is located functionally between cytochrome c_1 and cytochrome *a*. Since cytochrome *c* can be extracted from mitochondria as a lipid complex, the question has been raised whether the purified water-soluble cytochrome *c* represents a degraded form of the native protein. It is important, therefore, to emphasize that cytochrome *c* can be removed from liver mitochondria after treatment with hypotonic salt solutions, and that oxidative phosphorylation can be restored to the mitochondria by adding small amounts of water-soluble cytochrome *c*.[86] The efficiency of utilization of the added cytochrome *c* is in fact quite remarkable, since in many other cases the reassociation of a catalytic component with the parent structure, or even of a coenzyme with its apoenzymes (e.g., transketolase and thiamine pyrophosphate), is a sluggish process at dilute concentrations. It is usually necessary to add the agent at relatively high concentrations in order to obtain rapid recombination.

CYTOCHROME c_1

Cytochrome c_1 is assigned a position between cytochromes *b* and *c* in the respiratory chain.[118] The purified preparation, isolated either as a lipoprotein or free of lipid, did not replace cytochrome *c* in several systems; e.g., succinate oxidase or DPNH-cytochrome *c* reductase.[119] The isolated cytochrome c_1 had a molecular weight of 360,000, and it was cleaved in the presence of Triton X-100 and thioglycolate into single heme-containing units of a molecular weight of about

[118] I. Sekuzu, Y. Orii, and K. Okunuki, *J. Biochem. (Tokyo)* **48**, 214 (1960).

[119] D. E. Green, J. Järnefelt, and H. D. Tisdale, *BBA* **31**, 34 (1959).

51,000.[108] Since detergents were used in the initial extraction of cytochrome c_1, it is not known whether it exists within the respiratory chain as a monomer or a polymer.

CYTOCHROME b

Cytochrome b, the next catalyst in the chain, has been quite controversial. Purified preparations of cytochrome b have been obtained by various procedures, including enzymic digestion of particles and the use of detergents.[120] Unlike cytochrome c_1, whose very existence was at first doubted, cytochrome b has been known for a long time. However, its participation in the main respiratory chain has been challenged in view of its sluggish reactivity in Keilin-Hartree preparations, which are rather harshly treated particles obtained from heart mitochondria. In contrast to these particles, and to liver mitochondria that had been exposed to hypotonic solutions, freshly isolated mitochondria were shown to include cytochrome b as a respiratory catalyst in oxidative phosphorylation.[121] It was proposed that mistreatment of the particles results in a dislodging of cytochrome b from the main pathway with substitution of an alternative electron pathway which must be considered an artifact. More of this later.

Cytochrome b_5 will not be discussed, since it does not appear to be in the major pathway. However, it appears to be present in mitochondria,[122] not merely as a contaminant from microsomes but as a participant in another alternative pathway, the so-called "external pathway" of DPNH oxidation which is not linked to phosphorylation processes.

FLAVOPROTEINS

The next enzymes in the respiratory chain are the flavoproteins. In the chain of succinate oxidation there is succinate

[120] R. Goldberger, A. L. Smith, H. Tisdale, and R. Bomstein, *JBC* **236**, 2788 (1961).

[121] B. Chance and G. R. Williams, *JBC* **217**, 409 (1955).

[122] I. Raw, N. Petragnani, and O. C. Nogueira, *JBC* **235**, 1517 (1960).

dehydrogenase, and in the chain of DPNH oxidation there is DPNH dehydrogenase, both of which transfer electrons to cytochrome *b*. These two flavoproteins have been obtained from mitochondria in a highly purified state.[123] Without going into great detail, I should like to point again to the numerous indications that some properties of the highly purified enzymes are at variance with the properties of the catalysts in the intact respiratory chain. Of particular interest are the observations that relatively minor differences in extraction procedure (e.g., whether the enzyme is extracted at 30° or at 37°) profoundly alter the interaction of the protein with different electron acceptors.[124,125] Such experiments, as well as reconstruction experiments,[126-128] help to elucidate the relationship between the structure and function of the respiratory enzymes. Highly purified DPNH dehydrogenase from mitochondria is not inhibited by antimycin A,[129] whereas the oxidation of DPNH in mitochondria is highly sensitive to this agent. This is not just a difference between the soluble and the particulate enzyme, since antimycin sensitivity is lost in mitochondria exposed to hypotonic solutions at pH 6.0. What is particularly significant is that sensitivity to antimycin can be restored by readjustments in pH and ionic strength of the medium; and that the capacity of the mitochondria to couple phosphorylation to oxidation of DPNH is lost and regained parallel to antimycin A sensitivity.[86]

PYRIDINE NUCLEOTIDES

Diphosphopyridine nucleotide is the first hydrogen acceptor in electron transport. Although its molecular weight

[123] T. P. Singer, E. B. Kearney, and V. Massey, *Advan. Enzymol.* **18,** 65 (1957).
[124] T. E. King and R. L. Howard, *BBA* **59,** 489 (1962).
[125] H. Watari, E. B. Kearney, T. P. Singer, D. Basinski, J. Hauber, and C. J. Lusty, *JBC* **237,** PC1731 (1962).
[126] D. E. Green, *Discussions Faraday Soc.* **27,** 206 (1959).
[127] D. Keilin and T. E. King, *Proc. Roy. Soc.* **B152,** 163 (1960).
[128] Y. Hatefi, *in* "The Enzymes," 2nd ed. (P. D. Boyer *et al.*, eds.), Vol. 7, p. 495. Academic Press, New York, 1963.
[129] S. Minakami, T. Cremona, R. L. Ringler, and T. P. Singer, *JBC* **238,** 1529 (1963).

is small, it is retained by the mitochondria during the isolation and washing procedures, which take place in an isotonic
medium. It can be removed from mitochondria by special
procedures such as exposure to inorganic phosphate, which
also induces swelling.[130,131] Either DPN or DPNH can be
reincorporated into these depleted mitochondria. Structural
integrity is thereby restored, together with the ability to
catalyze oxidative phosphorylation.[132,133] In the case of liver
mitochondria, the incorporation of DPN requires either ATP
or ethylenediamine tetraacetate together with glutamate. It
is rather curious that compounds such as inorganic triphosphate can substitute for ATP. If ATP is added to mitochondria some time before the DPN, the incorporation of the
pyridine nucleotide is actually prevented. It appears as if
ATP induces the mitochondria to close their doors to the
entrance of DPN. This is somewhat reminiscent of the behavior of ghosts of red blood cells, which can be induced by
ATP to close up and to incorporate into the cell relatively
large molecular compounds such as hemoglobin or hexokinase.[134] Mitochondria that have been induced to incorporate
DPN retain it through several washing procedures as firmly
as freshly isolated mitochondria.[132,133]

The oxidation of DPNH added to freshly isolated mitochondria is not accompanied by phosphorylation unless the
mitochondria are pretreated in hypotonic solution. It appears,
therefore, that the shuttling of pyridine nucleotides in and
out of mitochondria is not a normal physiological process. In
spite of the fact that transhydrogenase is present in mitochondria, extramitochondrial DPNH or TPNH is not effectively utilized for energy production. This phenomenon can
be looked upon as a precautionary measure by nature to
preserve the important and multiple functions of extra-

[130] J. Raaflaub, *Helv. Physiol. Pharmacol. Acta* **11,** 142 and 157 (1953).
[131] F. E. Hunter, Jr., and L. Ford, *JBC* **216,** 357 (1955).
[132] R. L. Lester and Y. Hatefi, *BBA* **29,** 103 (1958).
[133] F. E. Hunter, Jr., R. Malison, W. F. Bridgers, B. Schutz, and A.
      Atchison, *JBC* **234,** 693 (1959).
[134] J. F. Hoffman, *FP* **19,** 127 (1960), and personal communication
      (1961).

mitochondrial reduced pyridine nucleotides for the synthesis of fatty acids, the reduction of glutathione, detoxification mechanisms, etc. On the other hand, small penetrating substrates can overcome, at least partially, this apparent permeability barrier by participating in cyclic processes which may assume specific physiological roles. As shown in Scheme 8.1, such a cycle depends on an interplay of a DPN-linked

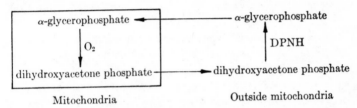

Over-all reaction: DPNH (glycolytic) + H^+ + O + 2ADP + P_i →
DPN + H_2O + 2ATP

Scheme 8.1

The α-Glycerophosphate Cycle

dehydrogenase which is outside of the mitochondria and which reduces a substrate with the aid of DPNH. The reduced substrate enters the mitochondria and is reoxidized by a mitochondrial enzyme that channels the electrons to molecular oxygen. The cycle illustrated in Scheme 8.1 has been called the α-glycerophosphate cycle, and was proposed to play an important role in activities, such as insect flight, that depend on the rapid production of energy.[135-137] The enzymes required for the operation of this cycle are indeed present in flight muscle in remarkably high amounts. On the other hand, the cycle cannot possibly operate as the major energy pathway in flight. Krimsky, in our laboratory, has calculated that if it were the major pathway, half of the total dry weight of the fly should accumulate as pyruvate after 5 minutes of flight. Kind-hearted Krimsky did not calculate

[135] E. Zebe, A. Delbrück, and T. Bücher, *Rona's Ber. Physiol.* **189,** 115 (1957).

[136] R. W. Estabrook and B. Sacktor, *JBC* **233,** 1014 (1958).

[137] M. Klingenberg and T. Bücher, *Ann. Rev. Biochem.* **29,** 669 (1960).

what would happen after 10 minutes of flight. Another fly in the ointment is that the α-glycerophosphate cycle as written does not produce CO_2, whereas measurements of the respiratory quotient during flight yield RQ values close to 1. Moreover, earlier measurements indicating rather low values for pyruvate oxidation have been replaced by more plausible ones, and the significance of the α-glycerophosphate cycle has been questioned.[138] It seems to me that the operation of the α-glycerophosphate cycle in conjunction with the Krebs cycle is exactly what is needed for the rapid production of energy. Glycolysis is dependent on the availability of DPN, and pyruvate is customarily written in the equation as hydrogen acceptor. However, lactate, the product of this reduction, must be reoxidized to pyruvate before entrance into the Krebs cycle. Such a procedure seems rather cumbersome compared to a coordinated operation of the α-glycerophosphate and Krebs cycles. Reduced DPN formed by the oxidation of glyceraldehyde 3-phosphate can be rapidly oxidized by the other half of the glucose molecule, dihydroxyacetone phosphate, in the presence of the potent α-glycerophosphate dehydrogenase. This step would have three important consequences. First, it would eliminate any lag in glycolysis due to lack of DPN. Second, it would yield α-glycerophosphate, which, in contrast to DPNH, can readily enter mitochondria and yield energy by oxidation. At the same time, dihydroxyacetone phosphate is returned to the system ready to accept hydrogen from DPNH, and when the appropriate steady state of this triose phosphate and pyruvate is reached, the entire glucose molecule becomes available for fermentation. Third, by having temporal priority in the utilization of DPNH, the α-glycerophosphate cycle serves as an important competitor for lactate dehydrogenase and thus helps to maintain a steady-state concentration of pyruvate for oxidation and energy production in the Krebs cycle.

Another cycle of this type was proposed by Devlin and Bedell[139] to overcome permeability problems of DPNH in

[138] S. G. Van den Bergh and E. C. Slater, *BJ* **82,** 362 (1962).
[139] T. M. Devlin and B. H. Bedell, *BBA* **36,** 564 (1959).

liver mitochondria. As shown in Scheme 8.2, β-hydroxy-butyrate and acetoacetate act as shuttle substrates in this cycle (DPN_M = mitochondrial DPN; DPN_G = glycolytic DPN). The authors visualized that DPNH and β-hydroxy-butyrate dehydrogenase reduced external acetoacetate to β-hydroxybutyrate; the latter entered the mitochondria and was oxidized by the respiratory chain to acetoacetate. They observed a four- to sixfold stimulation of the oxidation of added DPNH on addition of catalytic amounts of aceto-acetate to intact rat liver mitochondria. This oxidation of external DPNH was coupled to phosphorylation. However, Lehninger *et al.* have shown [140] that the β-hydroxybutyrate dehydrogenase of the intact mitochondria does not react with acetoacetate and DPNH, and no evidence for a soluble de-hydrogenase was obtained. Since Lehninger has found that hypotonicity or swelling agents such as GSH, inorganic phosphate, or thyroxine make at least some of the dehydro-genases available to the extramitochondrial substrates, he suggested that the acetoacetate–β-hydroxybutyrate shuttle may perhaps operate under certain physiological conditions when changes in mitochondrial permeability occur. However, since the swelling of mitochondria also changes the per-meability to DPNH, it is difficult to see what the additional function of the substrate cycle might be. Devlin agrees that there is no soluble β-hydroxybutyrate dehydrogenase which functions in this cycle, but his recent work suggests the presence of a β-hydroxybutyrate dehydrogenase on the sur-face of the mitochondria, which appears to have properties different from the well-known β-hydroxybutyrate dehydro-genase. It is quite apparent from these discussions that the β-hydroxybutyrate–acetoacetate cycle requires further work.

In the preceding lecture, it was mentioned that a cycle might be operative with mitochondrial and extramitochon-drial malate dehydrogenase.[111] A cycle with the aid of steroid dehydrogenase was invoked in the regulation of reduced and

[140] A. L. Lehninger, H. C. Sudduth, and J. B. Wise, *JBC* **235**, 2450 (1960).

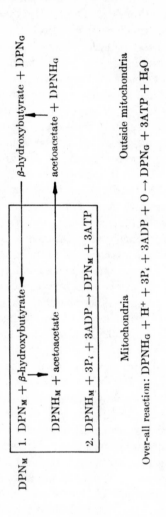

Scheme 8.2

The β-Hydroxybutyrate Cycle

oxidized nucleotides.[141] It would be of interest to learn what function the glycolate-glyoxalate cycle[142,143] fulfills in the physiology of plants. The oxidation of the reduced pyridine nucleotide accomplished by the reactions shown in Scheme 8.3 might be of particular interest in view of recent work by

$$Glycolate \longleftarrow Glycolate + TPN$$
$$\downarrow Oxidase \qquad\qquad \uparrow Dehydrogenase$$
$$Glyoxalate \longrightarrow Glyoxalate + TPNH$$

Over-all reaction: $TPNH + H^+ + O \rightarrow TPN + H_2O$

Scheme 8.3

Glycolate Cycle in Plants

Zelitch which points to a role of this cycle in the opening and closing of the stomata of green leaves.

Mitochondria contain a DPN-linked isocitrate dehydrogenase,[144] whereas most of the TPN-linked enzyme is found outside mitochondria. We mentioned in the last lecture how a substrate shuttle might be operative, in conjunction with extramitochondrial aconitase, that could function in TPN reduction. Heart mitochondria do not readily oxidize externally added citrate, but oxidize α-ketoglutarate.[145] Thus an extramitochondrial oxidation of citrate to α-ketoglutarate could provide TPNH for heart muscle, which is low in glucose-6-phosphate dehydrogenase.

UBIQUINONE-COENZYME Q

When ubiquinone-coenzyme Q_{10} (hereafter referred to as "Q_{10}") was discovered in large amounts in mitochondria,[146,147]

[141] P. Talalay and H. G. Williams-Ashman, *Recent Prog. Hormone Res.* **16,** 1 (1960).

[142] I. Zelitch and S. Ochoa, *JBC* **201,** 707 (1953).

[143] I. Zelitch, *JBC* **234,** 3077 (1959).

[144] G. W. E. Plaut and S. C. Sung, *JBC* **207,** 305 (1954).

[145] G. W. E. Plaut and K. A. Plaut, *JBC* **199,** 141 (1952).

[146] R. A. Morton, *CIBA Found. Symp., Quinones in Electron Transport, 1960* p. 5 (1961).

[147] D. E. Green, *CIBA Found. Symp., Quinones in Electron Transport, 1960* p. 130 (1961).

the interest of biochemists shifted from the possible role of vitamin K in respiration to the possible function of Q_{10}. The structure of this quinone[148], with 10 isoprenoid residues in the side chain, is as follows:

$$CH_3O \underset{O}{\overset{O}{\bigcirc}} CH_3 \quad \begin{bmatrix} CH_2-CH=\overset{CH_3}{\underset{|}{C}}-CH_3 \end{bmatrix}_{10} H$$

Similar quinones with varying isoprenoid residues have been found ubiquitously distributed in nature. A quinone with 6 isoprenoid residues is found in yeast and its chemical synthesis has been accomplished.[149]

The role of Q_{10} in electron transport has been the subject of considerable controversy. Data both in favor of and against its participation in electron transport have been published. The best experiments in its favor have been obtained with mitochondria that have been extracted with acetone.[150] These preparations are incapable of oxidizing succinate unless both Q_{10} and cytochrome c are added. These experiments have been confirmed in our laboratory. We found, however, that even a very brief exposure of mitochondria to acetone destroys the ability to catalyze oxidative phosphorylation, and thus far we have not been able to restore this ability by adding various soluble factors or crude extracts. Furthermore, it is well known that the quinones, like many other oxidoreduction dyes, chemically oxidize reduced flavoproteins, and that reduced quinones reduce cytochrome c. It is therefore possible that Q_{10} functions nonenzymatically as a shuttle for electrons in mitochondria

[148] D. E. Wolf, C. H. Hofmann, N. R. Trenner, B. H. Arison, C. H. Shunk, B. O. Linn, J. F. McPherson, and K. Folkers, *JACS* **80**, 4752 (1958).

[149] U. Gloor, O. Isler, R. A. Morton, R. Rüegg, and O. Wiss, *Helv. Chim. Acta* **41**, 2357 (1958).

[150] R. L. Lester and S. Fleischer, *BBA* **47**, 358 (1961).

which have been damaged with acetone. On the other hand, the presence of Q_{10} in the mitochondria speaks in favor of a function in electron transport and the important experiment by Lester and Fleischer should be (and will be) explored further. On the negative side are (*a*) the consistent failure of attempts to restore DPNH oxidation by Q_{10} in mitochondria treated with acetone, and (*b*) the quantitative evaluations of the participation of Q_{10} in the respiratory chain of phosphorylating mitochondria. The rates of Q_{10} turnover appear to be considerably slower than would be expected from an electron carrier in the main path of electron flow. Chance, therefore, proposed[151] that at least the bulk of mitochondrial quinone is on a side path of electron transport. This concept is strengthened by the observations that in nonphosphorylating mitochondria Q_{10} turnover is considerably more rapid than in phosphorylating particles, apparently by-passing the phosphorylating pathway via cytochrome *b*. Since negative experiments are obviously not decisive, Chance has included in his scheme of electron transport the possibility that a small amount of Q_{10} which has escaped detection by direct spectroscopic measurements may participate as carrier between the flavoprotein and cytochrome *c*.

PHOSPHOLIPIDS

More than 90% of the lipids in mitochondria are phospholipids. The most striking example of a requirement of a phospholipid for the activity of an enzyme is β-hydroxybutyrate dehydrogenase, which depends on unsaturated lecithin.[152] Stimulation of other mitochondrial enzymes by phospholipids has been recorded, but in no other case was there specificity. Mitochondria extracted with 90% acetone require cytochrome *c*, Q_{10}, and phospholipid for the reduction of cytochrome *c* by succinate.[153] The role of phospholipid is

[151] B. Chance, *CIBA Found. Symp., Quinones in Electron Transport 1960* p. 327 (1961).

[152] I. Sekuzu, P. Jurtshuk, Jr., and D. E. Green, *JBC* **238**, 975 (1963).

[153] S. Fleischer, G. Brierley, H. Klouwen, and D. B. Slautterback, *JBC* **237**, 3264 (1962).

partly solubilization of Q_{10} and partly "to act as a bridge between hydrophilic and hydrophobic areas and between functional groups." Specificity for such a function should perhaps not be expected. As much as 40% of the respiratory activity of acetone-treated particles was restored by substituting Triton X-100 for phospholipids.

Mitochondria treated with acetone lose the capacity to catalyze oxidative phosphorylation.[153] Submitochondrial particles obtained by sonic oscillation of mitochondria in the presence of 2% phospholipids catalyzed the oxidation of DPNH or succinate without phosphorylation. When two coupling factors were added, phosphorylative activity was restored.[154] Phospholipids may therefore play an important role in the orientation of the phosphorylating catalysts in relation to the respiratory enzymes.

STRUCTURAL PROTEIN

Before closing the discussion of the components of the respiratory chain, we must consider the elements of structure that allow for the proper organization of the respiratory catalysts. Green and his collaborators encountered considerable difficulty in the purification of the various components of the respiratory chain because of contamination with a rather insoluble protein. Instead of despairing over these difficulties, they turned to a systematic study of this insoluble protein and published a most interesting account of its properties.[108] Solubilization was achieved by treating mitochondria with a mixture of detergents. The protein was precipitated with ammonium sulfate at 12% saturation and was washed with butanol and methanol to remove residual lipids and detergents. This structural protein (SP) is an insoluble polymeric aggregate which could be dissociated by anionic detergents into monomers of a molecular weight of about 22,000. Cytochromes c_1 and a combined with SP in a maximal ratio of 1 cytochrome per monomer, but interactions with dimer $(SP)_2c_1$ and trimer $(SP)_3c_1$ were also encountered. The

[154] T. E. Conover, R. L. Prairie, and E. Racker, *JBC* **238**, 2831 (1963).

complex had the expected molecular weights of the sum of the components; e.g., the molecular weight of $(SP)c_1$ was 76,000. Cytochrome a monomer (70,000) reacted with SP to yield a complex of 91,000. Interaction between cytochrome b and SP was sluggish, requiring the presence of detergents. During this interaction of 4 to 5 hours, the redox potential of cytochrome b rose steadily until it reached that observed in intact mitochondria. Multiple complexes, containing, e.g., $(SP)_2c_1a$, were also obtained. Structural protein did not show interaction with a large number of glycolytic and other enzymes. Nor did it interact with cytochrome c itself, but after interaction of SP with phospholipids, cytochrome c was readily bound. Structural protein contained leucine as carboxy terminal amino acid. However, in view of the difficulties of determining the amino terminal amino acid and other analytical complications, it seems advisable to postpone a definite verdict on the homogeneity of this preparation. In a later lecture, the relationship of SP to two other rather insoluble proteins that we have isolated from mitochondria will be discussed. One is required for phosphorylation and the other is required to confer oligomycin sensitivity on soluble mitochondrial ATPase. Structural protein, prepared according to Criddle *et al.*,[108] did not substitute for either one of these proteins.

ELECTRON CARRIERS

In view of the uncertainties of the specific role of SP, phospholipids, Q_{10}, and nonheme iron in the respiratory chain of phosphorylating mitochondria, the scheme drawn up by Chance has been used in its simplest form (Scheme 1.5). Although it may be incomplete, it shows the electron carriers that undergo rapid changes in oxidation-reduction on addition of ADP to phosphorylating mitochondria. One phosphorylation site is between DPNH and flavoprotein (Site 1); one is between cytochromes b and c (Site 2); and one is between cytochrome c and oxygen (Site 3). The similarities of the three phosphorylation sites of the respiratory chain will be discussed in greater detail.

LECTURE 9

LOCALIZATION OF PHOSPHORYLATION SITES IN MITOCHONDRIA

You might as well fall flat on your face as lean over too far backward.
— James Thurber

Among the various approaches to the analysis of multienzyme system which I mentioned in Lecture 1, the most popular has been the use of inhibitors. This is particularly true of studies in oxidative phosphorylation, and it may therefore be appropriate to start this lecture by discussing the use of inhibitors and the concept of the crossover point.

THE CROSSOVER POINT

When antimycin is added to actively metabolizing mitochondria the respiratory catalysts shown in Scheme 9.1 undergo

$$\text{Antimycin A}$$
$$\downarrow$$

DPNH → F_P → (Q_{10}) cyt b → cyt c_1 → cyt c → cyt a → cyt a_3 → O_2

↑	↑	↑
Site 1	Site 2	Site 3
(state 4)	(state 4)	(state 4)
(with cyanide)	(with azide)	(no inhibitor)

Scheme 9.1

Effect of Antimycin on the Respiratory Chain and Crossover Points

characteristic changes in the steady state levels of the oxidized and reduced forms.[155–57] There is complete oxidation of cyto-

[155] K. Ahmad, H. G. Schneider, and F. M. Strong, *ABB* **28**, 281 (1950).
[156] V. R. Potter and A. E. Reif, *JBC* **194**, 287 (1952).
[157] B. Chance and G. R. Williams, *Advan. Enzymol.* **17**, 65 (1956).

chromes a_3, a, and c, whereas cytochrome b and DPN become fully reduced. The inhibitor acts, therefore, between cytochrome b and cytochrome c. The step at which one carrier becomes more reduced and the other more oxidized is called the crossover point.[157] Mitochondria prepared with certain precautions are tightly coupled; that term implies that respiration is dependent on phosphates and ADP,[158] and such mitochondria exhibit "respiratory control." Since respiration ceases when these mitochondria become depleted of ADP, Chance and Williams have used this "inhibition" to localize the crossover points of oxidative phosphorylation.[159] The state of respiration in the presence of substrate and ADP is called the active state (state 3). When ADP is exhausted and respiration ceases, mitochondria enter into the controlled state (state 4). It was observed that on transition from the active state to the controlled state, all respiratory carriers from DPN to cytochrome c became reduced, whereas cytochrome a became more oxidized. The crossover point was therefore localized between cytochrome c and cytochrome a (Site 3 in Scheme 9.1). In the presence of a low concentration of sodium azide (0.1 M) the crossover point on exhaustion of ADP was shifted toward the substrate and was localized between cytochromes b and c (phosphorylating Site 2). In the presence of larger concentrations of sodium azide or in the presence of cyanide, a further shift was observed in the direction of the substrate, the crossover point now lying between DPNH and flavoprotein, corresponding to the first phosphorylation site.

Thus, by ingeniously taking advantage of the phenomenon of respiratory control, the three sites of phosphorylation were localized, which confirmed and strengthened the scheme shown in Scheme 1.5, which was based on functional separation.

The use of crossover points to localize the site of action of an inhibitor is not without its pitfalls, however, and it should be emphasized that the procedure indicates the reaction that

[158] H. A. Lardy and H. Wellman, *JBC* **201,** 357 (1953).
[159] B. Chance and G. R. Williams, *JBC* **221,** 477 (1956).

is inhibited but not the reagent. For example, BAL, which inhibits between cytochrome b and cytochrome c, may affect either the oxidation of reduced cytochrome b or the reduction of cytochrome c, or may affect an unknown intermediate factor, e.g., the one proposed by Slater.[160] Another example is antimycin A, which also has a crossover point between cytochromes b and c and was proposed to act on reduced cytochrome b, rather than to inhibit the reaction by interacting with cytochrome c. The fact that ascorbate reduced cytochrome c in a system inhibited by antimycin was the principal experimental evidence for this conclusion.[157] Although the conclusion may be reasonable and correct, the experiments are not decisive. The chemical reduction may take place with an inhibited carrier, whereas the enzymatic reaction may not; moreover, there is still the possibility of an intermediate carrier that may have escaped identification.

An example of an alteration in crossover point between phosphorylating and nonphosphorylating mitochondria is amytal. The crossover point of the inhibition by amytal in phosphorylating mitochondria lies between flavoprotein and cytochrome b,[161] but in nonphosphorylating mitochondria it lies between DPNH and flavoprotein.[162] Because of this and other findings, it was necessary to invoke an inhibitory action by amytal on energy transfer as well as on electron transport.[161] This example illustrates some of the difficulties in interpreting crossover points, and also reemphasizes the changes in catalytic properties that may occur when mitochondria are mistreated. Such changes may be due to the unmasking of latent activities, or to the displacement of a carrier from its normal place of residence, or perhaps to an alteration in the protein itself. A depth analysis of the inhibition by, e.g., amytal or antimycin at various degrees of degradation of the mitochondrial structure might prove more profitable than a horizontal survey with a staggering number of different uncouplers and inhibitors. Inhibitors of

[160] E. C. Slater, *BJ* **45**, 14 (1949).
[161] B. Chance and G. Hollunger, *JBC* **238**, 418 (1963).
[162] R. W. Estabrook and B. Mackler, *JBC* **229**, 1091 (1957).

the respiratory catalysts are widely used in studies of the mechanism of respiration and phosphorylation. Cyanide, CO, and azide inhibit the terminal steps, and, therefore, like anaerobic conditions, cause the respiratory chain to become reduced. The deprivation of substrate or the addition of inhibitors of the dehydrogenases (e.g., malonate for succinate oxidation) induces all the catalysts of the chain to become oxidized. As was shown in Scheme 1.5, numerous inhibitors appear to act between cytochromes b and c, and to affect both succinate and DPNH oxidation. In contrast, amytal, rotenone, chloropromazine, and progesterone at appropriate concentrations inhibit the oxidation of DPNH but not of succinate.

These differential effects have been most useful in studies of the individual sites of oxidative phosphorylation and of partial reactions. Amytal and rotenone are used to inhibit the steps between DPNH and cytochrome b, and antimycin A and 2-alkyl-4-hydroxyquinoline-N-oxide to inhibit the steps between cytochromes b and c.

MEASUREMENTS OF THE THREE PHOSPHORYLATION SITES

To determine the contribution of the individual sites frequently involves using inhibitors together with dyes that serve as suitable electron acceptors. For example, Site 1 is being measured with phenazine methosulfate as electron acceptor, with DPNH or a DPNH-regenerating system as electron donor, and with antimycin to stop the electron flow via the cytochrome system.[163] Since phenazine methosulfate reacts chemically with DPNH, and since reduced phenazine methosulfate is oxidized not only directly by oxygen but also via cytochrome c and cytochrome oxidase, appropriate controls and precautions are required to minimize errors due to these side reactions. In our hands, the method has been very useful, particularly with submitochondrial preparations in which the last phosphorylation step between

[163] A. L. Smith and M. Hansen, *BBRC* **8**, 136 (1962).

cytochrome c and oxygen is lacking, so that the antimycin inhibition cannot be short-circuited. In particles that catalyze phosphorylation at Site 3 this procedure is not without ambiguity. The best procedure for the analysis of coupled phosphorylation with DPNH is to use fumarate as acceptor in the presence of cyanide.[164a] Although the reaction is slow the procedure is the least ambiguous. The first phosphorylation site can also be analyzed in the reverse reaction, with succinate as electron donor, DPN as acceptor, ATP as energy donor, and Na_2S as inhibitor of respiration.[154]

The second phosphorylation site can be measured anaerobically with succinate as electron donor and added cytochrome c as an acceptor, or, more conveniently, in submitochondrial particles that are inactive at the third site. The third phosphorylation site is usually measured with ascorbate as reductant of cytochrome c; but again, complicating factors have been encountered. In most submitochondrial particles, cytochrome c is not accessible to ascorbate, and an auxiliary dye must be added, such as tetramethyl p-phenylenediamine[164b] or phenazine methosulfate. It appears, however, that more than one phosphorylation site is brought into action by the reduced p-phenylenediamine, since at low dye concentration (60 mM) about 50% of the phosphorylation is very sensitive to antimycin.[164] Apparently, the most reliable measurements of Site 3 are with reduced cytochrome c in particles that are permeable to this electron carrier.

The various difficulties in the analysis of the individual phosphorylation sites have given further impetus to the attempts to perform physical separations of sections of the electron transport chain and their phosphorylating machinery.

The successful preparation of phosphorylating submitochondrial particles from animal tissues has been achieved only recently. The first publication appeared in 1955, when it was briefly reported that digitonin-treated liver mitochondria yielded "extracts" that catalyzed phosphorylation coupled to electron transport between DPNH and cytochrome c.[165]

[164] J. L. Howland, *BBA* **77**, 419 (1963).
[164a] D. R. Sanadi and A. L. Fluharty, *Biochemistry* **2**, 523 (1963).
[164b] E. E. Jacobs, *BBRC* **3**, 536 (1960).
[165] I. Raw, *JACS* **77**, 503 (1955).

Independently, Lehninger and his collaborators started systematic investigations on digitonin particles from rat liver mitochondria.[166,167] In various laboratories, mitochondria were disrupted with ethanol,[168] by sonic oscillation,[169,170] with Triton,[171] and by mechanical fragmentation[93] to obtain phosphorylating particles. The properties of these submitochondrial particles varied considerably with regard to the substrates which they utilized as well as in their relative efficiency of phosphorylation at the three phosphorylating sites. The digitonin particles yielded ATP only when β-hydroxybutyrate was oxidized. Succinate oxidation was observed also but there was little or no phosphorylation. Other Krebs cycle intermediates were not oxidized under the test conditions. Reduced DPN was oxidized via the external, antimycin-resistant, and nonphosphorylating pathway. From the relative efficiency of phosphorylation during electron transport from β-hydroxybutyrate to cytochrome c, from ferrocytochrome c to oxygen, and from succinate to cytochrome c, it was estimated that the phosphorylation sites operate at the efficiencies shown in Table 9.I. It can be seen that in contrast to digitonin

TABLE 9.I
EFFICIENCY OF PHOSPHORYLATING SITES

Treatment of submitochondrial particles	Percent efficiency		
	Site 1	Site 2	Site 3
Digitonin	90	20	70
Sonic oscillation	40	75	0
Mechanical fragmentation	trace	75	0

particles, the particles prepared by sonic oscillation show relatively low efficiency at Site 1, higher efficiency at Site 2, and little or no activity at Site 3. The particles obtained by

[166] C. Cooper and A. L. Lehninger, *JBC* **219**, 489, 519 (1956).
[167] T. M. Devlin and A. L. Lehninger, *JBC* **219**, 507 (1956).
[168] D. Ziegler, R. Lester, and D. E. Green, *BBA* **21**, 80 (1956).
[169] W. W. Kielley and J. R. Bronk, *JBC* **230**, 521 (1958).
[170] W. C. McMurray and H. A. Lardy, *JBC* **233**, 754 (1958).
[171] L. G. Abood, E. Brunngraber, and M. Taylor, *JBC* **234**, 1307 (1959).

mechanical fragmentation of mitochondria have little or no activity in Site 1 and Site 3; most of the phosphorylating activity was accounted for by the reaction between cytochromes b and c. Besides these differences in efficiency of the individual phosphorylating sites, there are other striking differences in the properties of particles obtained by different means. The digitonin particles, as well as those obtained by ethanol treatment, contain bound DPN and Mg^+, whereas the fragments obtained sonically or mechanically require DPN and Mg^+ for oxidative phosphorylation with DPN-linked substrates. The sonically prepared particles are capable of oxidizing added DPNH and this process is linked to phosphorylation, whereas all other particles give little or no phosphorylation under similar conditions.

Fractions that catalyze segments of the respiratory chain have been prepared by treatment of beef-heart mitochondria with various detergents and solvents. DPNH-Coenzyme Q reductase, succinate-coenzyme Q reductase, coenzyme QH_2-cytochrome c reductase, and cytochrome oxidase were prepared and recombined to yield particles with DPNH oxidase and succinate oxidase activities.[172] Although no phosphorylation took place during these oxidations, further attempts to reactivate oxidation phosphorylation in these systems seem warranted.

The localization of the three sites permitted an approach to the study of the properties of the individual phosphorylation sites. For example, it was observed that the oxidation of reduced cytochrome c was more readily uncoupled by gramicidin than other steps of DPNH oxidation. A marked uncoupling of oxidative phosphorylation with DPNH as donor and ferricyanide as acceptor was noted in liver mitochondria of thyrotoxic rats, whereas only a moderate inhibition of phosphorylation linked to the oxidation of reduced cytochrome c was noted.[173] Promethazine was described as an uncoupler of Site 3. It inhibited, but did not uncouple, the

[172] Y. Hatefi, A. G. Haavik, L. R. Fowler, and D. E. Griffiths, *JBC* **237**, 2661 (1962).
[173] G. F. Maley and H. A. Lardy, *JBC* **215**, 377 (1955).

reactions between DPNH and cytochrome *c*.[174] These and similar studies will undoubtedly help us to characterize the individual steps of phosphorylation sites that are linked to electron transport, but I should like to emphasize that they do not yet allow us to draw any conclusions regarding possible differences in the mechanism of the coupling process at the three different sites. As we shall see later, coupling of phosphorylation to oxidation depends on several soluble factors. The availability of these coupling factors, the relative rate of oxidation, and other kinetic properties that determine the rate-limiting factor at each phosphorylation site may influence the properties of the individual phosphorylating steps. Observed differences in susceptibility, therefore, do not necessarily imply any fundamental differences in mechanism.

With the exception of β-hydroxybutyrate, substrates that are not members of the Krebs cycle have not been sufficiently used in studies of oxidative phosphorylation. For example, an exploration of the oxidation of choline[175] and sarcosine,[176] which have been reported to be linked to phosphorylation, should be of particular interest. There are bacteria which exploit a single oxidation step (e.g., from glucose to gluconate) as a source of energy. Exploration of such systems may yield important new findings and a purer system than can be obtained by fractionation of the more complex animal mitochondria.

THERMODYNAMIC CONSIDERATIONS

In the field of oxidative phosphorylation, thermodynamic considerations have been of limited value. This has been mainly because of the lack of precise information regarding the oxidation-reduction potentials of several of the respiratory catalysts. More meaningful calculations than had pre-

[174] J. D. Judah, K. R. Rees, and M. J. R. Dawkins, *Nature* **183,** 821 (1959).

[175] H. A. Rothschild, O. Cori, and E. S. G. Barron, *JBC* **208,** 41 (1954).

[176] W. R. Frisell, J. R. Cronin, and C. G. Mackenzie, *JBC* **237,** 2975 (1962); *FP* **19,** 37 (1960).

viously been possible were made from the steady state values of the respiratory catalysts, and with these data, attempts were made to assign probable phosphorylation steps from the calculations of Gibb's free energy changes of the individual oxidation-reduction steps.[157] The steps between flavoprotein and cytochrome b and between cytochromes c and a are considered improbable sites of phosphorylation. The sites between DPNH and flavoprotein, between cytochromes b and c, and between cytochrome a and oxygen are considered the most probable sites, in line with the conclusion from the studies of functional separations and crossover points. Perhaps the most severe restriction of the significance of these considerations is still the ambiguity of the oxidation-reduction potential of several respiratory catalysts. It is well known that the oxidation-reduction potential of prosthetic groups varies with different protein carriers. Flavoproteins in particular show considerable variation, as illustrated by the striking example of lipoate dehydrogenase. The differences in potential of cytochrome b in the presence and absence of structural protein have been mentioned previously. Further discussions of the limitations of thermodynamic calculations have been presented in review articles.[157,177]

[177] E. C. Slater, *Rev. Pure Appl. Chem.* **8,** 221 (1958).

LECTURE 10

EXCHANGE REACTIONS IN OXIDATIVE PHOSPHORYLATION

This is a long story, which shouldn't be long, but it will take a long time to make it short.

—Henry David Thoreau

The following exchange reactions are used in studying the mechanism of oxidative phosphorylation: the P_i-ATP exchange; the ADP-ATP exchange; and the H_2O^{18}-P_i and H_2O^{18}-ATP exchanges.

Before entering into a discussion of these reactions, I must draw attention to some important restrictions which have been pointed out by Boyer, Koshland, Cohn, and Lehninger. Some of these restrictions apply to the study of exchange reactions in general; some of them have specific application to exchanges in oxidative phosphorylation. The most important conclusions that have been reached are the following: 1: The presence of an exchange reaction does not necessarily prove the existence of the covalent enzyme substrate intermediate, since an exchange reaction could occur between Michaelis complexes. 2: The lack of an exchange reaction does not rule out the existence of a covalent enzyme substrate intermediate. A compulsory order of substrate addition may be operating, or a cofactor or a cosubstrate may be necessary for the proper configuration of the active site of the enzyme.

In the specific instance of mitochondrial exchange reactions there is considerable uncertainty about the relative contribution of the three different phosphorylating sites. It is possible that one site contributes primarily to one exchange reaction, while another site might contribute to another reaction. It is quite apparent that the three phosphorylating sites are different in their physical behavior, as most strikingly illustrated by their differences in susceptibility to various procedures of fragmentation, which I mentioned in the last lecture. A further complication in the interpretation of exchange data is the presence in mitochondria of enzymes that are apparently unrelated to oxidative phosphorylation, yet catalyze either a P_i^{32}-ATP or an ADP-ATP exchange reaction. Although there does not seem to be unanimous agreement among the investigators, I should like to add one further restriction. I don't believe that one can safely draw conclusions, from quantitative changes in an exchange reaction, regarding the mechanism of the over-all reaction. This is a rather severe limitation, but it is based on the experience that the ratio of exchange to net activity may differ by several orders of magnitude. The ratio approaches infinity in the case of the $C^{14}O_2$ incorporation into oxaloacetate, an exchange reaction catalyzed by oxaloacetate carboxylase, which does not catalyze net CO_2 fixation. Moreover, the exchange to net activity ratio is subject to great variation depending on experimental conditions, and it is obviously treacherous to draw any conclusion regarding the mechanism of the net reaction unless one already knows a great deal about it and the variables are fully controlled.

THE P_i^{32}-ATP EXCHANGE

We discussed the principle of the P_i^{32}-ATP exchange reaction in the first lecture, and concluded that at least two steps are involved, with an $X \sim P$ compound as an intermediate (Scheme 1.6). Some of the experimental findings obtained by measurements of the P_i^{32}-ATP exchange will be discussed now. First, a brief description of how these measurements are carried out. Mitochondria or fragments thereof are incubated in the presence of P_i^{32}, ATP, and Mg^{++}. After deproteinization, ATP^{32} is separated from P_i^{32}, either with a suitable solvent or by adsorption on charcoal, and counted. These procedures are so simple and rapid that they have gained considerable popularity. They are also adequate as long as ample ATP is left at the end of the experiment to saturate the system. As will be seen, this is not always the case. A rapid P_i^{32}-ATP exchange was first observed in liver mitochondria.[178,179] The reaction did not require net electron transport since neither oxygen nor an oxidizable substrate was required. To demonstrate the relationship of this reaction to oxidative phosphorylation, therefore, considerable circumstantial evidence was obtained. The exchange reaction is inhibited by a vast number of uncouplers, and numerous observations have been recorded in the literature indicating that the rate of oxidative phosphorylation declines parallel with the ability to catalyze the exchange reaction.

QUANTITATIVE EVALUATION

It soon became apparent, however, that differences in the ratio of the rates of the two processes may be induced experimentally either by uncouplers or inhibitors or by fragmentation of the mitochondria. Whereas in liver mitochondria the rate of the P_i^{32}-ATP exchange was several times as rapid as net phosphate uptake, the exchange rate in digitonin particles was only a small fraction of oxidative phosphorylation.[180] Even in intact mitochondria, differential inactivations were observed. Short exposure of mitochondria to dinitrophenol[181] or aging at $4°$[182] damaged the exchange more than oxidative phosphorylation.

One interpretation for these findings was offered by Löw et al.[181], who proposed that the first phosphorylation site (between DPNH and flavoprotein) was mainly responsible for this exchange reaction, since amytal at concentrations which inhibited DPNH oxidation but not succinate oxidation

---

[178] P. D. Boyer, W. W. Luchsinger, and A. B. Falcone, *JBC* **223**, 405 (1956).

[179] M. A. Swanson, *BBA* **20**, 85 (1956).

[180] C. Cooper and A. L. Lehninger, *JBC* **224**, 561 (1957).

[181] H. Löw, P. Siekevitz, L. Ernster, and O. Lindberg, *BBA* **29**, 392 (1958).

[182] E. C. Weinbach, *JBC* **234**, 1580 (1959).

almost completely suppressed the P_i^{32}-ATP exchange. Digitonin particles, however, which have an excellent efficiency at Site 1, exhibit a low rate of P_i^{32}-ATP exchange.[181] Moreover, it was recently shown that amytal affects the phosphorylation mechanism as well as electron transport.[161] Although none of these findings eliminate the possibility that in intact mitochondria Site 1 is a major contributor to the exchange reaction, they weaken the evidence in its favor.

A second consideration that applies to this as well as to other exchange reactions is the difficulty of evaluating a partial reaction in a complex multi-enzyme system with many unknown components. The optimal conditions for a partial reaction, and the rate-limiting factors, need not be identical (and frequently are not) with those for the over-all reaction. Moreover, it must be remembered that the exchange reaction requires a step in the reversal of oxidative phosphorylation: the formation of a high-energy intermediate from ATP. In line with these considerations are observations that variations in experimental conditions (e.g., in the concentration of ATP, which is not added for measurements of oxidative phosphorylation) greatly influenced the exchange in digitonin particles.[180] At low ATP and high P_i concentrations the exchange was dependent on the addition of ADP, whereas at high ATP concentrations, ADP actually inhibited. The requirement for ADP is difficult to understand in view of the ATPase activity, which is considerably higher than the exchange activity. It was pointed out[60] that the stimulation by ADP which inhibits ATPase is therefore most likely due to ATP preservation.

This brings us to a third aspect of the exchange reaction, an aspect that has not received enough attention. It is rather unfortunate that in most reported studies of the P_i^{32}-ATP exchange the ATP concentrations at the end of the experiments were not recorded. Without this information it is virtually impossible to evaluate some of these data. To mention an extreme case, it is obvious that no P_i^{32}-labeled ATP can be measured if no ATP is left. Measurements of total counts in ATP are subject to great variation depending on the ATPase activity, on the amounts of ATP added, on the time of incubation, etc. Submitochondrial particles have been prepared in our laboratory[183] that had almost no P_i^{32}-ATP exchange activity, yet catalyzed oxidative phosphorylation provided a very active trapping system (a large excess of hexokinase and glucose) was added. When the potent ATPase of these particles was inhibited either by a mitochondrial ATPase inhibitor[184] or by a low concentration of sodium azide, the exchange activity was restored. This finding may explain similar earlier observations,[179] namely, that low concentrations of azide stimulate the P_i^{32}-ATP exchange, which at the time seemed inconsistent with the known uncoupling property of this compound. It was subsequently demonstrated[92] that azide inhibits ATPase at concentrations which have little effect on oxidative phosphorylation. Analysis of the specific radioactivity of the ATP at the end of the P_i^{32}-ATP exchange experiments showed, in many instances, that a low P_i^{32} incorporation could be accounted for by a decreased level of ATP, since the specific radioactivity of the ATP remained unchanged.[184] Thus, the level of ATPase activity is more critical for measurements of the exchange than of oxidative phosphorylation, which includes an effective ATP trap (hexokinase and glucose). Bearing in mind these objections to the significance of the total counts incorporated into ATP, a number of apparent discrepancies recorded in the literature can be eliminated. Yet there remain numerous experimental observations that cannot be readily explained. The findings that mitochondrial ATPase inhibitor[184] or atractylate[185] can severely depress the P_i^{32}-ATP exchange in submitochondrial particles without seriously affecting oxidative phosphorylation remain unexplained. In the case of atractylate, the Mg^{++}-activated ATPase activity was unaffected while the dinitrophenol-activated ATPase activity was, in fact, inhibited, so that depletion of ATP could not account for the effect. Suggestive evidence is available, how-

[183] E. Racker, *Proc. Natl. Acad. Sci. U. S.* **48**, 1659 (1962).
[184] M. E. Pullman and G. C. Monroy, *JBC* **238**, 3762 (1963).
[185] P. V. Vignais, P. M. Vignais, and E. Stanislas, *BBA* **60**, 284 (1962).

ever, indicating a competition between the drug and ADP.[185] Since ADP must be available for the incorporation of P^{32} at the terminal phosphate of the adenosine nucleotide, it was thought that the drug, as well as the mitochondrial inhibitor of ATPase, might act by preventing the generation of an effective ADP concentration. Yet, in the case of the mitochondrial inhibitor, the addition of ADP did not reverse the inhibition of exchange.[184] It should be pointed out, however, that in all these experiments, and in all others recorded in the literature and properly documented, the P_i^{32}-ATP exchange, though low, was not entirely absent. It should be reemphasized that the exchange requires a step in the forward reaction as well as in the reversal of oxidative phosphorylation, and undoubtedly conditions exist that do not favor this cyclic reaction.

There is another apparent discrepancy that has been encountered with submitochondrial particles prepared by sonic oscillation of beef-heart mitochondria that have been depleted of cytochrome *c*. These particles catalyzed a very active P_i^{32}-ATP exchange without catalyzing oxidative phosphorylation. Submitochondrial particles with this property were also obtained by treatment of mitochondria with EDTA or by exposure of submitochondrial particles to an alkaline pH.[186] This phenomenon is not difficult to understand, however, if we examine the scheme shown in Scheme 1.6. The formation of the intermediate $X \sim Y$ in the exchange reaction requires ATP, whereas in oxidative phosphorylation it arises from reactions coupled to electron transport. A defect in this primary step from the respiratory chain to the phosphorylating mechanism need not affect the exchange reaction. The numerous apparent and real discrepancies between the rates of the exchange and the over-all reaction have left doubts in the minds of some investigators regarding the significance of the exchange reaction.

The interest in exchange reactions was given a new impetus

[186] T. E. Conover, M. E. Pullman, and I. Krimsky, Unpublished observations (1962).

by the important findings[187] that the $P_i{}^{32}$-ATP exchange in liver mitochondria and in digitonin particles was maximal when the respiratory carriers were in the oxidized state. Addition of succinate and β-hydroxybutyrate in the presence of cyanide resulted in a strong inhibition of the exchange. Since, in mitochondria, the exchange rate is faster than oxidative phosphorylation, the latter could not have contributed greatly to the incorporation of $P_i{}^{32}$ into ATP in the absence of cyanide. The experiments with digitonin particles are less convincing on this point, since the exchange is considerably slower than net phosphorylation and it is difficult to compare the reactions in the presence and absence of cyanide. The striking effects of the oxidation state of the carrier on the exchange rate are reminiscent of the requirements for oxidized DPN in phosphate transfer by glyceraldehyde-3-phosphate dehydrogenase. The significance of these findings in regard to the oxidation-reduction state of the high-energy intermediates will be discussed in a later lecture.

I should like to summarize my views on the present status of the $P_i{}^{32}$-ATP exchange reaction. There is very strong evidence that in mitochondria and in submitochondrial particles the $P_i{}^{32}$-ATP exchange represents a partial reaction of oxidative phosphorylation. This conclusion is supported not only by numerous similarities between the exchange and the over-all reaction with respect to uncouplers and exposure of particles to damage, but also by the findings, to be discussed later, that several soluble protein factors which are required for oxidative phosphorylation are also needed for the exchange reaction. On the other hand, there is evidence for differential loss of activities; and furthermore, some phosphorylations linked to electron transport (e.g., in chloroplasts) do not seem to be associated with an exchange activity.

Perhaps the presence of the exchange is correlated with the ease of reversal. As we shall see later, electron transport coupled with phosphorylation at Sites 1 and 2 is readily reversed. It seems almost mandatory that these sites must

[187] C. L. Wadkins and A. L. Lehninger, *JBC* **233**, 1589 (1958).

also, under appropriate conditions, catalyze an exchange. No evidence has thus far been obtained for a reversal of electron transport at Site 3, or of electron transport coupled with photophosphorylation. It will be of considerable interest to analyze these systems for variations on the mechanisms of oxidative phosphorylation.

THE ADP-ATP EXCHANGE

The exchange reaction between ADP and ATP, which can be measured with either C^{14}- or P^{32}-labeled ADP, has been subject to controversy. The first measurements of this exchange reaction in connection with oxidative phosphorylation were carried out with preparations from *Acetobacter vinelandii*.[188] Particles capable of oxidative phosphorylation were dried with acetone, and a soluble enzyme was extracted which catalyzed the ADP-ATP exchange reaction. Its relation to oxidative phosphorylation, however, was left open. It was pointed out that other ADP-ATP exchange reactions may have been responsible for the observations. Indeed, several enzymes are known[60] that catalyze an ADP-ATP exchange reaction, and there may be others of which we are still unaware. The enzymes involved in the synthesis of glutathione and some other peptides, in the activation of succinate, and in the phosphorylation of casein, all catalyze an ADP-ATP exchange. One could include also the biotin-dependent carboxylation reactions since enough carbon dioxide is usually present to permit the ADP-ATP reaction catalyzed by these enzymes to take place. None of these reactions are directly involved in oxidative phosphorylation. One enzyme in particular has caused difficulties in studies of the ADP-ATP exchange in mitochondria, namely adenylate kinase. Recent experiments in our laboratory have shown that under conditions that are generally used for the measurement of the ADP-ATP exchange reactions in mitochondria, adenylate kinase catalyzes the formation of C^{14}-ATP with little or no accumulation of AMP. In intact mitochondria,

[188] I. A. Rose and S. Ochoa, *JBC* **220,** 307 (1956).

it is possible to minimize interference by adenylate kinase simply by not adding Mg^{++} (a sufficient amount of this ion is present in mitochondria to support oxidative phosphorylation but apparently is not available for adenylate kinase), and to demonstrate a dinitrophenol- and oligomycin-sensitive ADP-ATP exchange reaction.[189] With most submitochondrial particles this is not possible since phosphorylation occurs only on addition of Mg^{++}.

In intact mitochondria, numerous observations have linked the ADP-ATP exchange to oxidative phosphorylation.[97,189,190] Sensitivity to dinitrophenol was lost on aging at a rate strikingly parallel to the loss of oxidative phosphorylation. The exchange was inhibited if the respiratory carriers were kept in the reduced form by substrate, particularly succinate.

An enzyme catalyzing the ADP-ATP exchange has been purified from liver mitochondria.[191] The soluble enzyme was not inhibited by dinitrophenol but sensitivity was conferred on the exchange when the enzyme was added to fresh digitonin particles. Damaged particles conferred sensitivity poorly, but were activated by yet another protein fraction, called M factor. The possible relationship of the ADP-ATP exchange enzyme to the coupling factor at Site 3 of oxidative phosphorylation will be discussed in a later lecture.

Another enzyme that catalyzes an ADP-ATP exchange as well as P_i^{32}-ATP exchange was isolated from liver mitochondria.[192] These exchanges are not influenced by dinitrophenol or oligomycin, but are sensitive to arsenate. The possible role of this protein in oxidative phosphorylation is still obscure. No direct evidence for a stimulation of oxidative phosphorylation by this factor has yet been observed.

As in the case of the P_i^{32}-ATP exchange, a relationship between the ADP-ATP exchange and oxidative phosphorylation is gradually being more firmly established. It is curious,

---

[189] C. L. Wadkins and A. L. Lehninger, *JBC* **238**, 2555 (1963).

[190] J. R. Bronk and W. W. Kielley, *BBA* **29**, 369 (1958)

[191] C. L. Wadkins and A. L. Lehninger, *Proc. Natl. Acad. Sci. U. S.* **46**, 1576, 1582 (1960).

[192] M. Chiga and G. W. E. Plaut, *JBC* **234**, 3059 (1959).

however, that numerous attempts in our laboratory to demonstrate a dinitrophenol-sensitive ADP-ATP exchange in submitochondrial fragments obtained by sonic oscillation have been unsuccessful, although the reaction was readily demonstrable in the intact mitochondria from which the particles were derived. Furthermore, experimental conditions that brought about the incorporation of P_i[32] into ATP failed to reveal a dinitrophenol-sensitive incorporation of C^{14}-ADP into ATP. These recent findings induced us to reexamine the problem of the exchange, and I shall return to it again after our discussion of ATPase.

THE H_2O^{18}-P_i AND H_2O^{18}-ATP EXCHANGES

Cohn[193] made the important discovery that during oxidative phosphorylation inorganic phosphate labeled with O^{18} rapidly lost its label to water. This O^{18} exchange was dependent on oxidative phosphorylation and was abolished by dinitrophenol. Extension of this work[8,194,195] revealed a second exchange reaction which occurs between O^{18}-labeled water and ATP. Since the incorporation of the isotope into ATP is actually faster than its incorporation into inorganic phosphate, it was proposed by Cohn that an additional site of O^{18} entry into ATP is present. Boyer gave an alternative interpretation, namely, a compartmentation of intramitochondrial and extramitochondrial phosphate and nucleotides, which may give rise to an apparent preference for the incorporation into ATP.[8] It was pointed out, however, by Cohn[194] that the experiments would also require the assumption of a compartmentation of water, which is somewhat more difficult to visualize than compartmentation of phosphorylated compounds. In favor of a second site of entry is the recent observation[196] that in photophosphorylation

[193] M. Cohn, *JBC* **201**, 735 (1953).
[194] G. R. Drysdale and M. Cohn, *JBC* **233**, 1574 (1958); M. Cohn, Personal communication (1961).
[195] P. C. Chan, A. L. Lehninger, and T. Enns, *JBC* **235**, 1790 (1960).
[196] M. Avron and N. Sharon, *BBRC* **2**, 336 (1960).

O^{18} exchange from water does occur into ATP but not into inorganic phosphate, indicating that there is, in chloroplasts at least, a site of water entry at the nucleotide level. In digitonin particles, there is also a more a rapid labeling of of ATP than of phosphate, the rate of exchange exceeding that of oxidative phosphorylation severalfold.[195] With these simpler particles, the H_2O^{18}-P_i exchange was catalyzed by respiration without addition of ATP. However, the presence of catalytic amounts of nucleotides was not excluded. Both the ATP- and the respiration-activated exchanges were inhibited by azide and arsenate, and deteriorated, similar to oxidative phosphorylation, on aging.

An exchange between H_2O^{18} and phosphate occurs in crude extracts, but Cohn has pointed out that these activities can probably be accounted for by the presence of inorganic pyrophosphatase, which catalyzes such an exchange. Myosin also catalyzes an H_2O^{18}-P_i exchange in the presence of Mg^{++} and ATP.[197,198] Thus far, there is no evidence for a soluble protein from mitochondria that catalyzes an H_2O^{18}-P_i exchange that is clearly related to oxidative phosphorylation. Recent experiments in our laboratory have in fact shown a dependency on submitochondrial particles and coupling factors (F_1 and F_4) for the exchange reaction.[199]

A few final comments should be made regarding the usefulness and significance of the three types of exchange reactions that have been discussed in this lecture. There seems to be little doubt that the P_i^{32}-ATP exchange is closely related to the process of oxidative phosphorylation. The similarities in susceptibility to inhibitors, uncouplers, and physical fractionation are impressive. But why do we study exchange reactions? Can we learn from them anything that we could not learn from analysis of the over-all system? There are two areas in which the exchange reactions have been invaluable:

[197] H. M. Levy, N. Sharon, E. Lindemann, and D. E. Koshland, Jr., *JBC* **235**, 2628 (1960).
[198] R. G. Yount and D. E. Koshland, Jr., *JBC* **238**, 1708 (1963).
[199] P. Hinkle, H. S. Penefsky, and E. Racker, Unpublished observations (1964).

(*a*) They have been used for the rapid assay of soluble factors which participate in oxidative phosphorylation. (These tests, however, should be looked upon only as laboratory aids; the final analysis must be carried out on the over-all reaction, the net uptake of P_i.) (*b*) The analysis of a partial reaction such as an exchange carries with it the advantages of a simpler system. It is particularly useful for the study of the mode of action of uncouplers and inhibitors. But again, it must be stressed that the exchange reactions, which often include a step in the reversal, may have kinetic properties quite different from the process of oxidative phosphorylation. Moreover, structural changes that accompany the preparation of submitochondrial particles influence the steady-state concentration of intermediates which become more accessible to water. A decrease in the level of the intermediates due to hydrolysis may seriously affect exchange reactions, whereas in the over-all system the high-energy intermediates are efficiently removed by a suitable ATP-trapping system. We must, therefore, conclude by saying that, in the final analysis, oxidative phosphorylation must be studied by analyzing oxidative phosphorylation.

LECTURE 11

PARTIAL REACTIONS OF OXIDATIVE PHOSPHORYLATION

A little knowledge is a dangerous thing; but we must take that risk because a little is as much as our biggest heads can hold.
—G. B. Shaw

ATPase

The first suggestion that the ATPase activity of mitochondria might be associated with oxidative phosphorylation was made as early as 1945.[200] At the same time, it was reported that the ATPase activity of minced rat muscle was stimulated by dinitrophenol, and the proposal was made that the drug acted either by catalyzing the breakdown of an intermediate in oxidative phosphorylation, similar to the action of arsenate in glycolysis, or by dissociating oxidation from phosphorylation. It took several years, however, before it was shown experimentally that dinitrophenol uncouples oxidative phosphorylation.[201] The problem was pursued in the laboratories of Kielley,[202] Hunter,[38] and Lardy.[203] Procedures were developed for the isolation of mitochondria with little ATPase activity. The latent ATPase was unmasked by dinitrophenol, by aging, or by mistreatment of the mitochondria. Liver mitochondria were fragmented in a Waring blender and particles were obtained that catalyzed an Mg^{++}-dependent cleavage of the terminal phosphate of ATP.[202] This ATPase was inhibited by ADP and it was proposed that the low ATP-

---

[200] H. A. Lardy and C. A. Elvehjem, *Ann. Rev. Biochem.* **14,** 1 (1945).
[201] W. F. Loomis and F. Lipmann, *JBC* **173,** 807 (1948).
[202] W. W. Kielley and R. K. Kielley, *JBC* **191,** 485 (1951).
[203] H. A. Lardy and H. Wellman, *JBC* **195,** 215 (1952).

ase activity in fresh mitochondria was due to the presence of ADP. This important property of mitochondrial ATPase will be discussed further.

The literature has been virtually flooded with papers on the properties of mitochondrial ATPase, and I shall not attempt to cover this vast material. You may have found some of this literature rather confusing, and I believe that one particular question requires clarification before we can deal with these data. Is there more than one ATPase associated with the process of oxidative phosphorylation? There are many references in the literature to the so-called dinitrophenol-stimulated and to the Mg^{++}-activated ATPase. Since striking differences in properties were recorded, these two activities have sometimes been discussed as if they were catalyzed by distinct and separable enzymes. Statements have been made that the dinitrophenol-sensitive ATPase is associated with oxidative phosphorylation, whereas the Mg^{++}-activated ATPase is not. There is no compelling evidence, however, that mitochondria contain more than one protein which hydrolyzes ATP. On the other hand, the isolated ATPase is a single protein which requires Mg^{++} and exhibits different properties under different experimental conditions. Most of the discrepancies in the literature can be clarified by taking into consideration three aspects of the problem.

(a) Submitochondrial particles obtained by sonic oscillation[204] or by mechanical fragmentation[92] require Mg^{++} for ATPase activity. These particles, which catalyze oxidative phosphorylation, show little or no dinitrophenol-activated ATPase activity. Mitochondria and digitonin particles, which both exhibit dinitrophenol-stimulated ATPase activity, contain bound Mg^{++}. Apparently this Mg^{++} participates in the ATPase activity when the mitochondria are mistreated, aged, or treated with certain uncoupling agents such as dinitrophenol. There are several agents which chelate Mg^{++} and inhibit the dinitrophenol-stimulated ATPase, but do not inhibit ATPase when excess Mg^{++} is added. All agents that

[204] J. R. Bronk and W. W. Kielley, *BBA* **24**, 440 (1957).

inhibit the Mg^{++}-activated ATPase also inhibit the dinitro-phenol-activated ATPase.

(b) The ATPase activity of intact mitochondria represents a reversal of the process of oxidative phosphorylation. As in the case of glyceraldehyde-3-phosphate dehydrogenase, uncoupling may occur at different levels, thus accounting for some of the apparent differences in properties of the ATPase activities.

(c) Mechanical fragmentation of mitochondria releases a soluble ATPase with properties that have been ascribed to both the Mg^{++}-activated ATPase and the dinitrophenol-activated ATPase. This enzyme was isolated and shown to be a single protein which is required for oxidative phosphorylation at all three sites.[204a] The interaction of the protein at the different phosphorylation sites may well result in alteration of its properties, which may account for some of the differences in ATPase activities recorded in the literature.

I would like to turn now to the description of the soluble ATPase from beef-heart mitochondria. In the beginning of our work on the resolution of the enzymes that participate in oxidative phosphorylation, we encountered a soluble fraction that was required for the coupling of phosphorylation to oxidation and contained a considerable amount of ATPase activity. Since there had been no report in the literature up to that time on an ATPase from mitochondria which was truly soluble, we thought it worth while to purify the ATPase, hoping that eventually it would somehow be relevant to the process of oxidative phosphorylation. Two properties of the ATPase encouraged us in this hope. One was a 60% stimulation of the activity by dinitrophenol; the second was an inhibition by ADP, reminiscent of ATPase activity in mitochondria. This latter property actually presented some difficulties at the start, since it interfered with a dependable assay. On removal of ADP by a regenerating system of ATP consisting of phosphoenolpyruvate and pyruvate kinase, a

[204a] E. Racker and G. Monroy, *Abstr. 6th Intern. Congr. Biochem.*, *New York*, *1964* p. 760. Intern. Union Biochem. (Publ. Ser. Vol. 32), Washington, D.C., 1964.

4- to 5-fold stimulation of ATPase activity in mitochondria was observed.[205] This procedure yielded a more accurate and reproducible assay for the soluble enzyme.[92] Proceeding with the purification was not a simple matter, because the enzyme, which was relatively stable in the crude extract, became increasingly labile on purification. In order to analyze this lability, a procedure was used that is quite customary in our laboratory: The enzyme was incubated for an hour at 37° at a variety of pH's, usually covering the range between 5 and 9. Stability data from such experiments often yield an immediate clue to how to proceed further in the purification. This test revealed, surprisingly, that at neutral pH the enzyme was not only stable at 37° but actually increased slightly in activity. When the enzyme was returned to 0°, however, the activity disappeared quite rapidly. With this observation, the stability problem was solved. All we had to do was to forget the usual rules of enzymology and proceed with purification at room temperature. Fortunately, the enzyme was found to be stable for months in the cold when it was kept as a precipitate in 2 *M* ammonium sulfate. The major steps of the purification procedure are shown in Table 11.I.

TABLE 11.I
ATPase Purification

Preparation	Specific activity		Yield
	− DNP	+ DNP	
Crude extract	1.35	2.35	100
Protamine precipitate	9.36	14.4	78
After heating at 65°	76.5	114.0	214

The highly purified preparation was homogenous in the ultracentrifuge. The molecular weight was 280,000 and the turnover number 15,000. The enzyme cleaved the terminal phosphate of ATP with ADP as the end product. The purified

[205] S. Gatt and E. Racker, *JBC* **234**, 1015 (1959).

enzyme as well as crude preparations exhibited a small stimulation (60%) by dinitrophenol. Adenosine triphosphate, ITP, GTP, and UTP were hydrolyzed by the purified enzyme, but only ATP hydrolysis was stimulated by dinitrophenol. Cytidine triphosphate was not hydrolyzed, nor were any of the nucleotide di- or monophosphates. Other phosphorylated compounds, such as fructose 6-phosphate, glucose 6-phosphate, glucose 1-phosphate, ribose 5-phosphate, carbamyl phosphate, and pyrophosphate, were similarly inactive as substrates. The possibility that the cleavage of ITP, UTP, and GTP involved a second enzyme (e.g., nucleoside diphosphokinase) was explored. If the splitting of these compounds occurred through the intermediary formation of ATP, the addition of glucose and hexokinase should be expected to produce a competitive inhibition. As shown in Table 11.II,

TABLE 11.II

NUCLEOTIDE SPECIFICITY (COMPETITION EXPERIMENT)

| | Micromoles ATP cleaved | |
Substrate	− Hexokinase	+ Hexokinase
ATP	2.4	1.1
ITP	3.0	3.0
GTP	1.7	2.0
UTP	1.1	1.4
CTP	0	0

hexokinase and glucose affected only the cleavage of ATP, whereas the cleavage of other nucleotides remained unaffected, strongly suggesting that the cleavage of these other compounds did not occur via ATP formation. I have chosen to show you this experiment in greater detail because it represents a very useful application of an effective competing system. It may be used in many other systems where the role of ATP or of energy need in general is being explored.

It was somewhat disturbing to note that the protein which we felt participated in oxidative phosphorylation had such a lack of specificity toward the triphosphonucleotides, whereas

it was well known that oxidative phosphorylation in intact
mitochondria is highly specific for adenosine nucleotides.

On the other hand, the highly purified enzyme was markedly inhibited by ADP, as shown in Fig. 11.1, but not by any

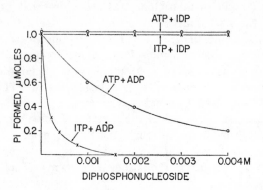

FIG. 11.1. Effect of ADP and IDP on ATP and ITP hydrolysis. The
test system contained either 0.004 M ATP or 0.004 M ITP; 0.002 M
$MgCl_2$; 24 μg of ATPase; and the indicated diphosphonucleoside, in a
final volume of 1.0 ml. After incubation for 3 minutes at 30°, the reaction
was stopped with 0.1 ml of 50% trichloroacetic acid. After centrifugation, 0.5 ml of the supernatant solution was removed for P_i determination (scaled down to 2.5 ml final volume).

of the other diphosphonucleosides, such as IDP, GDP, CDP,
or UDP, nor by any of the monophosphonucleosides. Since
the dinucleotide rather than the trinucleotide is the substrate in oxidative phosphorylation, the striking specificity
of the ATPase inhibition by ADP was a welcome discovery
at a time of doubt.

Purified ATPase showed a complete dependency on Mg^{++}
but other divalent ions such as Mn^{++}, Co^{++}, Ca^{++}, and Fe^{++}
substituted with varying degrees of effectiveness. Stimulation
by dinitrophenol was observed only in the presence of Mg^{++}
and to a lesser extent in the presence of Co^{++}. Many of these
observations on the purified enzyme resemble those on
ATPase in submitochondrial particles.[180,204]

The effect of various inhibitors on the ATPase activity is
shown in Table 11.III. In these experiments, the reagents
were added directly to the assay system without preincuba-

tion with the enzyme. The most striking effects were exhibited by azide, guanidine, and *p*-mercuribenzoate. Azide and guanidine inhibited the activity to a greater extent in the absence of dinitrophenol than in its presence, with the result that the stimulation by this compound was increased from about 60 to 300 or 400%. The opposite effect was observed with *p*-mercuribenzoate, which eliminated the stimulation by dinitrophenol. Other SH reagents, such as iodoacetate or *N*-ethylmaleimide, had little or no effect on ATPase activity,

TABLE 11.III

EFFECT OF INHIBITORS ON ATPASE

Experi- ment	Inhibitors		Micromoles P_i formed	
	Additions	Concentration (M)	− DNP	+ DNP
1	None	—	1.6	2.4
	p-Mercuribenzoate	5×10^{-4}	1.6	1.7
	N-ethylmaleimide	5×10^{-3}	1.6	2.5
2	None	—	2.9	4.5
	Azide	4×10^{-5}	0.5	2.2
3	None	—	1.9	2.9
	Guanidine	2×10^{-2}	0.42	1.3
4	None	—	1.44	1.81
	Bilirubin	3.2×10^{-4}	0.74	0.80
	Biliverdin	3.2×10^{-4}	1.20	1.38

either with or without dinitrophenol. Of interest is the ineffectiveness of 20 mM fluoride, which is often used in studies of oxidative phosphorylation; increasing the concentration to 60 mM did not increase the inhibition. Thyroxine analogs, known to be potent uncouplers of oxidative phosphorylation, inhibited the ATPase activity markedly. Bilirubin, an uncoupler of oxidative phosphorylation, strongly inhibited the enzyme, whereas biliverdin, which is ineffective as an uncoupler, was similarly ineffective as an inhibitor of the ATPase activity. The very small inhibition noted with biliverdin can be attributed to the presence of some contaminating bilirubin.

A particularly interesting compound is oligomycin. This compound has no effect on purified ATPase, but strongly inhibits ATPase activity in submitochondrial particles. When highly purified ATPase was added to particles that lacked ATPase activity, the enzyme was adsorbed and regained its sensitivity to oligomycin. We shall return to this problem shortly. The highly purified ATPase from the beef-heart mitochondria did not catalyze a P_i^{32}-ATP exchange, an ADP-ATP exchange, nor an exchange between O^{18}-labeled water and inorganic phosphate.

There are three properties of the purified ATPase which I should like to discuss in greater detail, because they illustrate how a purified enzyme may differ from the enzyme in its natural matrix and how these aberrations in properties may serve as important guides to our understanding of the operation of the enzyme under physiological conditions. The three properties are (a) its cold lability, (b) its interaction with water, and (c) its insensitivity to oligomycin. In contrast, the ATPase activity of mitochondria is insensitive to cold but sensitive to oligomycin, and carefully prepared mitochondria actually show little or no hydrolytic activity. The changes in the properties of the purified enzyme have served a useful purpose in allowing us to devise assay systems for the isolation of mitochondrial components which are responsible for the difference in properties. These components may or may not have catalytic activities of their own and yet may be essential components of the structural organization required for the efficient operation of the phosphorylation process.

Cold Lability of the Purified ATPase

Various compounds such as adenine nucleotides, Mg^{++}, p-mercuribenzoate, glutathione, ascorbic acid, and 1.2 M ammonium sulfate were tried as possible protectors of ATPase solutions against cold inactivation and found to be ineffective. However, high concentrations of glycerol (20%), as well as several other alcohols, protected the enzyme against cold inactivation. Attempts to reactivate cold-inactivated enzyme have been unsuccessful with preparations of less than highest purity. Dr. Penefsky has recently obtained reactivation of cold-inactivated enzyme with ATPase preparation of highest purity provided the exposure to cold was brief.

Many of the earlier studies of the cold inactivation of the enzyme were greatly hampered by a disconcerting variability of the lability from experiment to experiment. In due time, the variability was traced to two major factors: the age of the enzyme solution and the ionic composition during cold inactivation. Usually, solutions of ATPase were prepared by centrifuging an aliquot of the stock suspension in 2 M ammonium sulfate to remove excess salt and dissolving the precipitate in a buffered solution containing EDTA and ATP. Such solutions of the enzyme are stable at room temperature for several days. In the course of aging in the presence of ATP, the enzyme gradually lost cold sensitivity, as shown in Figure 11.2. After 15 minutes at 0°, a fresh solution of

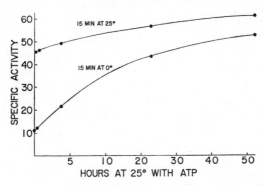

Fig. 11.2. Increased cold stability of aged ATPase solutions. Solutions of ATPase (100 μg per ml) in sucrose-Tris-EDTA buffer were aged in the presence of 4 mM ATP at 25°. To 0.12 M potassium bicarbonate (saturated with CO_2) were added 5 μg of various ATPase samples, and the mixtures were incubated for 15 minutes at 25° or 0° and then analyzed for residual ATPase activity.

ATPase showed 80% inactivation compared to the control at 25°, whereas a solution 2 days old showed less than 20% cold inactivation under the same conditions. The second important influence on the cold lability was the ionic composition of the medium of incubation. Under identical conditions the half-life of the enzyme at 0° in the presence of Tris-HCl buffer (pH 7.4) was 10 minutes, but with Tris-H_2SO_4 buffer (pH 7.4) it was more than 1 hour. In general, the cold lability was greater in the presence of monovalent anions than of divalent, but exceptions were noted, e.g., bicarbonate buffer was well tolerated and in fact accelerated the hydrolytic activity of the enzyme. Recent experiments have shown that ATPase solutions freed of salts by passage through a Sephadex column were only slowly inactivated in the cold. Loss of activity was greatly accelerated by addition of salts, particularly chlorides.

At least four mitochondrial components afford some protection to ATPase against cold inactivation. One is an unidentified substance of small molecular weight, which is soluble in 90% acetone and dialyzable; the second is a phospholipid mixture isolated from mitochondria; the third is an inhibitor of ATPase;[184] and the fourth is the oligomycin sensitivity factor (F_o). The last two factors will be discussed in greater detail in a later lecture. It is difficult to decide which of these factors plays a decisive role in intact mitochondria which have cold-stable ATPase activity. A large fraction of the potential ATPase activity is in the masked form, presumably in combination with a mitochondrial inhibitor. On the other hand, the unmasked ATPase is also stable and presumably protected by a combination of the three other factors. Of these, F_o is the most effective, but also the most complex, since it contains phospholipids and several proteins.

A great acceleration in the rate of cold inactivation was observed in the presence of relatively low urea concentrations, as shown in Figure 11.3. The half-life of an aged ATPase solution at 0° was less than 10 minutes in the presence of 0.8 M urea and about 2 hours in the absence of urea. At 25°, the enzyme was stable and even in the presence of urea the half-life was more than 2 hours. Inactivation of ATPase activity by urea in the cold proved particularly useful because it took place even with ATPase bound to mitochondria, though at a slower rate than with solutions of the enzyme.

Finally, a few words about the mechanism of cold inactivation. Recent experiments[206] have shown that the enzyme is

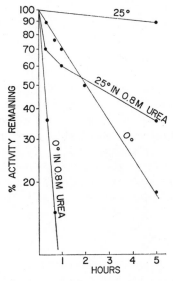

FIG. 11.3. Acceleration of cold inactivation of ATPase solutions in the presence of 0.8 M urea. Solutions of ATPase (100 μg per ml) in sucrose-Tris-EDTA buffer were exposed to 0.8 M urea and analyzed at intervals as described in Fig. 11.2.

broken into subunits in the cold and that 7 to 8 SH groups which are masked in the native enzyme become accessible for colorimetric determination. Similar changes occur by treatment of the enzyme with detergents. Amino acid analysis, kindly carried out by Dr. S. Moore, revealed 9 half cystine per mole of enzyme, 4 times as much histidine, and 5 times as much methionine. Besides these somewhat low values and the apparent absence of tryptophan, the composition of the amino acids showed no striking deviation from average pro-

206 H. S. Penefsky, *FP* **23**, 533 (1964).

teins. The formation of subunits in the cold, the physical chemists tell us, is most likely due to breaking of hydrophobic bonds.

INTERACTION WITH WATER

Freshly isolated mitochondria have little ATPase activity. This low reactivity with water is the basis of the phenomenon called respiratory control. In intact mitochondria neither $X \sim Y$ nor $X \sim P$ (Scheme 1.6) is readily hydrolyzed by water. On aging, respiratory control is lost and ATPase activity becomes manifest. A soluble protein obtained from mitochondria[184] was shown to combine with mitochondrial ATPase to yield an ATPase-inhibitor complex which did not react with water but was capable of coupling oxidation to phosphorylation. This inhibitor is a very interesting protein of small molecular weight (about 15,000) which is highly sensitive to proteolysis but rather stable to heat. It can be precipitated with trichloroacetic acid and redissolved without much loss in activity, and it is relatively soluble in ethanol (a nice protein to work with, except that there is not much of it in mitochondria). Addition of this inhibitor to submitochondrial particles blocked the entrance of water, presumably at $X \sim P$, but these particles remained "loosely coupled," i.e., they respired without a phosphate acceptor system. Presumably, water can still enter at site $X \sim Y$ at a rate sufficient to satisfy the rate of electron flow. It is therefore apparent that the inhibitor of ATPase cannot be the sole controlling mechanism operating in mitochondria, but it seems reasonable to assume that it may play an important role.

The content of ATPase activity in mitochondria is much greater than had been assumed on the basis of maximal stimulation by dinitrophenol. Treatment of submitochondrial particles with trypsin results in unmasking of an ATPase with a specific activity 10 times as high as that obtained with dinitrophenol in intact mitochondria.[107] Thus the

ATPase in mitochondria exposes, like an iceberg, less than 10% of its bulk to the surface.

INSENSITIVITY TO OLIGOMYCIN

This antibiotic has become a rather important tool in the study of oxidative phosphorylation and will be discussed in the next lecture. It inhibits ATPase activity in mitochondria or submitochondrial particles, but does not inhibit the purified enzyme. This fact indicated to us an important alteration in the property of the ATPase which required elucidation. Submitochondrial particles which were depleted of ATPase activity by sequential treatment with trypsin and urea (T-U-particles) conferred oligomycin sensitivity on the purified enzyme. Moreover, a factor which confers oligomycin sensitivity[107] can be extracted from T-U-particles by sonic oscillation. This factor (F_o) is similar in some respects to the structural protein of mitochondria, but the latter does not affect the oligomycin sensitivity of ATPase.

We can see from the foregoing that the three properties characteristic of the ATPase in intact mitochondria—the cold stability, the lack of reactivity with water, and the oligomycin sensitivity—can be conferred on the soluble ATPase by various soluble factors. Yet we still cannot tell how close we are to duplicating the proper structural environment of the ATPase by the addition of these various factors. We shall return to this difficult problem when we deal with experiments on reconstruction.

I should like to make a few comments regarding an ATPase which we have purified from yeast. At one time, we had difficulties in preparing ATPase from beef-heart mitochondria on a large scale, and we searched for a more suitable source. Our favorite source for enzyme purification is baker's yeast, and, in collaboration with W. Pricer at the National Institutes of Health, we purified ATPase from this source with properties remarkably similar to those of the beef-heart enzyme. The dependency of Mg^{++}, the substrate specificity, stimulation by dinitrophenol, inhibition by ADP, cold lability, sensitivity to mitochondrial inhibitor, and protection by glycerol were essentially the same. Both enzymes were insensitive to oligomycin when tested in solution, but sensitive in particulate preparations. Although we have not yet succeeded in preparing submitochondrial particles from yeast that show a dependency on yeast ATPase, it seems likely that the enzyme plays a similar role in oxidative phosphorylation in yeast and in beef-heart mitochondria.

I would like to draw your attention to certain similarities between myosin and mitochondrial ATPase.[60] Both hydrolyze only triphosphonucleotides (ATP, ITP, CTP, and UTP), although at different rates. Both are slightly stimulated by dinitrophenol or pentachlorophenol, and the stimulation by dinitrophenol is abolished by p-mercuribenzoate. It is tempting to consider the possibility that mitochondrial ATPase, in addition to its role in oxidative phosphorylation, is part of a contractile structure that participates in the phenomena of shrinkage and swelling of mitochondria, which we shall deal with in a later lecture.

REVERSAL OF ELECTRON TRANSPORT

Chance, Klingenberg, and their associates have demonstrated an energy-dependent reversal of electron transport.[206a,206b] It was shown with the double-beam spectrophotometer that mitochondrial DPN was reduced either by succinate or ferrocytochrome c, and that the reductive process was sensitive to uncouplers of oxidative phosphorylation. An alternative procedure to measure reversal is to add an acceptor for DPNH, such as acetoacetate,[206c] oxaloacetate,[206d] or α-ketoglutarate $+$ NH_4.[206e] With submitochondrial

[206a] B. Chance and G. Hollunger, *Nature* **185**, 666 (1960).

[206b] M. Klingenberg and W. Slenczka, *BZ* **331**, 486 (1959).

[206c] L. Ernster, *Proc. 5th Intern. Congr. Biochem., Moscow, 1961* Vol. 5, p. 115. Macmillan (Pergamon), New York, 1963.

[206d] M. Klingenberg and P. Schollmeyer, *Proc. 5th Intern. Congr. Biochem., Moscow, 1961* Vol. 5, p. 46. Macmillan (Pergamon), New York, 1963.

[206e] E. C. Slater and J. M. Tager, *BBA* **77**, 276 (1963).

particles, reduction of added DPN by succinate or other hydrogen donors can be measured spectrophotometrically,[206f] provided that the oxidation of DPNH is prevented by a suitable respiratory inhibitor.

Either ATP or respiratory energy can drive the reductive process. When ATP is used as energy source, either dinitrophenol or oligomycin inhibits; but when a high-energy intermediate of respiration provides the energy, the reduction is still sensitive to dinitrophenol but insensitive to oligomycin.[206c] These observations are important clues to the localization of the action of the inhibitors to be discussed later.

In some systems, the reduction of pyridine nucleotides (particularly TPN) by succinate can take place via formation of malate rather than by reversal of electron transport. This complication can readily be avoided by using chlorosuccinate as substrate.[206g]

The expenditure of energy in the reductive process was analyzed in several laboratories. It appears that one $\sim$ equivalent (ATP) is required for each step, in accordance with the expectation of a reversal of oxidative phosphorylation.[206c,206e] Yet some uncertainties still exist regarding the exact pathway of reversal. Differential susceptibility to antimycin has been reported,[206f] and participation of coenzyme Q_{10} is more readily demonstrable in the reduction of DPN than in the oxidation of DPNH.

In view of these considerations, some caution is indicated in the evaluation of data comparing the forward and reverse reactions of oxidative phosphorylation. Measurements of reaction rates under different conditions (e.g., in the presence or absence of Mg^{++}), of susceptibility to inhibitors, and of stimulation by coupling factors, have revealed differences between the forward and back reactions which have complicated the simple picture of reversal. This is unfortunate because the reduction of DPN by succinate represents the most convenient system for the study of the first site of

[206f] H. Löw, I. Vallin, and B. Alm, *in* "Energy-linked Functions of Mitochondria" (B. Chance, ed.), p. 5. Academic Press, New York, 1963.

[206g] R. L. Prairie and E. Racker, Unpublished observations (1963).

phosphorylation in the electron transport chain. Neverthe-less, the rapidly mounting data on the reversal of oxidative phosphorylation continue to yield very important information about the energy-producing and energy-utilizing mechanisms in mitochondria.

LECTURE 12

UNCOUPLERS AND INHIBITORS OF
OXIDATIVE PHOSPHORYLATION

Where is the knowledge we have lost in information?
—T. S. Eliot

There are literally hundreds of compounds that affect oxidative phosphorylation in one way or another. The effects of these various reagents have been tested, singly and in combination, on the P:O ratio, on crossover points, on exchange reactions, and on ATPase activity. These studies have been carried out with fresh mitochondria, with aged mitochondria, and with fragmented mitochondria. The amount of literature is staggering. It was once said that only uninhibited persons use inhibitors, and just now I wish that investigators in the field of oxidative phosphorylation were more inhibited. However, as I have emphasized before, inhibitors have played a decisive role in the elucidation of metabolic pathways. I shall therefore discuss some representative uncouplers and inhibitors of oxidative phosphorylation that have been most valuable in the study of its mechanism.

In view of their various actions, it may help to distinguish four categories: (*a*) the true uncouplers, which at appropriate concentrations limit phosphorylation and either stimulate or do not affect respiration; an example in this group is dinitrophenol; (*b*) inhibitory uncouplers, agents which depress respiration but inhibit phosphorylation even more (they lower the P:O ratio); an example in this group is progesterone; (*c*) inhibitors of oxidative phosphorylation which depress oxidation steps only when they are coupled to phosphorylation but not in an uncoupled system; an example in

145

this group is oligomycin; and finally, (d) inhibitors of oxidation such as cyanide or antimycin—compounds which block respiration in uncoupled as well as in coupled systems. These compounds may also sometimes affect phosphorylation more than oxidation, particularly if the system is capable of using an alternative pathway of electron transport.

TRUE UNCOUPLERS OF
OXIDATIVE PHOSPHORYLATION

The first uncoupler which we shall discuss is dinitrophenol. I mentioned in the last lecture the speculations of Lardy and Elvehjem in 1945 on the mode of action of dinitrophenol.[200] Their proposal received experimental support a few years later[201] when dinitrophenol was shown to uncouple oxidative phosphorylation and to eliminate the requirement of inorganic phosphate for respiration. Early interpretation of the mechanism of action of dinitrophenol by Hunter, Green, Lardy, and their collaborators centered around a dinitrophenol-induced cleavage of a high-energy phosphorylated intermediate. Soon thereafter, however, most investigators began to favor the idea that dinitrophenol facilitates the hydrolysis of a nonphosphorylated high-energy intermediate. Drysdale and Cohn[194] attempted to differentiate between these two possibilities of the mode of action of dinitrophenol, and after reporting their own studies on the H_2O^{18}-inorganic phosphate exchange, they presented a penetrating discussion of the difficulties arising from either of the two concepts mentioned above. At concentrations of dinitrophenol below 0.05 mM, which completely inhibited ATP formation, the O^{18} content of inorganic phosphate corresponded to the number of oxygen atoms expected to be introduced by hydrolysis of an $X \sim P$ intermediate. Also favoring an $X \sim P$ site of hydrolysis was the lower sensitivity of the O^{18} incorporation as compared to oxidative phosphorylation, since the H_2O^{18} may then enter via an earlier intermediate, such as $X \sim Y$, and via $X \sim P$ be incorporated into phosphate. A third point in favor of the $X \sim P$ site is the fact that dinitrophenol stimulated the soluble ATPase. Experiments with chloropromazine were also interpreted to indicate a cleavage of an $X \sim P$ compound by dinitrophenol.[174]

On the other hand, concentrations of dinitrophenol above 0.05 mM were found to reduce the level of O^{18} incorporation considerably below the 1 atom per mole of P_i expected if $X \sim P$ were the only site of dinitrophenol action.[194] The failure of mitochondria to catalyze the cleavage of synthetic dinitrophenyl phosphate, a hypothetical intermediate in the dinitrophenol-induced hydrolysis of $X \sim P$,[8] as well as their inability to catalyze an O^{18} exchange between O^{18}-labeled dinitrophenol and the medium,[194] seemed to eliminate O—P cleavage of a dinitrophenyl phosphate intermediate. Moreover, an acetone-dried preparation of liver mitochondria which contained dinitrophenol stimulated ATPase activity and did not catalyze an H_2O^{18}—P_i exchange. I have mentioned that the soluble ATPase from mitochondria also did not catalyze this exchange but was required for it in submitochondrial particles. The previously mentioned experiments[201] on the replacement of inorganic phosphate by dinitrophenol in respiration—a phenomenon more recently extensively investigated by Ernster, Slater, and their collaborators—are in favor of an $X \sim Y$ intermediate. These studies, as well as experiments with oligomycin which favor the $X \sim Y$ rather than the $X \sim P$ site of dinitrophenol action, will be discussed when I deal with the reversal of oxidative phosphorylation.

When two or more eminent investigators disagree and apparently obtain results that lead to divergent conclusions, it usually turns out that the experiments were correct but the interpretations can be challenged. Often an important link is missing and in the last analysis both investigators turn out to be right or, if you wish to put it less politely, to be wrong. In the case of the mode of dinitrophenol action, there are two ways out of the dilemma. Dinitrophenol induces the hydrolysis of both $X \sim Y$ and $X \sim P$, or it hydrolyzes neither. According to the second proposal,[60] dinitrophenol interacts with the coupling factors in such a manner as to cause a dissociation of phosphorylation from respiration and both systems thus become accessible to water. Electrons flow through the respiratory chain and ATP is hydrolyzed, as illustrated in Fig. 12.1.

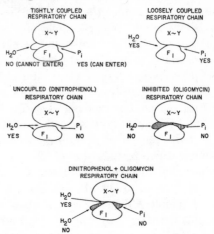

FIG. 12.1. Proposed mechanism of uncoupling of oxidative phosphorylation.

The alternative explanation of multiple sites of action of dinitrophenol (on $X \sim P$ and $X \sim Y$) deserves consideration, in view of the fact that this compound even affects some nonphosphorylative oxidative processes. Moreover, with certain other inhibitors, evidence for multiple sites of action is becoming increasingly convincing. Nevertheless, I still favor the view that dinitrophenol affects the structural relationship rather than catalyzes the hydrolysis of an intermediate, for the following two reasons: (*a*) The experimental observation, that dinitrophenol uncouples oxidative phosphorylation at concentrations that do not induce ATPase activity, is readily explained by a differential accessibility to water. On the other hand, if dinitrophenol catalyzes the hydrolysis of the intermediates, it should also release ATPase activity. (*b*) Submitochondrial particles that had been treated with the ATPase-inhibitor catalyzed oxidative phosphorylation which was uncoupled by dinitrophenol, yet this compound did not elicit ATPase activity. This again can be explained by a differential accessibility to water, but is more difficult to visualize in terms of a hydrolysis of an intermediate.

An uncoupler similar to dinitrophenol is carbonyl cyanide *m*-chlorophenyl hydrazone (CCP), which is a very useful agent because it is much more potent than dinitrophenol and also very effective as an uncoupler of photophosphorylation.[207] An interesting and useful aspect of CCP is that its action, at least in submitochondrial particles, was readily reversed by addition of certain substituted SH compounds. Cysteine, cysteamine, and homocysteine were very effective, but all other SH compounds that were tested, including dithiols, were relatively ineffective.

Arsenate, the classical uncoupler of substrate level oxidative phosphorylation, is also effective as uncoupler of electron transport-linked oxidative phosphorylation in mitochondria.[208] At relatively high concentrations of arsenate, both phosphorylation and the P_i^{32}-ATP exchange were markedly depressed. Wadkins[209] has recently studied the effect of arsenate on the ATPase activity and observed a pronounced Mg^{++}-dependent stimulation. The arsenate effect exhibited two pH optima, one at 6.5 and one at 7.5, similar to the peaks which Slater and his collaborators had reported[210,211] for the dinitrophenol-stimulated ATPase activity in mitochondria. The differences in pH optima in the presence of dinitrophenol are difficult to interpret in view of the effect of pH on the equilibrium of the different ionic species of the drug and on their ability to permeate the particles. On the other hand, it is quite conceivable than an uncoupler such as arsenate could affect the same coupling factor at one phosphorylation site at one pH and at another site at a different pH. Such studies are informative with

[207] P. G. Heytler, *Biochemistry* **2**, 357 (1963).
[208] R. K. Crane and F. Lipmann, *JBC* **201**, 235 (1953).
[209] C. L. Wadkins, *JBC* **235**, 3300 (1960).
[210] D. K. Myers and E. C. Slater, *BJ* **67**, 558, 572 (1957).
[211] H. C. Hemker and W. C. Hülsmann, *BBA* **48**, 221 (1961).

regard to the properties of the individual sites, but do not serve to indicate the operation of different coupling factors. It will be shown later that a single protein (ATPase) serves as a coupling factor at all three phosphorylation sites.

The mode of action of arsenate is still unknown. It is tempting to propose that it acts by competing with phosphate for a high-energy intermediate, $X \sim Y$, which is formed during electron transport, similar to the thiol ester in glyceraldehyde 3-phosphate oxidation. However, the large amounts of arsenate necessary, the time lag required for its action,[208,212] the need for ADP for stimulation of respiration,[213] and the inhibitory action of arsenate on dinitrophenol-stimulated ATPase activity,[214] all suggest that perhaps arsenate also affects a structural displacement rather than the hydrolysis of an intermediate. As in the case of dinitrophenol, quantitative differences can be discerned with regard to the site of action. For example, the effect of arsenate on the ATPase and P_i^{32}-ATP exchange occurred without lag, whereas the depression of oxidative phosphorylation was time-dependent.[212]

There is a long list of other agents that can uncouple oxidative phosphorylation. Among them are many oxidation-reduction dyes such as 2,6-dichlorophenolindophenol and methylene blue, which may act by virtue of their ability to short-circuit the electron pathway. Some of these dyes also affect the ATPase activity and the P_i^{32}-ATP exchange,[181,215] and therefore may act more directly on the phosphorylation mechanism. That an electron acceptor does not necessarily act as an uncoupling agent is illustrated by the fact mentioned previously, that ferricyanide or phenazine methosulfate can act as electron acceptors without seriously disturbing the phosphorylation process.

[212] G. F. Azzone and L. Ernster, *JBC* **236**, 1510 (1961).
[213] R. W. Estabrook, *BBRC* **4**, 89 (1961).
[214] P. Siekevitz, H. Löw, L. Ernster, and O. Lindberg, *BBA* **29**, 378 (1958).
[215] A. L. Lehninger, C. L. Wadkins, and L. F. Remmert, *CIBA Found. Sympos., Regulation of Cell Metabolism, 1958* p. 130 (1959).

There is one feature that complicates studies on the effect of uncouplers on oxidative phosphorylation or ATPase activity in mitochondria; namely, that small changes in the structural integrity of the mitochondria lead to uncoupling and to unmasking of the ATPase. For example, hypotonicity, Ca^{++}, azide, bile salts, and several detergents all elicit ATPase activity, and it is often difficult, therefore, to decide what represents a direct action on the phosphorylation mechanism and what is due to a change in the structural integrity of the mitochondria. It seems, moreover, that some of the agents may act in both ways. Bilirubin quite visibly alters the mitochondrial structure, but it also uncouples oxidative phosphorylation in submitochondrial particles and strongly inhibits the soluble ATPase.[92] Another compound is thyroxine, which is a potent uncoupling agent. Lehninger has been a proponent of the idea that thyroxine acts on the structure of the mitochondria and thereby uncouples oxidative phosphorylation,[216] since it was observed that phosphorylation in digitonin particles is not susceptible to thyroxine. Other submitochondrial particles, however, are quite sensitive to triiodothyronine,[93,217] and soluble ATPase is inhibited at low concentrations.[92] Sodium azide also has a double action, by stimulating ATPase activity of mitochondria first and then inhibiting it.[210,218] The first action, presumably due to structural changes of the mitochondria, may have considerable bearing on the frequently observed inhibition of assimilatory processes. In recent experiments on the effect of azide on muscle,[219] the primary effect was that of ATPase stimulation followed by an inhibition.

The question arises, how can small structural changes in mitochondria eliminate phosphorylation, while sonication or mechanical disintegration yields actively phosphorylating submitochondrial particles? There are probably several an-

[216] A. L. Lehninger, C. L. Wadkins, C. Cooper, T. M. Devlin, and J. L. Gamble, Jr., *Science* **128,** 450 (1958).
[217] J. H. Park, B. P. Meriwether, and C. R. Park, *BBA* **28,** 662 (1958).
[218] H. E. Robertson and P. D. Boyer, *JBC* **214,** 295 (1955).
[219] M. K. Gould and E. Racker. In preparation.

swers to this question, but perhaps the most important one leads us directly to our next point on the agenda, namely, the release of the so-called natural uncoupling agents. Pressman and Lardy discovered[220] that natural uncoupling agents, which were identified as long-chain fatty acids, can be released from microsomes or mitochondria. A particulate and heat-labile uncoupler was isolated from mitochondria;[221] and a soluble protein called mitochrome[222] and a U-factor with uncoupling activities[223] were also obtained in various laboratories. It seems likely now[224] that the active agent is a long-chain fatty acid, since all these natural uncouplers have in common the property of being effectively counteracted by serum albumin.

Liver mitochondria tested shortly after preparation yielded good P:O ratios. After storage for 1–2 days at 0° they respired but did not phosphorylate. Addition of serum albumin restored phosphorylation to a considerable extent, as shown in Table 12.I.[221] These data emphasize three points. One is to demonstrate a pitfall in the study of so-called coupling factors. Just looking at the data in Table 12.I, we might conclude that serum albumin is a coupling factor in oxidative phosphorylation. It is apparent, therefore, that in experiments with coupling factors we must be continuously aware of the possibility that we are dealing with a factor which counteracts an inhibitor from natural sources or even an inhibitor that was introduced during the preparation of the particles. A stimulation of oxidative phosphorylation by CoA was later traced to its participation in the esterification of long-chain fatty acids.[170,223] This brings us to the second point, the possible role of long-chain fatty acids as uncouplers of oxidative phosphorylation in metabolic regulation. Pressman and Lardy had proposed such a role[220] and recent studies on retrogressing mammary gland have yielded some direct experimental

[220] B. C. Pressman and H. A. Lardy, *BBA* **21**, 458 (1956).
[221] M. E. Pullman and E. Racker, *Science* **123**, 1105 (1956).
[222] B. D. Polis and H. W. Shmukler, *JBC* **227**, 419 (1957).
[223] A. L. Lehninger and L. F. Remmert, *JBC* **234**, 2459 (1959).
[224] W. C. Hülsmann, W. B. Elliott, and E. C. Slater, *BBA* **39**, 267 (1960).

evidence for such a function. Loss of oxidative phosphorylation was traced to the presence of long-chain fatty acids, primarily oleic acid, which probably accumulated because of marked decrease in the oleic acid-activating enzyme.[225] Unsaturated long-chain fatty acids are more effective uncouplers

TABLE 12.I

EFFECT OF SERUM ALBUMIN ON
OXIDATIVE PHOSPHORYLATION IN AGED MITOCHONDRIA

Additions	Δ O.D. $\times 10^3/10$ minutes[a]	
	Fresh mitochondria	Aged mitochondria (24 hours)
None	1357	87
+ Bovine serum albumin	1483	872
+ Bovine serum albumin + dinitrophenol (5×10^{-5} M)	35	0

[a] These measurements of oxidative phosphorylation were carried out spectrophotometrically, measuring TPN reduction in the presence of hexokinase, glucose, and glucose-6-phosphate dehydrogenase. This procedure can be used with liver mitochondria, but not with beef-heart mitochondria because of an active TPNH oxidase.

than saturated acids,[226] a fact we may wish to remember when we read advertisements on food containing large amounts of unsaturated fatty acids. We can easily understand that "calories don't count" in the presence of an uncoupler such as unsaturated fatty acids or dinitrophenol, but we should also remember that when we are exposed to a lethal dose of dinitrophenol,[227] we need not be concerned whether calories count or don't count. The third point that is apparent from Table 12.I is that the effect of the natural uncouplers is reversible, as shown by the considerable recovery of activity after 24 hours. Thyroxine, another natural un-

[225] R. A. Butow, A. Burg, and W. L. Nelson, *FP* **22,** 421 (1963).
[226] P. Borst, J. A. Loos, E. J. Christ, and E. C. Slater, *BBA* **62,** 509 (1962).
[227] E. Racker, *Am. J. Med.* **35,** 143 (1963).

coupler, which we discussed earlier, has also been used to make people thinner. Ca^{++} should also be listed as a natural uncoupling agent, as well as bile salts. The possible physiological role of these agents still needs elucidation. Obviously, the action of thyroxine cannot be explained on the basis of its uncoupling effect, for several reasons. The most apparent is the ineffectiveness of other uncoupling agents as substitutes for the hormone. But this argument is not quite as cogent as it may seem, since it does not and cannot take into account the possibility of highly selective effects of the hormone on target organs. Without more detailed information on the distribution of the hormone as well as on the differential sensitivity of various tissues or even cell population to its action as uncoupler, it is hardly worth while to extend the discussion of this interesting problem.

There are numerous naturally occurring uncoupling agents. Among them are various antibiotics.[228] Venoms and bacterial toxins have been shown to uncouple oxidative phosphorylation.[229,230] The effect of venom on the P:O ratio was prevented by lecithin and ascribed to phospholipase action. Recent experiments in our laboratory showed that phospholipase A rapidly inactivated one of the structural proteins of mitochondria (F_o), which we shall discuss later. The inactivation was completely prevented in the presence of EDTA. Longer exposure to phospholipase A was necessary to inactivate the respiratory chain.[231]

INHIBITORY UNCOUPLERS

Progesterone depressed respiration but also lowered the P:O ratio.[232,233] It inhibited the reduction of cytochrome *c*

[228] H. A. Lardy, D. Johnson, and W. C. McMurray, *ABB* **78,** 587 (1958); H. A. Lardy and W. C. McMurray, *FP* **18,** 269 (1959).
[229] J. H. Quastel, *Proc. Intern. Symp. Enzyme Chem., Tokyo and Kyoto, 1957* p. 510. Maruzen, Tokyo, 1958.
[230] I. Aravindakshan and B. M. Braganca, *BBA* **31,** 463 (1959).
[231] K. S. Ambe and F. L. Crane, *Science* **129,** 98 (1959).
[232] R. Wade and H. W. Jones, Jr., *JBC* **220,** 547, 553 (1956).
[233] K. L. Yielding and G. M. Tomkins, *Proc. Natl. Acad. Sci. U. S.* **45,** 1730 (1959).

by DPNH in mitochondria, had little effect with succinate as substrate, and actually stimulated ferrocytochrome c oxidation. Progesterone, therefore, acts as a true uncoupler at the third phosphorylation site and as an inhibitory uncoupler at the first site. Such differential effects, which are becoming increasingly apparent, do not necessarily indicate multiple modes of action but may be based on organizational differences of coupling factors, as I have pointed out earlier in the discussion of "multiple ATPases." Progesterone may interact with a coupling factor to form a rather nondissociable inhibitory complex at Site 1 but a dissociable complex at Site 3. It is of interest in this connection that progesterone did not inhibit the reduction of cytochrome c by DPNH in the presence of a soluble preparation of DPNH-cytochrome c reductase,[233] but did inhibit ATPase activity of disrupted mitochondria and of the soluble enzyme. Effects on structural organization similar to those noted with thyroxine are indicated by the elicitation of ATPase activity by progesterone in intact mitochondria.[232]

INHIBITORS OF OXIDATIVE PHOSPHORYLATION

There are four representatives in this group which I would like to discuss briefly: guanidine, oligomycin, amytal, and chlorpromazine. They inhibit respiration only when linked to phosphorylation; guanidine and oligomycin are counteracted by dinitrophenol, whereas amytal and chlorpromazine are not. Guanidine inhibits glutamate oxidation in kidney mitochondria without affecting the P:O ratio.[233a] Dinitrophenol, at 0.2 mM, completely reverses the inhibition of oxidation. Guanidine, which has no effect on uncoupled (calcium-treated) mitochondria, becomes inhibitory after coupling activity has been restored by treatment with Mn^{++} and ATP. Oligomycin is a very potent inhibitor of DPN-linked oxidation[228] and the inhibition is released by dinitrophenol, CCP, or oleate. The $P_i{}^{32}$-ATP and the H_2O^{18}-P_i exchange reactions, as well as the ATPase activity in the presence of dinitrophenol, are inhibited by oligomycin. In submito-

[233a] G. Hollunger, *Acta Pharmacol. Toxicol.* **11**, Suppl. 1 (1955).

chondrial particles that are loosely coupled, oligomycin does not affect oxidation but still inhibits ATPase as well as net phosphorylation and the P_i^{32}-ATP exchange reaction. It therefore seems that oligomycin acts on the phosphorylating apparatus rather than on the respiratory chain. We could visualize (Fig. 12.1) that oligomycin interacts with the complex coupling factor and respiratory chain as shown, in such a manner that the inhibited complex does not dissociate spontaneously; thus respiration is inhibited. When dinitrophenol is added, the coupling factor is dissociated and respiration can take place again. These schematic drawings are intended only as visual aids and should not be taken literally. In any event, from the experiments with dinitrophenol and oligomycin we could conclude that dinitrophenol acts on $X \sim Y$, and that oligomycin inhibits the formation of $X \sim P$ from $X \sim Y$ in the forward direction and from ATP in the reverse reaction.

There are indications that the action of amytal is not identical with that of chloropromazine. Chloropromazine inhibits the Mg^{++}-activated ATPase in mitochondria, but amytal does not. We have obtained similar data in our laboratory with the soluble enzyme, which is quite sensitive to chloropromazine and insensitive to amytal. I believe that all these variations can be explained with the least strain by an effect of the inhibitors on structural interaction.

Judah and his collaborators have come to the conclusion that chloropromazine and dinitrophenol do not act at the same site. Lardy and his collaborators have reached a similar conclusion with respect to oligomycin and dinitrophenol. However, the two groups of investigators have arrived at opposite conclusions regarding the site of dinitrophenol action. Whereas Lardy feels that $X \sim P$ is excluded as a site for dinitrophenol, Judah concludes from his data with chloropromazine that dinitrophenol acts on $X \sim P$. We are faced with the same dilemma that we discussed previously on the localization of action of dinitrophenol, and we might try to resolve it in a similar manner. We can postulate that amytal and chloropromazine react with a complex formed between the coupling factor and the respiratory catalysts at Site 1. Since a flavoprotein participates in this site, it can readily be visualized that chloropromazine, which is known to react chemically with FAD, may form an undissociable complex by interacting with both the coupling factor and the flavoprotein. Such a double complex might not be readily dissociated by dinitrophenol. An interaction between coupling factor and chloropromazine may also help to explain the uncoupling effect of this inhibitor on substrates such as succinate. However, the inhibition of cytochrome oxidase by chloropromazine, reported by Judah and his collaborators, cannot be fitted into this scheme. The conclusion that some of these inhibitors must have more than one mode of action appears to be almost inescapable, little as we favor such interpretations.

Oligomycin has emerged as the most useful representative of this group. It inhibits mitochondrial ATPase at very low concentrations, whereas much higher concentrations are needed to inhibit extramitochondrial ATPase.[234] Most important for theoretical consideration of the mechanism of phosphorylation is the finding [235,236] that oligomycin inhibits the energy-linked reduction of DPN by succinate when ATP is used as energy donor, but not when respiratory energy is used. Since the latter experiments were carried out with P_i-depleted mitochondria,[236a] a nonphosphorylated intermediate is implicated. The dinitrophenol-sensitive incorporation of C^{14}-labeled amino acids into proteins takes place in the presence of oligomycin.[237-239] The energy-dependent reduction of TPN not only proceeds in the presence of oligomycin but in loosely coupled systems is markedly accelerated

[234] H. E. M. Van Groningen and E. C. Slater, *BBA* **73**, 527 (1963).
[235] L. Ernster, *Proc. 5th Intern. Congr. Biochem., Moscow, 1961,* Vol. 5, p. 115. Macmillan (Pergamon), New York, 1963.
[236] A. M. Snoswell, *BBA* **60**, 143 (1962).
[236a] L. Ernster, Personal communication (1964).
[237] D. E. S. Truman and H. Löw, *Exptl. Cell Res.* **31**, 230 (1963).
[238] J. R. Bronk, *Proc. Natl. Acad. Sci. U. S.* **50**, 524 (1963).
[239] A. M. Kroon, *BBA* **72**, 391 (1963).

by oligomycin.[240,241] Of particular interest is the recent finding
that phospholipid synthesis shows the same pattern of differential susceptibility to dinitrophenol and oligomycin.[242]

It should be pointed out, however, that even potent inhibitors such as oligomycin do not eliminate the last traces
of oxidative phosphorylation. When a very slow reaction is
measured, such as the synthesis of phospholipid or of protein,
the small residual ATP-generating capacity may suffice to
drive the biosynthetic process. It is significant that at oligomycin concentrations that eliminated ATP synthesis, the
incorporation of $P_i{}^{32}$ into acid-soluble nucleotides still took
place.[242]

INHIBITORS OF OXIDATION

Among the inhibitors of respiration, probably the most
useful are cyanide, antimycin, and rotenone. Cyanide inhibits
at Site 3, antimycin at Site 2, and rotenone at Site 1. Thus,
functional separation of the sites in the respiratory chain is
possible, and numerous investigators have successfully used
these compounds. Under some conditions, however, these
compounds may interfere with phosphorylation, particularly
at concentrations higher than the minimal required for
blocking respiration. Adequate controls and caution in interpretation are required for the analysis of observations made
with these inhibitors.

[240] L. Danielson and L. Ernster, *in* "Energy-linked Functions of Mito-
    chondria" (B. Chance, ed.), p. 157. Academic Press, New York, 1963.
[241] E. Racker and T. E. Conover, *FP* **22**, 1088 (1963).
[242] J. Garbus, H. F. DeLuca, M. E. Loomans, and F. M. Strong, *JBC*
    238, 59 (1963).

LECTURE 13

SOLUBLE FACTORS AND
INTERMEDIATES OF OXIDATIVE
PHOSPHORYLATION

Get you home, you fragments.
—W. Shakespeare, *Coriolanus*

The Devil can quote Shakespeare for his own purpose.
—G. B. Shaw

Although brilliant deductions concerning metabolic pathways have been made from studies with intact tissues, the elucidation of detailed mechanisms requires the resolution of the multi-enzyme systems into separate components. Until recently very few successful attempts at physical separation of catalysts in the field of oxidative phosphorylation had been reported. The first submitochondrial system that catalyzed oxidative phosphorylation was obtained from *Escherichia coli*. Crude extracts catalyzed phosphorylation with a P:O ratio of 0.7 in the presence of alcohol and alcohol dehydrogenase as a DPNH regenerating system.[242a] Fractionation of this preparation revealed the requirement for a particulate fraction which catalyzed oxidation and a soluble fraction which was required for phosphorylation. Pinchot continued these studies with *Alcaligenes faecalis*, and obtained evidence for the participation of one particulate and two soluble fractions.[96] The particles catalyzed oxidation of DPNH, but the soluble fractions had to be added to obtain phosphorylation. One of the soluble fractions was heat-labile, the other was heat-stable. The latter was identified as polynucleotide which acted as a ligand between the heat-

[242a] G. B. Pinchot and E. Racker, *FP* **10**, 233 (1951).

labile soluble factor and the particles. From *Mycobacterium phlei*, one particulate and two soluble fractions were obtained which stimulated oxidative phosphorylation.[243] Of the soluble fractions, one was heat-labile, the other heat-stable and replaceable by vitamin K_1 and FAD.

With animal tissues, progress was delayed partly for psychological reasons. The preparation of mitochondria was tedious and phosphorylating capacity was lost at a discouragingly rapid rate. The development of large-scale preparation of stable beef-heart mitochondria[244] in 1957 encouraged the search for soluble factors. Shortly, thereafter, reports were published on two different protein factors that were required for the coupling of phosphorylation to oxidation.[245,246]

The discussion of the soluble factors in oxidative phosphorylation will be dealt with under two subheadings: nonprotein factors, and protein coupling factors.

NONPROTEIN FACTORS

Mg^{++} AND Mn^{++}

The role of the divalent metal ions is not easy to evaluate. Many particles, such as digitonin particles and intact mitochondria, contain enough Mg^{++} to make any further additions unnecessary. Some submitochondrial particles that show a dependence on Mg^{++} are loosely coupled and require an active phosphate acceptor system (hexokinase and glucose) to compensate for the ATPase activity. Since hexokinase requires Mg^{++}, the analysis of Mg^{++} requirement in these partly resolved particles is not without ambiguity. There are indications that Mg^{++} serves as a ligand between the soluble fraction required for phosphorylation and the particulate fraction required for oxidation. Linnane and Titchener described a requirement for Mg^{++} for the association of a soluble fraction with the particles.[94] A similar observation has been

[243] A. F. Brodie, *JBC* **234**, 398 (1959).
[244] D. E. Green, R. L. Lester, and D. M. Ziegler, *BBA* **23**, 516 (1957).
[245] M. E. Pullman, H. S. Penefsky, and E. Racker, *ABB* **76**, 227 (1958).
[246] A. W. Linnane, *BBA* **30**, 221 (1958).

made with bacterial fractions obtained from *Acetobacter vinelandii*.[247] We observed that ATPase from beef-heart mitochondria dissociated from the particles much more readily in the presence of EDTA. In some experiments addition of Mg^{++} appeared to aid the reconstitution, in others it did not seem to be necessary. The most striking evidence, though indirect, for the need of Mg^{++} for phosphorylation has been provided by experiments on the reversal of oxidative phosphorylation with resolved submitochondrial particles. A complete dependency of the reduction of DPN by succinate on Mg^{++} could be demonstrated[247a] when the energy required for this process was supplied by ATP.

RIBONUCLEIC ACIDS

Ribonucleic acid was reported to act as a ligand between a soluble coupling factor and oxidizing particles obtained from *A. faecalis*.[96] Allfrey and Mirsky observed a similar requirement for nucleic acid or other polyanions in nuclear phosphorylations.[99] Other investigators have noted inhibitory effects of ribonuclease on phosphorylating systems from both plant and animal tissues.[248,249]

QUINONES

The first suggestion that quinones participate in oxidative phosphorylation came from studies of liver mitochondria of animals that were fed a diet deficient in vitamin K.[250] A low P:O ratio was observed, and addition of vitamin K_1 at 10^{-5} M concentration stimulated phosphorylation linked to β-hydroxybutyrate oxidation. Since the P:O ratio appeared more depressed with β-hydroxybutyrate than with succinate as substrate, it was suggested that the quinone acted primarily on the first phosphorylation site. The sensitivity of vitamin K to ultraviolet light led to experiments on the effect of irradia-

[247] H. G. Hovenkamp, *Nature* **184,** 471 (1959).

[247a] R. L. Prairie, T. E. Conover, and E. Racker, *BBRC* **10,** 422 (1963).

[248] J. B. Hanson, *JBC* **234,** 1303 (1959).

[249] L. D. Wright, M. Rakowska, and R. Hanson, *FP* **19,** 38 (1960).

[250] C. Martius, H. Bieling, and D. Nitz-Litzow, *BZ* **327,** 163 (1955).

tion on oxidative phosphorylation. Both in animal tissues[251] and in bacteria,[252] inactivation of phosphorylation was observed, and in the case of bacteria, restoration of phosphorylation on addition of vitamin K was reported. Reduced vitamin K_3 was shown to be a substrate of oxidative phosphorylation,[253] an observation which was confirmed in our laboratory. The reduced quinone most probably serves, however, simply as a reductant of the respiratory chain. The great reactivity of quinones in oxidation-reduction reactions makes them, on the one hand, treacherous reagents for studies of mechanisms, but on the other hand, very attractive candidates as intermediate carriers at several sites of the respiratory chain. Chemical reactions take place between quinones and DPNH, flavoproteins, and cytochromes b and c, as well as with oxygen.

An interesting clue in favor of a possible participation of Q_{10} in oxidative phosphorylation has been obtained by Hatefi.[254] He observed that the addition of inorganic phosphate or arsenate to beef-heart mitochondria induced a reduction of Q_{10}. When ADP was added after inorganic phosphate, the reduced Q_{10} was reoxidized. Chance, however, could not observe an effect of inorganic phosphate on Q_{10} reduction,[255] and further work on this point is needed.

Experimental model systems of oxidative phosphorylation have been devised, demonstrating that the oxidation of quinolphosphates by oxidizing agents such as iodine or bromine in the presence of P_i gives rise to the formation of inorganic pyrophosphate; in the presence of AMP, to the formation of ADP.[256–258] Recent experiments have demonstrated a slow oxidation of Q_6-phosphate in mitochondria

[251] W. W. Anderson and R. D. Dallam, *JBC* **234,** 409 (1959).

[252] A. F. Brodie and J. Ballantine, *JBC* **235,** 226 and 232 (1960).

[253] J. P. Colpa-Boonstra and E. C. Slater, *BBA* **27,** 122 (1958).

[254] Y. Hatefi, *BBA* **31,** 502 (1959).

[255] B. Chance, *FP* **19,** 39 (1960).

[256] V. M. Clark, G. W. Kirby, and A. Todd, *Nature* **181,** 1650 (1958).

[257] V. M. Clark, D. W. Hutchinson, and A. Todd, *Nature* **187,** 59 (1960).

[258] T. Wieland and F. Pattermann, *Angew. Chem.* **70,** 313 (1958).

and in submitochondrial particles, which is accompanied by ATP synthesis.[259]

PROTEIN COUPLING FACTORS

The resolution of protein factors from the multi-enzyme system of oxidative phosphorylation in mitochondria has been progressing very slowly in spite of extensive efforts in several laboratories. There are three major impediments to progress in this area. (*a*) Resolution of the structurally firmly embedded coupling factors is usually not complete. The presence of residual activity in the submitochondrial particles (apo-particles) poses difficulties in the assay of the coupling factor. Sometimes, complete resolution can be achieved with respect to one phosphorylation site (e.g., between cytochrome *b* and cytochrome *c*) yet the same factor remains firmly anchored at another site. Thus, erroneous conclusions may be drawn regarding the specificity of the coupling factors for individual sites. (*b*) Reconstitution of the apo-particles with the factors to the active particles (holo-particles) is usually incomplete. Resolution often requires drastic procedures which result in damage to the submitochondrial particles. The potential phosphorylating activity of such particles, therefore, usually does not equal that of mitochondria. (*c*) The coupling factors separated from the mitochondrial matrix often exhibit pronounced changes in properties (e.g., alterations in their susceptibility to inhibitors or in their stability). It will be shown later that these changes in properties, although at times misleading, can be used as guides for the isolation of specific mitochondrial components that interact with the coupling factors.

Coupling Factor 1 (F_1)

This factor was purified from beef-heart mitochondria and was shown to catalyze the hydrolysis of ATP. The properties of this protein were dealt with in Lecture 11 and I shall confine myself here to discussing its relation to oxidative

[259] W. Gruber, R. Hohl, and T. Wieland, *BBRC* **12,** 242 (1963).

phosphorylation. I would like to tell you a little about the circumstances of its discovery, and the general approach we have taken to the problem of resolution of the system of oxidative phosphorylation.

At the time we made our first attempts to resolve a system of oxidative phosphorylation from animal mitochondria, several laboratories had just reported the successful preparation of submitochondrial particles that were capable of oxidative phosphorylation.[166,168] In no case, however, was there any indication of a resolution of the system into particulate and soluble fractions. Since, in the other laboratories, digitonin, alcohol, and sonic vibrations were being used for the fragmentation of the mitochondria, we decided to employ a different method. This is what you might call instrumental research: When you run out of ideas, use a new instrument. For several years, we had been breaking tumor cells or bacteria with glass beads in vacuum, and we now applied this procedure to beef-heart mitochondria. A suspension of mitochondria was placed, with glass beads, in a chilled Nossal tube, which was evacuated and then briefly shaken in the Nossal shaker. After intact mitochondria and mitochondrial debris had been removed at $26,000 \times g$, the supernatant solution was tested for oxidative phosphorylation and found to be active. It was then recentrifuged at $105,000 \times g$ for 30 minutes, and yielded a red-brown, gelatinous residue, which was referred to as "particulate fraction," and a faintly turbid yellow supernatant solution which was clarified by recentrifugation for an additional 30 minutes at $105,000 \times g$, and was referred to as "crude extract." The gelatinous particulate fraction was capable of catalyzing the oxidation of some intermediates of the Krebs cycle, but no phosphorylation accompanied this oxidation. On addition of the supernatant solution, esterification of phosphate took place,[93] as shown in Table 13.I. In this experiment, there was little or no phosphorylation associated with succinate oxidation in the presence of the particulate fraction, but, with increasing amounts of the extract, the phosphorylation increased until a P:O ratio of about 0.5 was obtained. Dinitrophenol uncoupled this system. The soluble factor was partially purified, but the assay was difficult because the dependency of the particles on F_1 was not too reproducible. Sometimes, almost complete dependency was obtained; sometimes, there was only a 50 to 300% stimulation of phosphorylation. Although this was sufficient to convince us that we were dealing with a real phenomenon, it was not really good enough for a reliable and convenient assay of the coupling factor. This misfortune actually turned out to be good fortune, since it induced us to

TABLE 13.I

EFFECT OF COUPLING FACTOR 1 ON OXIDATIVE PHOSPHORYLATION

Substrate	Coupling factor	P:O ratio
Succinate	−	0.0
	+	0.41
β-Hydroxybutyrate	−	0.05
	+	0.49
L-Glutamate	−	0.07
	+	0.46

take a chance and purify the ATPase, which was noted to fractionate parallel to F_1, and which turned out to be identical with the coupling factor. It was only considerably later that we learned how to obtain reproducible preparations that showed a complete dependency on F_1. The oxidation of DPNH yielded P:O ratios similar to those obtained with succinate as substrate, indicating that Site 1 did not contribute much to the phosphorylation process. Experiments with succinate as electron donor and cytochrome c as electron acceptor revealed that most of the phosphorylation obtained had occurred at Site 2, between cytochromes b and c. Tests with ascorbate of the phosphorylating activity at Site 3 in particles disrupted in the Nossal shaker were negative. In a sense, it was fortunate that the first resolved system of oxidative phosphorylation was active mainly at one site, thus permitting specific conclusions regarding the site under investigation.

Although the highly purified preparation of ATPase was

very effective as F_1, the question of whether the two activities really reside in the same protein had to be answered without ambiguity. One of the most unusual properties of the ATPase was its pronounced cold lability. We therefore looked into the cold lability of the coupling factor. As shown in Figure 13.1, the decline of ATPase activity was parallel to the

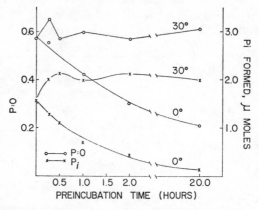

Fig. 13.1. Effect of incubation temperature on ATPase and coupling activity. The enzyme was incubated either at 0° or 30°. At the times indicated, aliquots were removed and the appropriate activity measured at 30°.

disappearance of coupling activity. At 30° both activities remained stable. Both coupling factor and ATPase were destroyed at 60°, but not in the presence of ATP. Inactivation due to dialysis, of both coupling activity and ATPase, was prevented by ATP in a similar manner. I have mentioned the effect of some uncouplers on ATPase. In Table 13.II, oxidative phosphorylation and ATPase activity are compared. Dinitrophenol ($5 \times 10^{-4} M$) is an effective uncoupler of oxidative phosphorylation and stimulates ATPase activity by about 50%. Pentachlorophenol, which is about 10 times as effective as dinitrophenol as an uncoupling agent, is also about 10 times as active as a stimulator of ATPase. All the other uncouplers in this Table (which contains only a partial list of compounds tested) were found to be potent inhibitors of ATPase activity. Of particular interest is azide, which is somewhat more effective as an inhibitor of ATPase activity than as an uncoupler of oxidative phosphorylation. Although it is quite apparent from these data that the correlation

TABLE 13.II
Effect of Uncouplers on ATPase and P:O Ratio

| | Percent of control | | | |
| Uncoupler | ATPase | | P:O ratio | |
	5×10^{-5}	5×10^{-4}	5×10^{-5}	5×10^{-4}
Dinitrophenol	108	152	36	0
Pentachlorophenol	161	22	0	0
Triiodothyronine	50	—	100	0
Dicoumarol	92	33	0	—
Chloropromazine	45	5	86	0
Atabrine	100	60	—	0
Azide	37	0	100	0

between uncoupling and ATPase is at best semiquantitative, a striking parallelism is apparent. In view of the complexity of oxidative phosphorylation, it is surprising that there is this much correlation.

The next aspect we looked into was the relationship between F_1 and the $P_i{}^{32}$-ATP exchange reaction. Neither F_1 nor the particles alone catalyzed an exchange reaction; both fractions were required. Although this finding of a parallel dependency of oxidative phosphorylation and $P_i{}^{32}$-ATP exchange on F_1 greatly supported the concept of a close association of the two processes, it was somewhat disappointing to us because we had hoped that a resolution of the exchange reaction might be achieved, as in the case of the ATPase activity.

Up to this point, all seemed well with the correlation between F_1 and ATPase activity. However, interpretation of experimental work is invariably complicated by observations which do not seem to fit. It usually pays to explore such discrepancies rather than to ignore them, because they often open up new avenues of approach. In the course of purification of F_1, it was observed that relatively more ATPase activity was recovered than F_1 activity.[92] One of the commonly used criteria for the presence of two different activities in a single protein is the constancy of the activity ratio throughout the purification procedure. As shown in Table 13.III, this criterion was not met. Whereas the activity of F_1

TABLE 13.III
PURIFICATION OF COUPLING FACTOR AND ATPASE

Preparation	Micromoles per minute per milligram		
	F_1	$P_i{}^{32}$-ATP	ATPase
Crude extract	3.1	1.7	0.25
Protamine precipitate	36.0	36	11.1
Heat step	91.0	71	39.8

for oxidative phosphorylation and for the $P_i{}^{32}$-ATP exchange reaction purified in a parallel manner, the ATPase activity was purified to a greater extent than the other two activities. This worried us at first, but we were relieved to find that the total yield of ATPase after purification was sometimes as high as 214% (Table 11.I). Although it was fashionable at the time to think in terms of protein synthesis, we refrained from this conclusion. It became clear later that the increase in total units was largely due to the removal of the ATPase inhibitor which I described in Lecture 11. In any case, it was obvious that an increase in the hydrolytic activity relative to coupling activity did not speak against the assumption that the two activities resided in the same protein. This experiment also illustrates the fact that the use of the activity ratio to establish the relationship between two reactions catalyzed by the same protein is not without ambiguity.

Coupling factor 1 was also shown to be required for other ATP-dependent processes in mitochondria, such as the reduction of DPN by succinate,[154] the reduction of TPN,[241] and the O^{18} exchange between H_2O and phosphate.[199] Oxidative phosphorylation at Site 1 as well as at Site 2 was shown to be dependent on F_1 in submitochondrial particles (P-particles) obtained by sonic oscillation in the presence of phosphatides.[154,241] Recently, it was shown that F_1 was required for phosphorylation at Site 3.[204a] F_1 from beef-heart mitochondria was found to act as a coupling factor in F_1-deficient rat liver submitochondrial particles.[260] However, F_1 was not required for the production of the high-energy intermediate formed during the oxidation of substrate, since the energy-dependent reduction of TPN took place in F_1-deficient particles if succinate oxidation was used to drive the reaction.[204a]

In view of these findings, it is visualized that F_1 catalyzes the transphosphorylation step from $X \sim P$ to ADP to form ATP at phosphorylation Sites 1 and 2.

COUPLING FACTOR 2 (F_2)

We had reported that submitochondrial particles that were exposed to sonic oscillation required a second coupling factor for phosphorylation associated with the oxidation of succinate.[93] A similar factor was described independently by Linnane and Titchener.[94] In both laboratories, difficulties were encountered because of the lability of the factor and the variability of the assay system.[261] However, our recent observations have eliminated some of these difficulties with regard to F_2. The partially purified factor was stabilized by the addition of ATP. A pronounced dependency on F_2 was achieved by exposing submitochondrial particles to pH 9.9 at 37° or by prolonged aging of P-particles. With such particles it was shown that F_2 was required for oxidative phosphorylation as well as for the $P_i{}^{32}$-ATP exchange.[204a] A crude preparation of the factor described by Linnane and Titchener[94] could be substituted for F_2 in these experiments.

COUPLING FACTOR 3 (F_3)

This factor was originally found to be required for the $P_i{}^{32}$-ATP exchange in submitochondrial particles that were exposed to trypsin.[183] Recent experiments in our laboratory

---

[260] R. L. Prairie, Unpublished experiments (1963).
[261] D. E. Green, R. E. Beyer, M. Hansen, A. L. Smith, and G. Webster, *FP* **22**, 1460 (1963).

have revealed a stimulation of phosphorylation associated
with the oxidation step between cytochrome b and cytochrome c by the addition of F_3. The factor described by
Linnane and Titchener[94] appears to contain F_3 as well as F_2.

COUPLING FACTOR 4 (F_4)

Submitochondrial particles obtained by exposing beef-
heart mitochondria to sonic oscillation in the presence of 2%
phosphatides require, in addition to F_1, another factor (F_4)
which can be extracted from mitochondria with $0.4\ N$ ammonia.[154] The protein is difficult to purify because of its low
solubility. It resembles in some respects the structural protein
described by Criddle *et al.*,[108] but the latter did not replace
F_4 in the system with P-particles. The low solubility of F_4
has the advantage that other soluble coupling factors, as well
as inhibitors of oxidative phosphorylation, can be readily
removed. This is mentioned because it points out the advis-
ability of assaying factors in multiple test systems. Crude
preparations of F_4 are suitable for studies of the P_i-^{32}-ATP
exchange but contain an inhibitor of oxidative phosphorylation. Purified F_4 preparations have been shown to be required
for oxidative phosphorylation at Sites 1 and 2[154] as well as at
Site 3.[204a] Recent experiments have shown an F_4 requirement
for the ATP-dependent reduction of DPN by succinate and
of TPN by DPNH,[241] as well as for the O^{18} exchange between
water and phosphate.[199] But F_4 is not required for the reduction of TPN when driven by respiration energy.[204a] It therefore
appears that F_4 is not concerned with the formation of the
nonphosphorylated high-energy intermediate but most probably with the formation of the phosphorylated intermediate.

A COUPLING FACTOR AT SITE 3

A rat liver enzyme which catalyzes an ADP-ATP exchange[191] has been shown[262] to act as coupling factor at Site
3. A coupling factor from beef-heart mitochondria was isolated which was said to be specific for Site 3.[261,262a] Since it

[262] C. L. Wadkins and A. L. Lehninger, *FP* **22**, 1092 (1963).
[262a] G. Webster, *BBRC* **7**, 245 (1962).

also catalyzes an ADP-ATP exchange reaction, it is possible that the liver and heart enzymes are similar, although no organ specificity study has yet been reported. Neither of the two preparations of the ADP-ATP exchange enzyme contained ATPase activity. The relationship of this factor to the other coupling factors that were shown to be required for oxidative phosphorylation[204a] remains obscure.

COUPLING FACTORS REQUIRED FOR PHOSPHORYLATION AT SITES 1 AND 2

These factors were briefly reported by Smith and Hansen[163] and Green *et al.*,[261] but no description of their properties was recorded. A stimulation of phosphorylation associated with DPNH oxidation by a crude extract (tentatively referred to as F_5) was observed in our laboratory with apo-particles prepared by exposing P-particles to mechanical fragmentation in a Nossal shaker. These various factors may be related to F_2 or F_3, but there is not sufficient information available for comparison. The large number of coupling factors that cannot be related to each other, and the many derivative submitochondrial particles which are used to test them, are no doubt a source of confusion for students and investigators.

A summary of some derivative submitochondrial particles obtained from mitochondria in our laboratory is presented in Table 13.IV, and a summary of the soluble factors from mitochondria in Table 13.V. One of the factors listed, F_0, has not yet been discussed. Although this factor has not been shown directly to be required for oxidative phosphorylation, it appears to play an important role in the structural orientation of coupling factors. Soluble ATPase (F_1) is not sensitive to oligomycin, whereas ATPase activity in phosphorylating particles is invariably very sensitive to this compound. In order to extract from submitochondrial particles the factor that confers oligomycin sensitivity, it was necessary to treat them first with trypsin, then with urea, and finally, to expose them to sonic oscillation. After 2 hours of centrifugation at $100,000 \times g$, the factor remained in the supernatant solution but was readily precipitated at low salt concentrations, and

TABLE 13.IV

DERIVATIVE SUBMITOCHONDRIAL PARTICLES

Preparation of particles	Name of particles	Properties
Shaking of mitochondria in Nossal disintegrator	N-particles	P_i^{32}-ATP exchange, and oxidative phosphorylation at Site 2 dependent on F_1
Sonic oscillation of N-particles	N-S-particles	P_i^{32}-ATP exchange, and oxidative phosphorylation at Site 2 dependent on F_1 and F_2
Sonic oscillation of mitochondria	S-particles	Oxidative phosphorylation at Sites 1 and 2 independent of coupling factors
Treatment of S-particles with 2 M urea	U-particles	P_i^{32}-ATP exchange, and oxidative phosphorylation at Site 2 dependent on F_1
Treatment of S-particles with trypsin	T-particles	P_i^{32}-ATP exchange dependent on F_3
Treatment of T-particles with 2 M urea	T-U-particles	Conferral of oligomycin sensitivity on added ATPase
Sonic oscillation of mitochondria in 2% phosphatides	P-particles ⎫	P_i^{32}-ATP exchange, and oxidative phosphorylation at Sites 1, 2, and 3 dependent on F_1 and F_4
Sonic oscillation of mitochondria in 0.02 N ammonia	A-particles ⎬	Reversal of oxidative phosphorylation dependent on F_1 and F_4
Treatment of S-particles at pH 9.9 at 37°	KOH-particles	P_i^{32}-ATP exchange and oxidative phosphorylation dependent on F_1 and F_2
Shaking of P-particles in Nossal disintegrator	P-N-particles	Stimulation of oxidative phosphorylation by F_5 with DPNH as substrate

TABLE 13.V

Soluble Factors from Mitochondria

Preparation of extract	Name of factor	Properties
Shaking of mitochondria in Nossal disintegrator	F_1	ATPase activity; required for oxidative phosphorylation, P_i^{32}-ATP exchange, and reversal of electron transport in P-particles
Extraction of acetone-dried mitochondria	F_2	Required for oxidative phosphorylation and P_i^{32}-ATP exchange in KOH-particles
Sonic oscillation of mitochondria	F_3	Stimulation of P_i^{32}-ATP exchange in P- or T-particles
Alkaline extraction of mitochondria	F_4	Required for oxidative phosphorylation, P_i^{32}-ATP exchange, and reversal of electron transport in P- or A-particles
Shaking of P-particles in Nossal disintegrator	F_5	Stimulation of oxidative phosphorylation with DPNH as substrate
Sonic oscillation of T-U-particles	F_o	Conferral of oligomycin sensitivity on ATPase
Alkaline extraction of mitochondria	ATPase-inhibitor	Inhibition of ATPase, but not of oxidative phosphorylation

exhibited properties of a structural protein. The treatment of submitochondrial particles with trypsin for the preparation of F_o resulted in a 10-fold activation of ATPase activity. Treatment with urea removed the ATPase activity and exposed F_o in such a manner that it became highly sensitive to trypsin. On addition of ATPase, F_o again became resistant to trypsin. I mention these experiments because they illustrate the intricate relationship between the various factors and suggest a topography of coupling factors governed by structural proteins such as F_o and F_4.[263]

We come now to the experimental evidence for intermediates in oxidative phosphorylation. The theoretical formulation (Scheme 1.7) which is widely accepted, with minor variations, requires a nonphosphorylated and a phosphorylated high-energy intermediate. There are two reports concerning nonphosphorylated high-energy compounds and two reports concerning phosphorylated intermediates, all capable of yielding ATP. Perhaps a few general comments should be made regarding these intermediates. Obviously, the discovery of an intermediate in oxidative phosphorylation represents a major contribution to biochemistry, and it is not surprising that the descriptions of such intermediates are presented with a great deal of enthusiasm. It is also apparent that the various interpretations of the role of these intermediates offered by different investigators are not compatible with each other. What should be emphasized is that a compound which was isolated from mitochondria, and which was shown to be capable of yielding ATP, may be an intermediate in oxidative phosphorylation, or it may not be. Let us remember that glucose 1-phosphate is a very important metabolite but it is not an intermediate between glucose and lactate. In bacteria, acetyl phosphate is formed from pyruvate and it can yield ATP, but it is not an intermediate in the combustion of pyruvate in the Krebs cycle. Carbamyl phosphate is formed in phosphorylating mitochondria but it is not an intermediate of oxidative phosphorylation. I should not

[263] E. Racker, *in* "Energy-linked Functions of Mitochondria" (B. Chance, ed.), p. 75. Academic Press, New York. 1963.

be surprised if the future reveals the presence of several other high-energy compounds which communicate with the system of oxidative phosphorylation. There is increasing evidence that important physiological processes, such as ion transport and synthetic reactions, can utilize the energy-producing machinery of mitochondria without the mediation of ATP. We should be prepared for multiple channels into oxidative phosphorylation, such as were found to enter glycolysis. If the production of two ATP molecules during glycolysis requires about a dozen enzymes, why should we assume that oxidative phosphorylation is a simple process?

In view of the probability that mitochondrial metabolites such as carbamyl phosphate will be claimed as intermediates of oxidative phosphorylation, it is necessary to apply criteria for intermediates such as have been used in other metabolic pathways. Without data both on the rate of formation of the intermediate and on its kinetic capacity to yield ATP, the possibility that they are formed in a side reaction remains open.

The first nonphosphorylated intermediate was found in a phosphorylating system of *A. faecalis*.[264,265] A heat-labile protein was obtained from DPNH-oxidizing particles that contained DPN and yielded ATP when supplied with P_i and ADP. It is of particular interest that this high-energy intermediate can be formed in a back reaction, with soluble factor, DPN, and ATP. This discovery indeed represents a breakthrough in oxidative phosphorylation, but numerous questions must be answered. Does this high-energy compound satisfy the kinetic criteria of an intermediate in oxidative phosphorylation? Is it a double-headed enzyme that catalyzes two reactions, one with P_i, the other with ADP? The rather sluggish formation of ATP from the intermediate suggests that the system is deficient and that perhaps additional transfer enzymes are required.

The second high-energy nonphosphorylated intermediate

[264] G. B. Pinchot, *Proc. Natl. Acad. Sci. U. S.* **46**, 929 (1960).
[265] G. B. Pinchot and M. Hormanski, *Proc. Natl. Acad. Sci. U. S.* **48**, 1970 (1962).

was isolated from beef-heart mitochondria.[266] In the presence of cytochrome oxidase containing particles and a soluble coupling factor, a dissociable intermediate was formed during the oxidation of reduced cytochrome *c*. The isolated intermediate yielded ATP on addition of ADP and P_i. The similarity of this system to that in *A. faecalis* is apparent, and the questions to be answered are identical.

A third compound implicated as an intermediate of oxidative phosphorylation is a phosphoprotein[267-269] from mammalian mitochondria that were exposed to highly radioactive solutions of P_i^{32} or to ATP^{32}. In both cases the label was shown to appear in the bound phosphohistidine group of the isolated proteins. The noted lack of sensitivity of the isotope incorporation to various uncoupling agents does not detract from these interesting findings, since we must apply different criteria when dealing with reactants than when dealing with catalysts, as I have pointed out previously. The kinetic behavior of the phosphoprotein appears compatible with an intermediate, since with P_i^{32} it is labeled more rapidly than intramitochondrial ATP, and more rapidly than P_i when ATP^{32} is used. The finding that a soluble enzyme from bovine liver mitochondria catalyzed the formation of bound phosphohistidine led to interesting studies of the properties of this protein. The relationship of all these observations to oxidative phosphorylation rests on two major assumptions. The first is that the phosphohistidine protein is indeed the only type of phosphoprotein in mitochondria; the second is that the histidine group is indeed the primary site of phosphorylation. Protein chemists have been plagued by artifacts

266 G. Webster, A. L. Smith, and M. Hansen, *Proc. Natl. Acad. Sci. U. S.* **49,** 259 (1963).

267 P. D. Boyer, M. DeLuca, K. E. Ebner, D. E. Hultquist, and J. B. Peter, *JBC* **237,** PC3306 (1962).

268 J. B. Peter and P. D. Boyer, *JBC* **238,** PC1180 (1963); J. B. Peter, D. E. Hultquist, M. DeLuca, G. Kreil, and P. D. Boyer, *ibid.* p. PC1182.

269 P. D. Boyer, D. E. Hultquist, J. B. Peter, G. Kreil, R. A. Mitchell, M. DeLuca, J. W. Hinkson, L. G. Butler, and R. W. Moyer, *FP* **22,** 1080 (1963).

due to shifts of groups during manipulations of the proteins. Moreover, two facts are disturbing and require further explanation: that only small amounts of bound phosphohistidine are observed in actively phosphorylating submitochondrial particles,[269] and that the formation of this intermediate is insensitive to dinitrophenol. In any case, the formation of a phosphoprotein during oxidative phosphorylation is a finding of great interest even if the intermediate should turn out to be on another pathway.

Similar considerations apply to the very interesting fourth compound considered to be a possible intermediate in oxidative phosphorylation.[270] A radioactive phosphorylated derivative of DPN was formed when mitochondria were exposed to succinate, DPN, and P_i.[32]. The isolated compound yielded ATP and DPNH when added, together with ADP and Mg^{++}, to suitable particles. The formation of the compound was inhibited by antimycin, the phosphate transfer to ADP was inhibited by oligomycin. Griffiths states that "the failure to demonstrate the formation of the phosphorylated derivative on incubation with DPN-linked substrates is not considered to be evidence against the participation of this compound in the main pathway of oxidative phosphorylation." Yet this failure suggests possibilities of alternative pathways, such as the energy-dependent reduction of TPN by DPNH, which is an attractive candidate for the participation of a phosphorylated pyridine nucleotide derivative.

It is apparent from the foregoing that in the recent past several important clues to intermediates of oxidative phosphorylation have been discovered. It is not yet clear which ones are the primary products of the electron-transport chain of mitochondria, and which ones are secondary derivatives that channel into various energy-requiring processes.

[270] D. E. Griffiths, *FP* **22,** 1064 (1963).

LECTURE 14

THEORIES AND SPECULATIONS

First get your facts; and then you can distort them at your leisure.
—Mark Twain

The secrecy and complexity of events that take place behind the iron-porphyrin curtain of oxidative phosphorylation have led to numerous and sometimes contradictory speculations. Schemes have emerged from different laboratories with various letter designations for hypothetical intermediates that extend almost through the entire range of the alphabet.

Since questions (according to Oscar Wilde) are never indiscreet, only answers are, I shall start out, at least, by raising some discreet questions on controversial points.

The first question deals with the most basic problem discussed in the first lecture: Does phosphate enter before or after the oxidative step? The second question concerns the relationship between members of the respiratory chain and the intermediates of oxidative phosphorylation: Are there high-energy intermediates that are distinct and separable from the respiratory catalysts, and how many are there? The third question is whether the primary high-energy intermediate contains a respiratory carrier in the oxidized or in the reduced form. The fourth question is almost multiple-choice: What is the significance of the many factors and intermediates that have been claimed as participants in oxidative phosphorylation?

Without doubt I shall give some indiscreet answers to these questions, but I shall attempt to justify them on the basis of experimental evidence available at this time.

The answer to the first question is that it now seems quite certain that oxidation precedes phosphorylation. Although

Slater proposed this sequence of events, in an analogy with glyceraldehyde 3-phosphate oxidation, as early as 1953, convincing evidence was obtained only rather recently. One of the most frequent arguments quoted earlier in favor of oxidation preceding phosphorylation was based on the well-known fact that in uncoupled systems oxidation takes place in the absence of phosphate. This argument had been used more than 10 years ago in the case of glyceraldehyde-3-phosphate dehydrogenase, when it was observed that substrates such as glyceraldehyde were oxidized in the absence of phosphate. However, just as the oxidation of glyceraldehyde in the absence of phosphate could have occurred, as proposed by Warburg, by the addition to the aldehyde of water instead of phosphate, so oxidation in mitochondria in the presence of dinitrophenol may have occurred by simple replacement of phosphate by water. It was therefore necessary to demonstrate in oxidative phosphorylation, as had been done in glyceraldehyde 3-phosphate oxidation, that a nonphosphorylated high-energy intermediate was actually formed. It also follows from such a formulation of the sequence of events (Formulation A, Scheme 1.7) that in the reverse direction phosphate transfer should take place in the absence of a reducing system, as was shown in the case of the reaction catalyzed by glyceraldehyde-3-phosphate dehydrogenase (*cf.* Lecture 2, p. 27). On the other hand, according to Formulation B, a reduction step should be an essential part of transphosphorylation. Since submitochondrial particles that were depleted of endogenous substrate still catalyzed a rapid P_i^{32}-ATP exchange, it appears that a reductive process is not required for the transphosphorylation step. In fact, reduction of the respiratory carrier by addition of substrate inhibited the P_i^{32}-ATP exchange,[187] a finding reminiscent of the requirement for DPN rather than DPNH in the transphosphorylation catalyzed by glyceraldehyde-3-phosphate dehydrogenase.

The most convincing evidence in favor of a nonphosphorylated high-energy intermediate has come from studies of the energy-driven reduction of DPN by succinate. When succinate oxidation was used to generate the required energy, the reduction of DPN took place in the presence of oligomycin in mitochondria that were depleted of P_i.[235,236] Furthermore, it was shown recently[204a,236a] that submitochondrial particles that were deficient in coupling factors 1 and 4 catalyzed, in the absence of P_i, the reduction of TPN by DPNH if the energy was provided by respiration. When ATP was used as energy source, both coupling factors were required. Thus, neither phosphate nor the transphosphorylation enzymes were required either for the formation of the nonphosphorylated high-energy intermediate or for the transhydrogenation step proper. Oligomycin actually markedly stimulated the rate of TPN reduction, presumably by inhibiting the breakdown of the high-energy intermediate in the loosely-coupled particles. Similarly, oligomycin did not impair the respiration-driven DPN reduction, whereas dinitrophenol inhibited it completely.

Although there is little biochemical evidence in favor of the alternative Formulation B, in which phosphate enters prior to oxidation, very attractive chemical models with quinol phosphate have been devised[257,258,271] that catalyze a process of oxidative phosphorylation according to such a mechanism. The utilization of either Q_6-phosphate[259] or DPNH-phosphate[270] for the formation of ATP might be used as an argument in favor of such a formulation, but neither of these compounds has yet been shown to be produced during oxidative phosphorylation in mitochondria.

In view of the fact that formation of a high-energy intermediate of oxidation has been demonstrated in the absence of phosphate, whereas the formation of a phosphorylated compound prior to oxidation has not, the answer to the first question must be in favor of Formulation A: oxidation preceding phosphorylation.

The answer to the second question must at present remain more ambiguous. Although it seems likely that respiratory catalysts participate in the formation of the primary high-energy intermediate, and some evidence for this is avail-

[271] M. Vilkas and E. Lederer, *Experientia* **18**, 546 (1962).

able,[265,266] the subsequent steps in energy transfer are still completely hypothetical. It thus seems advisable to reduce the number of steps to a minimum that is still compatible with most of the available experimental evidence. Therefore, in Formulation A, the high-energy intermediate was designated as $A \sim X$ indicating that a respiratory carrier (A) is part of the high-energy intermediate which is cleaved by phosphate. In support of this formulation, experiments have been cited[187] on the inhibition of the $P_i{}^{32}$-ATP exchange by the reduction of the respiratory chain with substrates, but these findings are subject to alternative explanations, as was pointed out previously.[60]

The answer to the third question is that in all probability the high-energy intermediate is in the oxidized form. This answer is also based on the facts that (a) in substrate-free submitochondrial particles the $P_i{}^{32}$-ATP exchange occurs without a reducing system; (b) a high-energy intermediate is formed from oxidized DPN and ATP[265]; and (c) in all instances in nature thus far examined, the conservation of energy is in the oxidized product.

Chance and Williams have proposed[157] that the primary high-energy intermediate contains the respiratory carrier in the reduced form; e.g., $DPNH \sim I$. Two objections may be raised with regard to this formulation. One is the need for the introduction of the symbol I, which stands for inhibitor. It was used because of the phenomenon of respiratory control which we have discussed before: DPNH in tightly coupled mitochondria in the controlled state (state 4) is not oxidized unless ADP is added. It is conceivable that an inhibitor of oxidation does exist, but direct evidence for such a compound is not available. It seems simpler and less confusing to assume that DPNH is not oxidized because of the lack of a phosphate acceptor system, just as glyceraldehyde 3-phosphate is not oxidized by the dehydrogenase in the presence of catalytic amounts of P_i unless a phosphate acceptor system is added. We do not assume the presence of glyceraldehyde 3-phosphate $\sim I$, and there is no compelling reason to invoke an inhibitor in oxidative phosphorylation. The second objection concerns the high-energy intermediate being in the reduced form. In so-called "jump experiments," the amount of energized intermediate that accumulated in intact respiring mito-chondria was estimated.[272] Addition of P_i^{32} and ADP to mitochondria that were kept in state 4 (controlled state) resulted in a sudden jump in ATP^{32} level, followed by a steady increase that corresponded to the expected rate of ATP synthesis. The height of the initial jump corresponded ap-proximately to the amount of DPNH present. These experi-ments are important since they represent the first approach to a quantitative evaluation of the high-energy intermediate, which is estimated to be about 1.5 mμmole per milligram of mitochondria. However, the correlation with DPNH does not seem to be a compelling reason for the assumption that the reduced nucleotide is actively part of the high-energy compound. Under conditions of tight coupling, a close cor-relation might be expected between processes of oxidation and phosphorylation. For example, in the oxidation of glycer-aldehyde 3-phosphate by the dehydrogenase in the absence of P_i there is a close correlation between acyl-enzyme forma-tion and DPNH formation, yet the nucleotide is not a com-ponent of the high-energy intermediate, the acyl-enzyme, which is a derivative of the oxidized substrate.

An attractive compromise formulation was recently pre-sented[273] based on observations of a fluorescence enhancement when DPNH was added to mitochondria. It was proposed that a charge-transfer complex is formed between DPNH and mitochondrial imidazole groups, whereby the hydrogen of the imidazole nitrogen is labilized and removed by the respiratory chain. Simultaneously, a lone-pair electron from the pyridine nitrogen is added to the imidazole ring, which is then prepared for nucleophilic attack on the phosphate. This interesting variant of the theory by Grabe (substituting imidazole for flavin)[274] accounts for observations of a phos-phorylated histidine in a mitochondrial protein[269] and in-

---

[272] L. Schachinger, R. Eisenhardt, and B. Chance, *BZ* **333**, 182 (1960).
[273] R. W. Estabrook, J. Gonze, and S. P. Nissley, *FP* **22**, 1071 (1963).
[274] B. Grabe, *BBA* **30**, 560 (1958).

cludes proposals on the function of imidazoles in electron transport.[275,276]

We come now to the last and most difficult question, concerning the role of the coupling factors. We have demonstrated a dependency on coupling factors 1 and 4 at each of the three phosphorylating sites,[93,204a] and, therefore, assume that the mechanism of the conversion of the high-energy intermediate into ATP is essentially similar in each case. The formation of $X \sim Y$ is likely to vary with the different oxidation-reduction catalysts.

Coupling factors 1 and 4 are required for ATP synthesis and for the ATP-dependent reductions of nucleotides (DPN and TPN). But they are not required for the reduction of TPN by DPNH when oxidative energy is the energy source.[204a] Coupling factors 1 and 4 are also required for the H_2O^{18}-P_i exchange when ATP is used as energy source.[199] Since F_1 catalyzes the hydrolysis of ATP, it is proposed that it catalyzes the last transphosphorylation step, $X \sim P + ADP \rightleftarrows X + ATP$. In line with this conclusion are experiments that demonstrate the formation of an ADP-F_1 complex which was isolated by precipitation with $2\,M$ ammonium sulfate.[277] Coupling factor 4 is visualized to be involved either in the formation of $X \sim P$ or in the structural organization of the coupling process. Coupling factor 2, which was shown to stimulate the reduction of TPN by DPNH when it is driven by respiratory energy,[204a] appears to participate in the formation of the nonphosphorylated high-energy intermediate.

A very tentative scheme based on these considerations is shown in Scheme 14.1. The essence of this scheme is that of Formulation A (Scheme 1.7), in which oxidation precedes phosphorylation. The assignment of F_o, the factor which interacts with oligomycin, as a component of the high-energy

[275] H. Theorell, *JACS* **63**, 1820 (1941).
[276] D. W. Urry and H. Eyring, *Proc. Natl. Acad. Sci. U. S.* **49**, 253 (1963).
[277] H. Zalkin, M. E. Pullman, and E. Racker, Unpublished experiments (1964).

intermediate, is entirely speculative. However, it would explain the observation that oligomycin markedly stimulated the reduction of TPN by DPNH when the energy was supplied by respiration in the absence of P_i, F_1, and F_4. It was inferred from this experiment that oligomycin interferes not only with the phosphorolysis but also with the hydrolysis of the high-energy intermediate.

Site 1

Step I $\quad \begin{array}{l} F_o\text{—}F_1\text{—}ADP \\ | \\ F_4\text{—}F_{2_{red}} \end{array} + \text{cyt. } b \rightleftarrows \begin{array}{l} F_o\text{—}F_1\text{—}ADP \\ | \\ F_4 \sim F_2 \end{array} + \text{cyt. } b_{red}$

Step II $\quad \begin{array}{l} F_o\text{—}F_1\text{—}ADP \\ | \\ F_4 \sim F_2 \end{array} + P_i \rightleftarrows \begin{array}{l} F_o\text{—}F_1\text{—}ADP \\ | \\ F_4\text{—}F_2 \sim P \end{array}$

Step III $\quad \begin{array}{l} F_o\text{—}F_1\text{—}ADP \\ | \\ F_4\text{—}F_2 \sim P \end{array} \rightleftarrows \begin{array}{l} F_o\text{—}F_1 \\ | \\ F_4\text{—}F_2 \end{array} + ATP$

Site 2

Step I $\quad \begin{array}{l} F_o\text{—}F_1\text{—}ADP \\ | \\ F_4\text{—}F_{2_{red}} \end{array} + \text{cyt. } c \rightleftarrows \begin{array}{l} F_o\text{—}F_1\text{—}ADP \\ | \\ F_4 \sim F_2 \end{array} + \text{cyt. } c_{red}$

Step II $\quad \begin{array}{l} F_o\text{—}F_1\text{—}ADP \\ | \\ F_4 \sim F_2 \end{array} + P_i \rightleftarrows \begin{array}{l} F_o\text{—}F_1\text{—}ADP \\ | \\ F_4\text{—}F_2 \sim P \end{array}$

Step III $\quad \begin{array}{l} F_o\text{—}F_1\text{—}ADP \\ | \\ F_4\text{—}F_2 \sim P \end{array} \rightleftarrows \begin{array}{l} F_o\text{—}F_1 \\ | \\ F_4\text{—}F_2 \end{array} + ATP$

Scheme 14.1

Hypothetical Roles of Coupling Factors at Sites 1 and 2
of Oxidative Phosphorylation

An attempt was made[263] to speculate on the spatial organization of the coupling factors with respect to each other. Analysis of the sensitivity of various derivative particles to trypsin served as the major guide line. For example, F_o and F_4 were found to be highly sensitive to trypsin, yet in submitochondrial particles they resisted tryptic digestion. Addition of F_1 to F_o conferred considerable resistance against tryptic inactivation of the oligomycin-sensitivity factor. In submitochondrial particles, ATPase inhibitor[184] is visualized to cover F_1. It is very readily attacked by trypsin, as indicated by the more than 10-fold stimulation of ATPase activity.[107]

The complexity of such a structural organization probably fulfills two purposes, efficiency and regulatory mechanisms. There is considerable evidence that energy-consuming processes may be linked specifically to certain energy-generating processes, and there are several indications that some high-energy intermediates of oxidative phosphorylation may be directly utilized without the aid of ATP for processes such as TPN reduction or P_i transport. As mentioned previously, both these processes can be driven by energy generated by electron transport before entrance of P_i under conditions (presence of oligomycin) which exclude the formation of significant amounts of ATP. Such specifically directed distribution of energy may well be expected to be controlled by a highly organized regulatory process.

The complex and intimate interaction between the various coupling factors and the structural core of the mitochondria has been largely responsible for the difficulties encountered in solving the problem of oxidative phosphorylation. The tenacity of the togetherness of the members of the phosphorylating family has made resolution difficult. A derivative particle that is only partly resolved is not a suitable tool for the analysis of a coupling factor. With each factor we had to go through a period of trial and error which we would rather have avoided. This has led us to an approach which for lack of a better word I call inhibition-resolution analysis, because it consists of using an inhibitor or an inactivator of a coupling factor, followed by a procedure of resolution. The advantage of such a procedure is simply this: When sonic oscillation of mitochondria results in submitochondrial particles which are only partly resolved (e.g., 40% with respect to a coupling factor), the assay is unsatisfactory because the residual activity (60%) leaves room for only a relatively small increase in activity (between 60% and 100%). However, if the coupling factor is inactivated first and then 40% of it is removed, the basal activity of the particles is close to zero and addition of coupling factor can restore up to 40% of the original activity. This concept has led to experiments with urea, which at relatively low concentrations inactivated F_1 at $0°$, and which became a most useful agent in the resolution of submitochondrial particles.

Finally, I should like to spend just a few minutes on a very important problem, namely the relationship between the physiology and the structural organization of mitochondria. Several reviews have been written on this subject,[60] and I shall select only two items for a very brief discussion, since they relate specifically to oxidative phosphorylation and have caused a great deal of interest as well as confusion. I am referring (a) to the phenomenon of swelling and contraction of mitochondria, and (b) to the relation of function to structures observed in the electron microscope. An analysis of the literature reveals that experiments on swelling and contractions have been compared that were not executed under comparable conditions. Moreover, there are two types of shrinkage phenomena with different time factors. The swelling and contraction phenomenon studied by most investigators is a relatively slow event which is strongly influenced by the constitution of the medium and the metabolic state of the mitochondria. It is often impossible to compare data in the literature because of lack of information, e.g., on the presence of endogenous substrate capable of sustaining some oxidative phosphorylation. It had been clearly recognized by Raaflaub[130] that the process of water uptake and swelling of mitochondria was associated with an active process of oxidation. Succinate induced swelling; malonate inhibited it, but amytal did not. However, swelling induced by β-hydroxybutyrate was inhibited by amytal and not by malonate. Swelling induced by thyroxine or by inorganic phosphate was apparently dependent on the oxidation of endogenous substrates, since it was counteracted by inhibitors of respiration.[278,279] Fatty acids are natural uncouplers that are re-

[278] F. E. Hunter, Jr., J. F. Levy, J. Fink, B. Schutz, F. Guerra, and A. Hurwitz, *JBC* **234**, 2176 (1959).

[279] J. B. Chappell and G. D. Greville, *Nature* **183**, 1525 (1959).

leased under certain conditions and promote swelling.[228] Dinitrophenol retarded swelling,[280] but prevented contraction that was associated with oxidative phosphorylation.[281] ATP-induced contraction[130] was particularly variable with experimental conditions such as the ionic environment.[280] The concentration of mitochondria influenced the rate of swelling,[282] perhaps due to release of a protein required for contraction.[283] What emerges from these observations is that the balance of uptake and extrusion of water is regulated by several factors, among which the following appear to be of particular importance: (a) the presence of electron flow due to either endogenous or exogenous substrate; (b) the energetic competence of the mitochondria; i.e., whether the electron flow is associated with phosphorylation; (c) the nature of the suspending media, which includes the presence of natural uncouplers released from the mitochondria and of proteins that favor the contractile process.

It is tempting to speculate that the soluble ATPase may be involved in this process of contraction. I have mentioned earlier the similarity between ATPase and myosin. Recently an actomyosin-like complex was isolated from mitochondria.[284] It is rather impressive how many agents that affect the swelling process, such as ATP, Mg^{++}, dinitrophenol, dicoumarol, azide, and oligomycin, also interact with mitochondrial ATPase. Even the previously mentioned effect of electron flow on swelling has its parallel in the inhibition of ATPase when the respiratory carriers are kept in the reduced form.

Perhaps it is appropriate to add to these considerations of uncertainties and theories yet another speculation. I have mentioned the puzzling feature that there appears to be much more potential ATPase in mitochondria than is elicited by dinitrophenol. This is a masked ATPase which presumably

[280] A. L. Lehninger, *JBC* **234**, 2187 (1959).

[281] M. N. Lipsett and L. M. Corwin, *JBC* **234**, 2448 (1959).

[282] Y. Avi-Dor, *BBA* **39**, 53 (1960).

[283] A. L. Lehninger and G. S. Gotterer, *JBC* **235**, PC8 (1960).

[284] T. Onishi and T. Onishi, *J. Biochem. (Tokyo)* **51**, 380 (1962).

is combined with ATPase inhibitor and manifested after trypsin action. I propose that it is this masked ATPase that may have a function in contraction and in the observed movements of mitochondria in intact cells.

Finally, we come to the question of the relation between function and electron-microscopic morphology. Textbook pictures of mitochondria show the presence of an outer and an inner membrane. Invaginations of the inner membrane, called cristae, extend into the interior. Recent advances in staining methods have revealed that the inner membrane is lined with round particles attached by a stalk.[285,286] Speculations have been offered suggesting that these inner membrane subunits represent integrated units of the respiratory chain,[287] and some evidence against this view has been presented.[288]

Submitochondrial particles were prepared by sonic oscillation and subsequently exposed to trypsin and urea. These particles were analyzed for electron transport activities, ATPase, and morphological characteristics.[289,289a] Treatment with urea eliminated ATPase activity and stripped the inner membranes of the subunits, whereas electron transport with DPNH was not affected. It was therefore concluded that the subunits of the inner membrane do not contribute an essential component to the electron transport chain. On the other hand, an excellent correlation was observed between the presence of the subunits and total ATPase activity (activated by trypsin). Recently, Dr. Kagawa has purified in our laboratory an insoluble mitochondrial ATPase which was sensitive to oligomycin but contained no respiratory pigments. Electron microscopy of this preparation revealed small membrane fragments with characteristic inner membrane subunits. Moreover, preparations of the pure, soluble mitochondrial

[285] H. Fernández-Morán, *Circulation* **26,** 1039 (1962).

[286] D. F. Parsons, *Science* **140,** 985 (1963).

[287] D. E. Green, P. V. Blair, and T. Oda, *Science* **140,** 382 (1963).

[288] B. Chance and D. F. Parsons, *Science* **142,** 1176 (1963).

[289] E. Racker, D. D. Tyler, R. W. Estabrook, T. E. Conover, D.F. Parsons, and B. Chance, *in* "Oxidases and Related Redox Systems," Wiley, New York. In press.

[289a] E. Racker, B. Chance, and D. F. Parsons, *FP* **23,** 431 (1964).

ATPase revealed the presence of round units 85 Å in diameter which were quite similar in appearance to the inner membrane subunits.

Submitochondrial particles that were virtually depleted of inner membrane subunits catalyzed oxidation but not phosphorylation. On addition of coupling factors (F_1 and F_2), a marked increase in the number of subunits on the membrane was observed. In one experiment, the stripped particles contained 6 units/μ and the reconstituted particles 30 units/μ, as compared to 60 units/μ in intact beef-heart mitochondria.

In view of these findings, it appears likely that the projection units are concerned with the phosphorylating process and that the inner membranes of the mitochondria carry the respiratory chain.

PART III

Regulation of Adenosine Triphosphate
Utilization in Multi-Enzyme Systems

LECTURE 15

STUDIES OF RECONSTRUCTED
MULTI-ENZYME SYSTEMS

He apprehends a world of figures here
But not the form of what he should attend.
—Shakespeare, *Henry IV*

The metabolism of the intact cells is carried out with the aid of a large number of enzyme catalysts, coenzymes, and inorganic ions. Every cell has many enzymes which require energy for the metabolic tasks they perform, and has several systems capable of producing energy. Some of these multi-enzyme systems share enzymes and coenzymes, as well as inorganic ions, with other multi-enzyme systems, and may compete for them. How is order established in this complex metabolic machinery? What are the means of communication and the regulatory mechanisms which control the individual processes?

The first degree of order is established by means of structure. The cell contains subcellular structures such as mitochondria, ribosomes, and nuclei, with specific functions and metabolic pathways. Communications between these intracellular compartments can take place with the aid of small molecular substances, such as the adenine nucleotides, that have the necessary mobility and permeability properties. Communications of graver significance and greater precision, concerning, for example, protein synthesis, are carried by large molecular substances such as nucleic acids.

The second degree of order is accomplished by a functional separation of anabolic and catabolic processes. Our concepts of the relationship between anabolic and catabolic processes have undergone some interesting cyclic changes. The sharp demarcation line once believed to exist between degradative

and synthetic processes began to fade about 20 years ago
when biochemists started to recognize the reversibility of
enzyme-catalyzed reactions; for example, the enzyme phosphorylase was shown to catalyze both the breakdown and
the synthesis of glycogen. At about the same time, experiments with isotopes led to the concept of a dynamic state of
metabolism, of a continuous flux of reversible reactions common to both anabolism and catabolism. As a consequence
of these ideas, even the names "catabolism" and "anabolism"
were banned from textbooks. However, in recent years the
pendulum has started swinging back again. Biochemists have
learned to interpret with greater caution experiments with
isotopes. They are discovering that synthetic and degradative
pathways are distinct and catalyzed by different enzymes and
multi-enzyme systems. Even when the same enzymes are
used for both anabolism and catabolism, the two pathways
are differentiated by at least one reaction which is essentially
irreversible and thus functions as a one-way gate. For example, in the breakdown of glycogen to glucose, the hydrolysis
of glucose 6-phosphate to glucose and phosphate is not readily
reversible. In the biosynthesis of glycogen, the transfer of
glucose from UDPG to glycogen is a one-way reaction. In
the Krebs cycle, the oxidative decarboxylation of α-keto acids
is irreversible.

A third degree of order is afforded by some of the properties
of the multi-enzyme systems themselves. We have reconstructed, with highly purified enzymes, the system of glycolysis which catalyzed the breakdown of glucose to lactic acid.[290]
We have put together purified enzymes of the oxidative
pentose-phosphate cycle which catalyzed the complete oxidation of glucose to CO_2 and water.[291] What knowledge have we
gained from these experiments?

The first lesson we have learned is that in a community of
enzymes such as the glycolytic system we are faced with many
problems of a socioeconomic nature—availability of raw
materials, delivery of and demands for products, availability

[290] S. Gatt and E. Racker, *JBC* **234,** 1024 (1959).
[291] D. Couri and E. Racker, *ABB* **83,** 195 (1959).

and transport of cofactors, etc. Perhaps the most striking fact emerging from these studies is that each multi-enzyme system has a character of its own, depending on the composition of its catalytic population and the character of its pacemaker. To beginning students of biochemistry who have read the textbook by Gertrude Stein, glycolysis is glycolysis is glycolysis. But this is an erroneous impression. Depending on the concentration and properties of the individual enzymes, the various systems may differ from each other to such an extent that one may just as well be facing a different pathway. To vary Bernard Shaw, we could say, for example, that brain and liver are separated by a common pathway of glycolysis. Since the concept of a pacemaker in a multi-enzyme system is a rather fundamental aspect of all control mechanisms, I would like to illustrate the problem with an experimental example from our studies on the reconstructed system of glycolysis.

In a reaction sequence from A to L, shown in Table 15.I, the enzymes (a) to (k) catalyze the over-all reaction. There are numerous parameters which influence the rate of the process. For example, the reaction

$$D \overset{d}{\rightleftharpoons} E$$

is affected by the amount and turnover of enzyme (d). Since the reaction is reversible, the reverse reaction must be considered also. Since the forward and reverse reactions are dependent on the steady-state concentration of their respective substrates D and E, the rate of the reaction $D \rightarrow E$ becomes dependent on the removal of E, and, therefore, on the catalytic properties of its functional neighbor (enzyme e), etc. Let us now assume that in this multi-enzyme system the reaction $C \rightarrow D$, catalyzed by (c), is rate-limiting. Therefore, shortly after addition of substrate A, it will be possible to demonstrate the accumulation of the intermediate C until a concentration is reached that saturates the enzyme, at which point maximal rates are obtained. If at saturation the enzyme is still rate-limiting, a steady state will be achieved

TABLE 15.I

Variable Properties of Multi-Enzyme Systems

$$
\overset{\text{I}}{\underset{A \rightleftarrows B \rightleftarrows C \rightleftarrows D}{\overset{a \quad b \quad c \quad d}{}}} \bigg| \overset{e \quad f \quad g}{\underset{\rightleftarrows E \rightleftarrows F \rightleftarrows G}{}} \bigg| \overset{\text{II}}{\underset{\rightleftarrows H \rightleftarrows I \rightleftarrows K \rightleftarrows L}{\overset{h \quad i \quad k}{}}}
$$

System	Rate-limiting	20 × excess	Fluoride	K_m of P_i
I	Glyceraldehyde-3-phosphate dehydrogenase	Enolase	Resistant	10^{-3} M
II	Enolase	Glyceraldehyde-3-phosphate dehydrogenase	Sensitive	$<10^{-4}$ M

and the pacemaker (c) now works at full capacity. If we introduce an inhibitor which eliminates as much as 90% of the activity of enzyme (g), this enzyme may now become the rate-limiting factor, and a shift in intermediates will occur. But it is also possible that nothing at all will happen to the over-all rate if enzyme (g) is present in large excess. This is illustrated by the examples in Table 15.I. We are dealing here with two systems of glycolysis with the same content of glycolytic enzymes, except that, in System I, glyceraldehyde-3-phosphate dehydrogenase is rate-limiting and there is a 20-fold excess of enolase, and, in System II, enolase is rate-limiting and there is a 20-fold excess of glyceraldehyde-3-phosphate dehydrogenase. How will these two systems behave in the presence of a typical glycolytic inhibitor such as fluoride, and how will a change in the concentration of a cofactor, such as P_i, affect the rates of glycolysis in these two systems?

When we selected a concentration of sodium fluoride that inhibited 90% of the enolase-catalyzed reaction, glycolysis in System I, in which enolase was present in 20-fold excess, was unaffected; whereas, in System II, glycolysis was blocked. This can be readily understood, since in System I an inhibition of 90% of enolase still leaves 10% of residual enolase active, which is more than sufficient to maintain the over-all rate of glycolysis. When we analyzed the effect of inorganic phosphate concentration on glycolysis in these two systems, we found that System I, with limiting glyceraldehyde-3-phosphate dehydrogenase, was very sensitive to changes in P_i levels below 10^{-3} M, which is the K_m value for inorganic phosphate for glyceraldehyde-3-phosphate dehydrogenase. On the other hand, System II did not change its glycolytic rate even when we lowered the steady-state concentration of P_i to 10^{-4} M. You may wonder, at this point, whether these artificially reconstructed systems are at all models for what might happen within the cell. Do we actually see multi-enzyme systems in which one enzyme exceeds another of the same pathway by a factor of 20? The answer to this is simply: Yes. Some enzymes may be present not only in 20-fold but in several 100-fold excess. The probable reason for such apparent waste will become clearer to you later on. What I would like to emphasize now is that the concept of the pacemaker is very important for our understanding of the mode of action of hormones, drugs, and poisons. If a hormone or drug acts by influencing an enzyme, it is more likely that it will affect an enzyme with a capacity close to the rate-limiting factor of the pathway than an enzyme present in large excess.

The second lesson we have learned from reconstructed systems is that the introduction of a competing multi-enzyme system may profoundly change the rate-limiting factor and character of a pathway. An illustration of this phenomenon is shown in Fig. 15.1. In Fig. 15.1a, a reconstructed system of glycolysis may be seen. In the experiment shown in the lower curve the glycolytic enzymes were present in excess, but adenine nucleotides and inorganic phosphate were added in catalytic amounts. Little lactic acid was formed in this system unless an enzyme was added which regenerated ADP and phosphate from ATP which was produced during the glycolytic process. This was accomplished by the addition of an ATPase. In this particular experiment, an excess of adenylate kinase, together with increasing amounts of apyrase, which converts ATP to AMP and phosphate, was used as a source of ATPase. Optimal production of ADP was obtained within a rather narrow range of ATPase activity, when the rate of ATP synthesis and breakdown was balanced. An excess of ATPase inhibited glycolysis because ATP required for glucose phosphorylation became limiting. I should like to draw your attention to the remarkably small tolerance for changes in the ATPase activity in the reconstructed systems, which not only made it necessary to titrate the optimal ATPase concentration for each experiment, but also greatly increased our respect for nature's capacity for operating with delicately balanced control systems.

In Fig. 15.1b, we see what happens when actively respiring and phosphorylating mitochondria are added to the reconstructed system of glycolysis. We shall discuss this experiment in detail later on, but here I should like to make two points.

We can see that glycolysis is markedly depressed by the mitochondria at optimal ATPase concentrations. In the presence of excess ATPase, mitochondria actually stimulated glycolysis by maintaining the level of ATP. Such a "negative

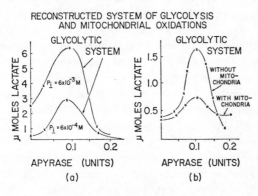

Fig. 15.1. (a) Effect of apyrase on glycolysis. Each test tube contained, in a final volume of 0.5 ml: 15 μmoles of DL-histidine; 0.25 μmole of K-fumarate; 0.25 mg of DPN; 12 μmoles of fructose; 10 μmoles of KCl; 0.15 μmole of ATP; 2.5 μmoles of $MgCl_2$; 0.3 or 3.0 μmoles of phosphate; 0.12 unit of hexokinase (assayed with glucose as substrate); 0.3 unit of phosphofructokinase; 2.4 units of aldolase; 2.4 units of glyceraldehyde-3-phosphate dehydrogenase; 4 units of phosphoglycerate kinase; 2 units of phosphoglycerate mutase; 2 units of enolase; 1.85 units of pyruvate kinase; 4 units of lactic dehydrogenase; 50 μg of adenylate kinase; 0.025 μmole of 2,3-diphosphoglycerate; and apyrase in varying amounts as shown in the figure. The final pH was 7.4. The mixtures were incubated for 30 minutes at 27° and deproteinized by the addition of 0.5 ml of 10% trichloroacetic acid. (b) Pasteur effect at various apyrase concentrations. Additions were the same as in a, except that 0.3 μmole of phosphate was used and each test tube contained either 0.05 ml of 0.25 M mannitol containing 1 mg per milliliter of neutral EDTA or 5.5 mg of mitochondrial protein suspended in this medium. The mixtures were incubated for 50 minutes at 28° and deproteinized by the addition of 1 ml of 0.3 N $Ba(OH)_2$ and 1 ml of 0.3 N $ZnSO_4$.

Pasteur effect" can, in fact, be observed in some tissues. This experiment clearly demonstrates the profound effect of one pathway on another. The second point not immediately apparent from inspection of these data is that the rate-limiting factor of glycolysis is changed by the presence of the mitochondria. I mentioned before that in the reconstructed system the enzymes of glycolysis were added in large excess. Thus, further addition of phosphoglycerate kinase, for example, had no effect on the rate of lactate production. On the other hand, in the presence of mitochondria and catalytic amounts of ADP, addition of phosphoglycerate kinase increased glycolysis by effectively competing for the available adenine nucleotide. This example illustrates how an enzyme may be present in large excess in comparison to other enzymes of its community, yet be rate-limiting in competition with another multi-enzyme system. Under such conditions of stress the physical-chemical properties of the enzyme, such as the turnover number and the affinity constants for substrates and coenzymes, which are of little consequence within its own enzyme community, become important factors in the competition with other multi-enzyme systems.

The third lesson we learned from studies of reconstructed systems is the significance of lag phenomena in the operation of metabolic cycles within a pathway. Very often a thorough investigation of a lag period had led to a better understanding of the pathway, and sometimes to the discovery of an unknown enzyme or cofactor. Probably the first example of lag phenomena was discovered about half a century ago in a fermenting cell-free extract of yeast.[292] We know now that this lag period is due to the operation of the hydrogen cycle in glycolysis. When glyceraldehyde 3-phosphate is oxidized to 3-phosphoglycerate, the hydrogen is accepted by DPN and reduced DPN must be oxidized before the process can continue. Acetaldehyde (or pyruvate), which serves as the physiological hydrogen acceptor in fermentation, is derived from phosphoglycerate. Thus, fermentation lags until a suitable steady-state concentration of hydrogen acceptor is built up. Long before the intimate details of this hydrogen cycle were understood, it was known that addition of acetaldehyde to a yeast extract eliminates the lag of CO_2 production.

[292] A. Harden, "Alcoholic Fermentation," 3rd ed. Longmans, Green, New York, 1923.

A similar phenomenon was observed in the operation of the oxidative pentose-phosphate cycle, which appears to be limited in many cells by the reoxidation of TPNH. Methylene blue,[293] other artificial electron acceptors,[294] pyruvate,[295] and α-ketoglutarate + ammonia[296] were shown to stimulate the oxidation of glucose via the oxidative pentose-phosphate pathway. Under conditions of growth, the task of accepting hydrogens from TPNH is taken over by biosynthetic processes, such as fatty acid synthesis, that require TPNH. The frequently noted stimulation of the pentose-phosphate cycle in bacteria during active growth may be at least partly due to an increased oxidation of TPNH.

Let us turn now to the discussion of another cycle that operates in glycolysis and not infrequently gives rise to a lag phenomenon. In the phosphate cycle (shown in Scheme

Glucose + 2 ATP → Fructose diphosphate + 2 ADP

Fructose diphosphate → 2 Glyceraldehyde 3-phosphate

2 Glyceraldehyde 3-phosphate + 2 P_i + 2 ADP

→ 2 Phosphoglycerate + 2 ATP

2 Phosphoglycerate + 2 ADP → 2 Lactate + 2 ATP

Glycolysis: Glucose + 2 ADP + 2 P_i → 2 Lactate + 2 ATP

"ATPase": 2 ATP → 2 ADP + 2 P_i

Sum: Glucose → 2 Lactate

Scheme 15.1

Phosphate Cycle in Glycolysis

15.1), ATP or ADP and P_i may be rate-limiting for glycolysis. Adenosine triphosphate, which is utilized in the first steps of

[293] E. Racker, *Ann. N. Y. Acad. Sci.* **63,** 1017 (1956).

[294] R. Wu and E. Racker, *in* "Control Mechanisms in Respiration and Fermentation" (B. Wright, ed.), p. 265. Ronald Press, New York, 1963.

[295] C. E. Wenner, *JBC* **234,** 2472 (1959).

[296] E. Holzer, *Cold Spring Harbor Symp. Quant. Biol.* **26,** 277 (1961).

glucose phosphorylation, is regenerated during later phases of the glycolytic pathway. We are dealing here with a positive feedback mechanism similar to that of the hydrogen cycle.

Adenosine diphosphate and P_i are not, however, generated stoichiometrically within the glycolytic process. Thus, in contrast to the hydrogen cycle, the phosphate cycle is not balanced. It requires the auxiliary system, which I would like to refer to as "ATPase in the broadest sense." This ATPase includes all reactions that produce ADP and phosphate from ATP, such as biosynthetic reactions, ion transport, and muscular contraction. I have mentioned earlier how difficult it is experimentally to achieve the proper balance between ATP synthesis and ATP breakdown in reconstructed systems, and I have expressed admiration for nature's precision of control. Actually, nature's method is a rather simple one. It reminds me of the story of the rabbi who was pressed by his admiring students to tell them the secret of his ability to make comparisons which always hit the bull's eye. "It is really very simple," the rabbi explained. "I first shoot off the arrow, and wherever it hits I draw rings around it." Nature's secret is that ATP production is geared to utilization, because both in the glycolytic system and in oxidative phosphorylation there is a tight coupling between oxidation and phosphorylation. When ATP is not utilized, oxidation ceases and ATP is not produced.

This brings us to a discussion of some of the differences between intact cells and reconstructed systems, and to the fourth lesson. Studies of reconstructed systems have taught us a great deal about multi-enzyme systems and how they might interact, but they did not tell us how control mechanisms operate in intact cells. In the experiment illustrated in Fig. 15.1, we have shown a phenomenon of competition between glycolysis and oxidative phosphorylation which superficially resembles the Pasteur effect. Further analysis, however, revealed important differences.[290] As Table 15.II, shows, both glucose utilization and lactate production were inhibited in the presence of mitochondria and catalytic amounts of ADP and phosphate. In the presence of actively

TABLE 15.II

EFFECT OF DEPLETION OF PHOSPHATE ON GLUCOSE UTILIZATION

System	Initial $P_i{}^a$	Final $P_i{}^a$	After 50 min		Pasteur effect	
			Lactate^a	Glucose^a	Lactate	Glucose
Glycolytic system	0.77	0.95	4.0	2.3	—	—
Glycolytic system + mitochondria	0.81	0.16	1.2	1.4	70%	40%

^{a} Values expressed in micromoles.

TABLE 15.III

COMPETITION BETWEEN GLYCOLYTIC AND MITOCHONDRIAL PATHWAYS

	O_2 uptake[a]	P_i esterification[b]	Δ Lactate[b]	Δ Fructose[b]	Δ HMP[b]	Δ HDP[b]
Mitochondria (5.5 mg)	3.8	—	—	—	—	—
Mitochondria + hexokinase						
+ phosphofructokinase	8.0	13.5	—	7.3	0.5	5.2
Mitochondria + glycolysis	5.5	13.5	6.0	10.8	2.0	3.1
Glycolysis alone	—	8.6	6.9	10.6	3.3	2.2
Mitochondria (10 mg)	6.1	1.5	—	—	—	—
Mitochondria + hexokinase						
+ phosphofructokinase	10.0	14.0	—	7.1	0.5	5.7
Mitochondria + glycolysis	10.7	16.5	1.7	10.9	1.0	6.3
Glycolysis alone	—	11.2	7.5	11.3	2.2	2.5

[a] Values expressed in microatoms.
[b] Values expressed in micromoles.

phosphorylating mitochondria, the concentration of inorganic phosphate became so low that glycolysis as well as oxidation were severely depressed. Analysis revealed that phosphorylated hexose esters, mostly fructose-1,6-diphosphate (HDP), accumulated, as shown in Table 15.III. On the other hand, in intact cells fructose-1,6-diphosphate does not accumulate, and intracellular phosphate, although lower under aerobic conditions, does not reach a level as low as in reconstructed systems.

We can see from Table 15.III, what happened in the reconstructed systems when the proportion of the competing systems was altered. In the first experiment only 5.5 mg of mitochondria were used, and an inhibition of respiration was observed in the presence of glycolytic enzymes. An inhibition of respiration by glycolysis was first described in 1929 by Crabtree,[297] who recognized its intimate relationship to the Pasteur effect. I have therefore referred to the phenomenon as the Crabtree effect.[293] In the first experiment in Table 15.III, glycolysis was hardly affected by the mitochondria. In the presence of 10 mg of mitochondria, however, the glycolytic enzymes had no effect on respiration, but lactate production was strongly depressed. Under these conditions, sugar utilization was not impaired as long as sufficient phosphate was available to sustain oxidative phosphorylation. Again, in contrast to intact cells, such a system leads to the accumulation of fructose-1,6-diphosphate, since mitochondrial ATP is readily available for hexokinase. We have not been able thus far to obtain conditions in the reconstructed systems that preclude the utilization of mitochondrial ATP for the phosphorylation of hexose. We therefore ended the discussion in our published paper on reconstructed systems[290] with the following sentence: "It remains to elucidate the true Pasteur effect where it was first observed, in cells."

Before leaving the subject of interaction between glycolysis and oxidative phosphorylation in reconstructed systems, I would like to touch briefly on another aspect of this relation-

[297] H. G. Crabtree, *BJ* **23**, 536 (1929).

ship, namely, the biosynthesis of carbohydrates. Whereas in most areas of metabolism we emphasize the division between biosynthetic and degradative pathways, in glycolysis there appears to be considerable overlapping. All enzymes in glycolysis catalyze reactions that were experimentally shown to proceed in both directions, but at three steps alternative enzymes participate in the reversal of glycolysis. The formation of phosphoenolpyruvate from pyruvate and ATP is catalyzed by pyruvate kinase, as well as by a combination of steps which include a carboxylation of pyruvate and decarboxylation of oxaloacetate. The dephosphorylation of fructose-1,6-diphosphate and of glucose 6-phosphate is catalyzed by specific phosphatases. On the other hand, the phosphorylation of phosphoglycerate by ATP, which at physiological pH is thermodynamically as unfavorable as the phosphorylation of pyruvate, is not known to be catalyzed by an alternative pathway. A reversal of glycolysis from lactate to fructose-1,6-diphosphate was accomplished in a reconstructed system with highly purified enzymes of glycolysis.[298] It emerges from these studies that the most important driving force controlling the direction of the glycolytic reactions is the ATP/ADP ratio. When a very high ratio was maintained with actively respiring mitochondria, reversal was readily achieved even though pyruvate kinase was used to catalyze the phosphorylation of pyruvate. The experimental demonstration of glycolytic reversal in a reconstructed system has eliminated theoretical objections to its feasibility, but it cannot be used as evidence for a participation of pyruvate kinase in gluconeogenesis in intact cells. Recent findings, in fact, clearly implicate the pathway via oxaloacetate as the physiological one.

The next interplay between multi-enzyme pathways which concerns us is that between glycolysis and the pentose-phosphate cycle.[291] These two pathways have four enzymes in common. Hexokinase acts in both systems in the same direction, namely, the synthesis of glucose 6-phosphate from glucose. However, three other enzymes—namely, triose

[298] I. Krimsky, *JBC* **234**, 228, 232 (1959).

phosphate isomerase, aldolase, and glucose-6-phosphate isomerase—proceed in glycolysis toward lactate production, but in the pentose-phosphate cycle toward glucose 6-phosphate synthesis. At these three points there is an interlocking of the metabolic wheels, and the enzymes may have to work in either direction. What events actually take place is governed by the availability of substrates of the forward and reverse reaction. Since the parent substrate glucose is common to both pathways, we must look for the steps at which the pathways part, a very critical crossroad in intracellular metabolism. In view of what was said, it is apparent that in this case we do not deal with competition for a common cofactor, but with competition for a common substrate. There is a curious phenomenon that appears to operate as a control mechanism at the crossroads of glucose 6-phosphate utilization. Several intermediates of the oxidative pentose-phosphate cycle—phosphogluconate,[299] erythrose 4-phosphate,[300] and sedoheptulose 7-phosphate[301]—were shown to be potent inhibitors of hexose isomerase, which channels glucose 6-phosphate into the glycolytic pathway. This phenomenon may be looked upon as a negative feedback of one pathway for another pathway, and it may be operating more frequently then we suspect at the moment. In principle, this practice is well known to occur among microorganisms that elaborate antibiotics, and it is not entirely unknown in our world of business.

A particularly interesting aspect of the interaction between glycolysis and the pentose-phosphate cycle is that inorganic phosphate is required for glycolysis, but inhibits the oxidation of glucose 6-phosphate by glucose-6-phosphate dehydrogenase.[302] A control mechanism based on this finding was proposed by Kravitz and Guarino.[303] Stimulatory effects of

[299] C. W. Parr, *BJ* **65,** 34P (1957).
[300] E. Grazi, A. DeFlora, and S. Pontremoli, *BBRC* **2,** 121 (1960).
[301] R. Venkataraman and E. Racker, *JBC* **236,** 1876 (1961).
[302] H. Thorell, *BZ* **275,** 416 (1935).
[303] E. A. Kravitz and A. J. Guarino, *Abstr. 132nd Meeting, Am. Chem. Soc., New York* p. 23C (1957).

phosphate on phosphofructokinase[304] and on hexokinase[305] have been demonstrated. In line with these findings are recent experiments carried out in our laboratory with reconstructed systems,[306] which revealed striking stimulatory effects of phosphate on the phosphorylation of glucose. I shall return to these findings in the last lecture.

[304] J. V. Passonneau and O. H. Lowry, *BBRC* **7,** 10 (1962).
[305] I. A. Rose, J. V. B. Warms, and E. L. O'Connell, *BBRC* **15,** 33 (1964).
[306] K. Uyeda and E. Racker, Unpublished experiments (1964).

LECTURE 16

APPROACHES TO THE METABOLISM OF INTACT CELLS AND TO THE RATE-LIMITING FACTORS IN ASCITES TUMOR CELLS

Knowledge comes; but wisdom lingers.
—Tennyson, "Locksley Hall"

We came to the conclusion in the previous lecture that the final analysis of control mechanisms must be conducted with intact cells. I shall therefore review very briefly the avenues that are open to the study of metabolic processes in cells. There are essentially only three approaches.

The first approach is the chemical analysis of metabolic events after exposing cells to a variety of environmental as well as intracellular conditions. For this purpose one can use selection of mutants, induction due to substrates, and repressions due to products; one can alter the environment by nutritional depletion, by changes in the atmosphere, by inhibitors, etc. Usually, only the beginning and the end of complex metabolic processes are measured in such experiments. In order to correlate changes in the over-all process with specific intracellular events, we disrupt the cells by suitable means and determine the intracellular constituents, such as enzymes and cofactors. Obviously, this approach has the disadvantage that the ultimate analysis is carried out on disintegrated cells.

The second approach consists of direct spectrophotometric and fluorometric measurements of intermediates in intact cells. Respiratory carriers and coenzymes undergo spectral changes during oxidoreductions and can frequently be quite successfully measured. Alterations in the environment (the presence of inhibitors, phosphate acceptor systems, etc.) can be used to force the system into different stages of metabolism. The disadvantages of this approach lie primarily in the restriction to light-absorbing or fluorescent compounds, as well as in possible interferences by overlapping spectra. These methods have nevertheless been used in ingenious experiments by Chance with intact cells, and recently even with intact mammalian organs.

The third procedure is based on the use of isotopes. The classic studies by Hevesy and Schoenheimer and their collaborators are described in textbooks and are familiar to all of you. Among the more recent developments are the use of isotopes for the study of intracellular compartmentation and the exploration of rate-limiting steps. Substrates specifically labeled with deuterium, which served via DPND as reductants in gluconeogenesis, were used by Hoberman and his collaborators.[307] Measurements of the distribution and rate of incorporation of deuterium into glycogen have yielded many fascinating observations. It should be emphasized that it would have been impossible to interpret some of these data—e.g., the preponderance of deuterium at carbon 4 and 6 in glycogen in animals receiving 2-deutero-DL-lactate were it not for the prior studies[308–310] on the mechanism of aldolase and triose phosphate isomerase, and on the exchange reactions which these enzymes catalyze.

A second use of isotopes, recently employed by Rose and his collaborators[311,312] to determine a rate-limiting step in carbohydrate metabolism, takes advantage of the isotope effect. From studies with deuterated glycerol administered to intact animals, it was concluded that the reaction catalyzed

[307] H. D. Hoberman and A. F. D'Adamo, Jr., *JBC* **235,** 514, 519, and 523 (1960).

[308] I. A. Rose and S. V. Rieder, *JBC* **231,** 315 (1958).

[309] S. V. Rieder and I. A. Rose, *JBC* **234,** 1007 (1959).

[310] B. Bloom and Y. J. Topper, *Science* **124,** 982 (1956).

[311] I. A. Rose, *JBC* **236,** 603 (1961).

[312] I. A. Rose, R. Kellermeyer, R. Stjernholm, and H. G. Wood, *JBC* **237,** 3325 (1962).

by triose phosphate isomerase is slow in the liver relative to the other glycolytic reactions, thus explaining earlier observations on the unequal incorporation of C^{14} into glycogen.[312]

Of these three approaches, we have mainly used the first one, and I shall describe how we have applied it to problems in energy metabolism and its control. But, before embarking on this subject, I should like to emphasize once more that most procedures for analyzing intracellular metabolites have pitfalls and represent artifacts of one kind or another. Nevertheless, we have no choice, and at least the artifacts produced by various approaches are different. We must hope that one day when we have collected enough artifacts we can extract from them the information relevant to intracellular events.

RATE-LIMITING FACTORS IN ASCITES TUMOR CELLS

We chose ascites tumor cells for our first studies[313] because they exhibit two phenomena of metabolic control, the Pasteur effect and the Crabtree effect. Moreover, ascites tumor cells can be washed with little damage, and are obtained as relatively homogeneous cell suspensions. This property not only permits accurate dispensing of uniform aliquots but also facilitates studies of ion transport, which are more difficult with tissue slices.

Our analytical procedure consisted essentially of three steps. First, the cells were broken by mechanical disintegration and the homogenate was analyzed either directly or after separation into a soluble and a particulate fraction. These fractions were analyzed for the presence of each of the individual glycolytic enzymes. Activities were measured uniformly at pH 7.4 in the presence of excess substrate, and a typical profile of ascites tumor enzymes is shown in Table 16.I.

We shall not dwell on the individual values of the enzyme activities, but I should like to discuss briefly four aspects in connection with these data: (1) the significance of enzyme

[313] R. Wu and E. Racker, *JBC* **234**, 1029, 1036 (1959).

activities measured in the presence of excess substrate; (2) the presence of large excesses of certain enzymes compared to the over-all process; (3) the distribution of glycolytic enzymes in the soluble and particulate fractions; and (4) the characteristic profiles of different cell populations.

TABLE 16.I

PROFILES OF GLYCOLYTIC ENZYMES IN TISSUE HOMOGENATES[a]

Enzyme	Ascites tumor	HeLa cells	Chicken leukocyte	Mouse brain
Hexokinase	4.8	3.7	2.4	12.5
Phosphofructokinase	5.0	7.6	7.0	25
Aldolase	17	6.7	7.8	8
Glyceraldehyde-3-phosphate dehydrogenase	121	110	19	18
Phosphoglycerate kinase	640	700	165	111
Phosphoglycerate mutase	41	41	30	43
Enolase	27	22	21	18
Pyruvate kinase	138	150	55	145
Lactate dehydrogenase	230	370	111	79
Lactate production (intact cells)—aerobic	0.58	0.5	0.13	0.14
—anaerobic	0.96	0.5	0.36	1.2
Oxygen uptake	0.16	0.05	0.17	0.86
Glyceraldehyde-3-phosphate dehydrogenase/ respiratory P_i esterification[b]	125	365	19	3.5

[a] All values expressed as micromoles of substrate per minute per 100 mg of protein at 26°.

[b] Calculated from oxygen uptake, assuming a P:O ratio of 3.

(1) When we measure enzymes of a multi-enzyme system in the presence of excess substrate, the information we obtain is usually not relevant to the functional activity of this enzyme within its own enzyme community. Very few enzymes operate under physiological conditions in the presence of saturating substrate concentration. What information do we actually gain from these measurements? First of all, they tell us a great deal about those enzymes that are not present in large excess in comparison with the rate of the over-all

process. These measurements also tell us which of the enzymes are in large excess and therefore are less likely to be influenced directly by control mechanisms.

(2) Are we permitted to raise the question of the purpose of such enzyme excesses? You may have noticed that there has been a gradual change in the attitude of biologists to such questions. A few decades ago, teleology was still defined as a lady of ill repute whom everybody uses but nobody wants to be seen with in public. Recent years have brought about a striking change in our morals. The writings of the modern biologist inform us that the lady has obtained a marriage license and even a new name, teleonomy.[314] We could say that the marriage was legalized by the "justices of the survival of the fittest." Although this expression may not be without ambiguity, it is just as appropriate as "justices of the peace." In any case, the lady is no longer a lady but a wife, and as far as I am concerned, a very charming one

It is probably not coincidental that those enzymes that are present in 100- to 200-fold excess over some of the other enzymes in the same pathway are enzymes involved in competition; e.g., lactate dehydrogenase competes with mitochondria for pyruvate and DPNH, phosphoglycerate kinase for ADP. Thus, the purpose of excess enzymes at important crossroads of metabolism is to provide a "metabolic buffer system" that is not readily disturbed by small changes in catalytic activities.

(3) We come now to the third point, the distribution of glycolytic enzymes within the cells. You may be aware of the position taken by some investigators, that glycolysis is associated with mitochondria. I shall not burden you with data on this point, but shall only state in summary that our evaluation of the enzyme profile in various cell fractions indicates that, at least in ascites tumors, the content of glycolytic enzymes in the particulate fractions can be largely accounted for by contamination with supernatant fluid, with one clear exception: hexokinase. This enzyme is found in various tissues associated to different degrees with particles that sedi-

[314] B. D. Davis, *Cold Spring Harbor Symp. Quant. Biol.* **26,** 1 (1961).

ment approximately like mitochondria. In ascites tumor cells, about half of the total enzyme found is recovered in the mitochondrial fraction. In brain, the proportion is even greater; in other cells, it is less. We must consider first the possibility that hexokinase is localized in the cell membrane and the association with mitochondria is an artifact, resulting from the disruption of cellular membranes into particles with similar sedimentation properties. Experiments could perhaps be designed to eliminate this possibility. A second possibility is that hexokinase is readily adsorbed by mitochondria following disruption of the cell. The third possibility is that part of the hexokinase is actually associated with the mitochondria within the cell. It will become clear later why I do not favor this alternative, but it cannot be ruled out with certainty.

(4) Let us inspect the character of the profile itself. As you can see from Table 16.I, there are striking differences in enzyme distribution in different cell types. For example, in ascites tumor cells, the ratio of glyceraldehyde-3-phosphate dehydrogenase to phosphofructokinase is over 20, whereas in brain it is about 0.7. Although some variations were noted in the enzyme profiles of the same tissue of individual animals, the essential character of the profile was remarkably reproducible. It therefore seems quite feasible to establish characteristic ratios of enzyme activities that will enable us to analyze an unknown tissue fragment and arrive at a diagnosis of its source without histological examination. Of even greater interest, however, is an examination of the profiles in relation to the physiological functions of the organ. Available data are not extensive, but even a broad evaluation of a few selected enzymes will serve to illustrate the point. The distribution of hexokinase, phosphofructokinase; phosphorylase, and glucose 6-phosphatase in three different organs—liver, brain, and muscle—is shown in Table 16.II. The activities of these enzymes seem to be consistent with the over-all carbohydrate metabolism and function of each organ. The liver, which is concerned with maintaining the blood sugar level from glycogen, has a very active phosphorylase and glucose 6-phosphatase, but phosphofructokinase and hexo-

kinase are relatively inactive. Brain, which is dependent on the blood glucose as the primary source of energy supply, has probably the highest hexokinase activity of all normal mammalian tissues, and has a very active phosphofructokinase; phosphorylase is low and there is little or no glucose 6-phosphatase. Muscle, which depends on the rapid delivery of glycolytic energy from its glycogen store, has very active

TABLE 16.II
ENZYME PATTERNS IN ORGANS

Organ	Hexo-kinase	Phospho-fructokinase	Phos-phorylase	Glucose 6-phosphatase
Liver	Low	Low	High	High
Muscle	Low	High	High	Absent (?)
Brain	High	High	Low	Absent (?)

phosphorylase and phosphofructokinase, but a low hexokinase, and little if any specific glucose 6-phosphatase. It should be noted that when phosphorylase activity is designated as high, it is compared to the phosphorylase activity of other organs. Within the community of glycolytic enzymes phosphorylase may still be rate-limiting, as we shall see later.

After completing the profile analysis, the second step was to study glycolysis in a homogenate or crude extract which was fortified with cofactors and ions. Data obtained with crude extracts allowed us to evaluate the potentials of the multi-enzyme system as a whole. We were no longer testing the enzymes at saturation levels of substrate, but under conditions presumably closer to intracellular events. Several procedures have been used to evaluate the rate-limiting factor in a soluble multi-enzyme system, but I believe that only one method is reliable. It consists of adding the individual components of the multi-enzyme system, one at a time, to the crude extract, and determining the effect on the over-all system. It is essential, of course, that the catalysts added should be highly purified, free of other contaminating enzymes of the same pathway. A crude extract from ascites tumor cells responded to the addition of glyceraldehyde-3-phosphate dehydrogenase and phosphofructokinase, and under certain conditions to hexokinase also, with an increase in lactate production; none of the other enzymes had much effect. I should like to emphasize that more than one enzyme can be rate-limiting under certain conditions.

The third step in our analysis consisted of comparing glycolysis of the intact cells and of the extract fortified with cofactors, as shown in Table 16.III. Glycolysis in the fortified

TABLE 16.III

COMPARATIVE RATES OF GLYCOLYSIS IN THE CELL-FREE EXTRACT
AND IN INTACT ASCITES CELLS

	Gas	Δ Glucose[a]	Δ Lactate[a]
Cells	Air	53	68
	N_2	92	120
Extract	Air or N_2	256	360

[a] Results expressed as micromoles per hour per milliliter of packed cells (or that amount of extract obtained from 1 ml of packed cells).

extract was about 5 times as rapid as aerobic glycolysis, and about 3 times as rapid as anaerobic glycolysis in intact ascites tumor cells. These findings, together with the determinations of the enzyme profiles, clearly indicated that in these cells the enzymes are present in excess and that a required cofactor or ion must be rate-limiting.

We then turned to the analysis of intracellular components under a variety of conditions that affected the over-all rate of glycolysis, such as the presence or absence of oxygen, and the presence of inhibitors such as dinitrophenol. It soon became apparent that major changes, which strikingly paralleled the rate of lactate production, occurred in the level of inorganic phosphate of the cell. Changes in the ADP concentration were less marked and less reproducible. In view of these findings, it seemed desirable to study the effect of added phosphate and adenine nucleotides on the intracellular concentration of these compounds and on the rate of glycolysis. It was found that high concentrations of P_i in the medium increased the intracellular P_i concentration as well as the rate of lactate production, as shown in Table 16.IV. Adenosine 5′-phosphate added in the medium had no effect on glycolysis, in spite of the fact that a distinctly increased level of intracellular adenine nucleotides, particularly ATP, was noted.

TABLE 16.IV
EFFECT OF ADDED PHOSPHATE ON GLYCOLYSIS

Extracellular P_i (mM)	Lactate produced (μmoles)	Intracellular P_i (mM)
4	50	4.6
40	104	7.7
80	130	9.9

Although phosphorylated compounds do not readily enter mammalian cells, the uptake of AMP by ascites tumor cells was not entirely unexpected, since it had been previously reported.[315] When both AMP and P_i were added, the stimulation of glycolysis was equal to that due to P_i. We shall see that in HeLa cells, AMP did have an effect on carbohydrate metabolism.

These experiments incriminated P_i as the rate-limiting factor in ascites tumor cells. Since a relatively high and unphysiological concentration of extracellular phosphate was required in order to increase the intracellular phosphate concentration to an appreciable extent, it was apparent (Table 16.IV) that a barrier to the entrance of phosphate was present. The transport of phosphate from the medium into the cells was therefore further investigated with $P_i{}^{32}$ and by measurements of the net phosphate uptake.[313] The presence of either glucose or air markedly stimulated the rate of $P_i{}^{32}$ uptake into the cell. When both were present together, the stimulation was almost additive. Iodoacetate prevented the stimulation by glucose; dinitrophenol eliminated the stimulation due to air. It appeared from these studies that the transport of phosphate into the cells requires energy which

[315] M. Edmonds and G. A. LePage, *Cancer Res.* **16**, 222 (1956).

can be supplied either by glycolysis or by respiration, both of them contributing about equally to the entry of phosphate during aerobic glycolysis under these conditions.

A comparison of phosphate transport in various cells has been made in our laboratory by Dr. R. Wu, and a few representative data are shown in Table 16.V. In general, it seems

TABLE 16.V
P_i Transport and the Pasteur Effect

Cells	Lactate[a] (aerobic)	P_i transport[a]	Percent Pasteur effect
HeLa cells	110	50	0
Ascites tumor cells	120	30	40
Chicken leukocytes	20	1	70

[a] Values expressed as micromoles per milliliter of packed cells.

that there is an inverse relationship between the rate of P_i transport and the Pasteur effect. In cells that have a very pronounced Pasteur effect, the rate of P_i transport was found to be slow, whereas the most rapid rate of P_i transport was observed in HeLa cells, which have little or no Pasteur effect. This finding makes sense: A barrier to the entrance of P_i is an essential feature of any regulatory mechanism that is based on phosphate as a controlling factor. It seems obvious that an unlimited flux of phosphate into the cell is incompatible with a theory which assumes that the intracellular P_i level is rate-limiting for aerobic glycolysis.

Since the discovery by Pasteur of the decreased utilization of glucose by yeast under aerobic conditions,[316] a large amount of experimental work has been published and numerous explanations of this very important and economical control mechanism have been put forward.[317] Many of the earlier theories were based solely on an effect of oxygen and had to be abandoned when it was discovered that addition of an uncoupler of oxidative phosphorylation (e.g., dinitrophenol)

[316] L. Pasteur, "Études sur la Bière." Gauthier-Villars, Paris, 1876.
[317] D. Burk, *Cold Spring Harbor Symp. Quant. Biol.* **7**, 420 (1939).

eliminated the Pasteur effect in the presence of oxygen. These experiments suggested that the Pasteur effect is a phenomenon of the regulation of energy metabolism.

A second aspect of the Pasteur effect, neglected in some of the theories but pointed out by Dixon as early as 1937,[318] is that the control mechanism affects not only lactate production but also the uptake of glucose. In a remarkable paper published in 1932, Engelhardt proposed a phosphate cycle that controlled aerobic energy metabolism.[80] Theories dealing more specifically with the role of P_i in the operation of the Pasteur effect were published independently by Lynen[319] and Johnson.[320] However, an important aspect of the phenomenon was not explained by these theories. It seemed reasonable enough to assume that the formation of lactate in animal tissues or of alcohol in yeast could be controlled by the availability of phosphate, but it was not clear how the phosphorylation of glucose by ATP was controlled under aerobic conditions. If oxidative phosphorylation takes place, ATP is produced in abundance and one might expect a stimulation of glucose utilization rather than an inhibition. This type of stimulation was in fact observed in some reconstructed systems, which I discussed in the previous lecture.

When we approached this problem experimentally, we considered three possibilities to explain the aerobic inhibition of glucose uptake: (*a*) that ATP was actually not produced under aerobic conditions (a dismal prospect after you have read fourteen lectures on its mode of formation); (*b*) that ATP is indeed formed, but its availability is restricted by compartmentation; (*c*) that ATP is formed, but is not used because of the presence of an inhibitor of hexokinase.

The first possibility was, fortunately, quickly eliminated. Analysis of ascites tumor cells revealed plenty of ATP under aerobic conditions. A kinetic analysis of the intracellular changes in P_i and ATP concentration following addition of glucose yielded the data shown in Fig. 16.1. Actually, some-

[318] K. C. Dixon, *Biol. Rev.* **12,** 431 (1937).
[319] F. Lynen, *Liebigs Ann.* **546,** 120 (1941).
[320] M. J. Johnson, *Science* **94,** 200 (1941).

what more ATP was present aerobically than anaerobically. The most striking change occurred in the P_i level, which dropped rapidly following glucose addition, until a new steady state was attained. After an initial spurt, the uptake of glucose came to a virtual standstill for 1 or 2 minutes and then proceeded at a slow rate, which was about one-half of

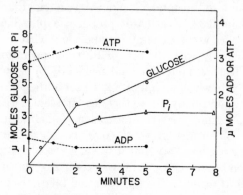

FIG. 16.1. Kinetic study of glucose uptake and variation of intracellular concentrations of ATP, ADP, and P_i. Tumor cells were washed and incubated in air. Glucose (3 μmoles per milliliter) was added after 5 minutes of incubation at 30°. Results are expressed as micromoles per milliliter of packed cells.

that observed under anaerobic conditions. The brief lag phase of glucose utilization was first described by Chance and Hess[321] and was confirmed in our laboratory. What is most remarkable is that for a brief interval there is no glucose utilization when ATP is present in large excess and glucose is freely available. In a second experiment, shown in Fig. 16.2, we see again the utilization of glucose in the control cells (Curve 1) with the characteristic inhibitory phase. In this experiment, samples were taken every 40 seconds, and a drop in ATP concentration was noted 40 seconds after glucose addition and was accompanied by increased ADP (not shown in the figure). A second sample of the ascites tumor cells was exposed to $10^{-4}\,M$ dinitrophenol prior to glucose addition. Adenosine triphosphate was not detectable at this point, and

[321] B. Chance and B. Hess, *Ann. N. Y. Acad. Sci.* **63**, 1008 (1956).

for about 90 seconds little or no glucose was taken up. After this lag phase, glucose was consumed at about twice the aerobic rate, in spite of the fact that the intracellular concentration of ATP was quite low. These experiments indicated either that ATP formed by glycolysis was more efficiently used for glucose phosphorylation than was mitochondrial

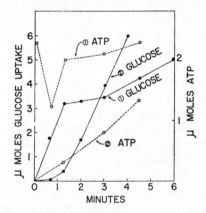

Fig. 16.2. Effect of 2,4-dinitrophenol on the kinetics of glucose uptake. Experimental conditions were the same as in Fig. 16.1, except that cells were incubated for 15 minutes with (Curve 2) or without (Curve 1) dinitrophenol (1×10^{-4} M) before addition of glucose.

ATP, or that an inhibitory effect was eliminated in the presence of dinitrophenol or under anaerobic conditions. It should be pointed out that in the experiments shown in Figs. 16.1 and 16.2, a rapid rate of glucose phosphorylation took place in the first minute following the addition of glucose to cells that were actively respiring and contained high ATP levels. In order to uphold the compartmentation theory, which imposes a restriction on the availability of mitochondrial ATP, it was necessary to assume that compartmentation was established only after glucose was added. Another unattractive feature of this theory was that it was difficult to approach it experimentally. I reemphasize that it is better to do experiments based on a wrong theory than no experiments based on a right one.

We therefore investigated the third possibility, namely, the inhibition of hexokinase. I had proposed in 1954 that glucose 6-phosphate, an inhibitor of hexokinase, might play a role in the Pasteur effect.[322] However, initial analysis with the ascites tumor cells did not look very encouraging. The intracellular concentration of glucose 6-phosphate appeared insufficient to account for the marked inhibition of glucose uptake according to calculations that were based on the K_i value of ascites tumor hexokinase for glucose 6-phosphate. Moreover, there was little difference between the steady-state concentration of glucose 6-phosphate aerobically and anaerobically. It also bothered us that glucose 6-phosphate is a very poor inhibitor of hexokinase from yeast, a cell that has paternal rights with regard to the Pasteur effect.

It is remarkable how aging often mellows hard facts as well as men. The facts are still with us, but we have become more tolerant of them because we have accumulated other facts. First of all, it was found[306] that the K_i of hexokinase from ascites tumors for glucose 6-phosphate was considerably lower when measured by the isotope method of Rose and O'Connell[323] than when conventional procedures for measuring glucose uptake were used. Moreover, the K_i value for glucose 6-phosphate was shown to be altered by ATP[324] as well as by phosphate.[305] Thus, the same steady-state concentration of glucose 6-phosphate may have a very different effect depending on the levels of these rather variable intracellular components. It may be suggested that glucose 6-phosphate can be joined in its inhibitory action by metabolically related compounds such as mannose 6-phosphate[325] or 6-phosphogluconate,[326] or even replaced by them (e.g., in yeast). Finally, we have become increasingly aware, in recent years, of changes in the properties of enzymes when they are removed from their physiological environment, as I em-

[322] E. Racker, *Advan. Enzymol.* **15,** 141 (1954).

[323] I. A. Rose and E. L. O'Connell, *JBC* **239,** 12 (1964). We are indebted to Dr. Rose for communicating this procedure prior to publication.

[324] H. J. Fromm and V. Zewe, *JBC* **237,** 1661 (1962).

[325] H. J. Fromm and V. Zewe, *JBC* **237,** 3027 (1962).

[326] R. Wu, Unpublished experiments (1960).

phasized in my discussion of mitochondrial ATPase. Yeast hexokinase may be regulated by mannose 6-phosphate, by ADP, or even by glucose 6-phosphate if the enzyme within the cell is altered.

I shall describe further experiments on the Pasteur effect and outline our present views in the last lecture. I should now like to turn briefly to another phenomenon which illustrates other difficulties in our approaches to the metabolism of intact cells. Crabtree observed[297] that the respiration of tissue slices from tumors, but not from normal tissues, was inhibited by glucose, and he regarded the phenomenon as a "reverse Pasteur effect." In the previous lecture, I mentioned reconstructed systems of glycolysis and mitochondria which compete with each other for phosphate or ADP, and exhibit phenomena similar to those described by Pasteur and Crabtree with intact cells. However, two experimental observations indicated that in intact cells the situation is more complex.

The first observation was that iodoacetate, at concentrations that completely blocked glycolysis, did not eliminate the Crabtree effect; in fact, it tended to increase it.[293] This did not at first look like a competition between glycolysis and oxidative phosphorylation, yet it was. The intracellular phosphate concentration decreased very markedly and fructose-1,6-diphosphate accumulated.[313] Thus glucose served as a trap for phosphate, which no longer cycled through the adenine nucleotides, and was unavailable for oxidation. Moreover, a rather unexpected and drastic loss in total nucleotides was observed when the cells were exposed to both glucose and iodoacetate. These conditions favored the dephosphorylation of ATP to AMP, which was deaminated and dephosphorylated, and finally diffused from the cell as inosine.[313] A similar phenomenon was noted with HeLa cells, which lost ATP when both an inhibitor of glycolysis (oxamate) and glucose were added.[327]

---

[327] J. Papaconstantinou, E. B. Goldberg, and S. P. Colowick, *in* "Control Mechanisms in Respiration and Fermentation" (B. Wright, ed.), p. 243. Ronald Press, New York, 1963.

The second observation was that the Crabtree effect, in contrast to the Pasteur effect, was not reproducibly influenced by the addition of phosphate to the medium.[313,328–330] Nevertheless, a lack of stimulation of respiration by phosphate could be compatible with a mechanism based on competition between glycolysis and respiration, since with high P_i in the medium the increased over-all glycolysis is likely to compete more effectively with respiration for ADP.

It has repeatedly been suggested in the literature that the Crabtree effect is simply due to a glycolytic lowering of the pH that inhibits respiration. This explanation appears quite inadequate, since the Crabtree effect was largely eliminated in the presence of dinitrophenol, which almost doubled the rate of glycolysis and considerably decreased the pH. The restoration of respiration by dinitrophenol was usually not complete, however, which might indeed be due to the very low pH in the medium or, as suggested by Kvamme,[330] to competition for phosphate between glyceraldehyde-3-phosphate dehydrogenase and α-ketoglutarate dehydrogenase.

Although it is apparent that pH changes in the medium cannot be responsible for the diminished respiration in the presence of glucose, it is difficult to rule out local accumulations of lactic acid which affect respiration. It is necessary in this case to assume that dinitrophenol prevents these local changes or eliminates the pH sensitivity of respiration. No experimental evidence for these possibilities has been forthcoming.

Most of the observations on the Crabtree effect have been made on endogenous respiration. How does glucose influence the oxidation of glucose? In collaborative experiments with Dr. Kvamme, this was tested by comparing the rate of oxidation of C^{14}-labeled glucose at low and at high concentrations.[293] Since ascites tumor cells have a pentose-phosphate cycle, it is necessary to differentiate between oxidation via

[328] M. Brin and R. W. McKee, *Cancer Res.* **16,** 364 (1956).

[329] K. H. Ibsen, E. L. Coe, and R. W. McKee, *Cancer Res.* **20,** 1399 (1960).

[330] E. Kvamme, *Acta Physiol. Scand.* **42,** 204 and 219 (1958).

the Krebs cycle and oxidation via phosphogluconate. Although a quantitative evaluation of these processes is difficult, C^{14}-glucose labeled at carbon 1 (C_1) and carbon 6 (C_6) can be used for an approximate evaluation. It was found that at low glucose concentrations, C_1 was oxidized about twice as fast as C_6. At high glucose concentrations, the rate of C_1 oxidation was markedly increased, whereas C_6 oxidation was actually depressed. A calculation of the $C_1:C_6$ ratio revealed that it could be changed from a value of 2 to about 8 simply by increasing the concentration of glucose. Dinitrophenol had little effect on C_1 oxidation, either at low or at high glucose concentration. However, it reversed the Crabtree effect (inhibition of C_6 oxidation) at high glucose concentration, and decreased the $C_1:C_6$ ratio from 4 to 2. These experiments clearly demonstrated that the inhibitory effect of glucose is not restricted to endogenous respiration, which is presumably fatty acid oxidation, but manifests itself also in the oxidation of pyruvate via the Krebs cycle.

A Crabtree effect has been observed only in tissues that have a high glycolytic rate compared to respiration, such as tumor cells and retina. In reconstructed systems, it was shown that a Crabtree effect based on competition for phosphate and ADP could be demonstrated only when an appropriate ratio between glycolytic enzymes and mitochondria was used. Although conceptually, the competition theory represents the most attractive explanation of the Crabtree effect, it must be admitted that the experimental evidence in its favor is weak. Therefore, it is quite conceivable that, as in the Pasteur effect, more complex regulatory mechanisms are superimposed on the simple regulation by competition. Perhaps intermediates of glucose metabolism are formed which interfere with respiration, but we must keep in mind that they would have an effect only on respiration coupled to phosphorylation, since in the presence of dinitrophenol only a very small Crabtree effect can be discerned.

LECTURE 17

METABOLISM OF INTACT CELLS

No generalization is worth a damn, including this one.
—O. W. Holmes

RATE-LIMITING FACTORS IN HeLa CELLS

Cells grown in tissue cultures or, stated more correctly, in cell cultures, offer obvious advantages for metabolic studies because of the possibility of varying the conditions of growth. In our earlier investigations, we did not fully appreciate the profound influence exerted on the activity of certain enzymes by the steady-state concentration of glucose in the medium. We were puzzled by the variability of the results until we found that the glucose concentration at the termination of growth was rather critical.[331] It was then possible to design experiments that would not have been feasible with mammalian cells grown *in vivo*, such as ascites tumor cells.

The profile of glycolytic enzymes in HeLa cells was, on the whole, remarkably similar to that of ascites tumor cells (Table 16.I). Hexokinase and phosphofructokinase were relatively low, whereas phosphoglycerate kinase was about 100 times as active. The over-all glucose metabolism was also similar. The rate of glucose utilization in fortified homogenates was much faster than in intact cells, indicating that here again the enzymes were present in excess. High phosphate concentration in the medium resulted in a marked stimulation of glucose utilization by the intact cells. In contrast to ascites cells, the HeLa cells exhibited endogenous fermentation due to the breakdown of glycogen. Whereas lactate production from glucose showed no Pasteur effect, the production of lactate from glycogen was much faster anaero-

[331] J. B. Alpers, R. Wu, and E. Racker, *JBC* **238**, 2274 (1963).

bically than aerobically.[331] This Pasteur effect on endogenous fermentation was of interest for two reasons. First, it eliminated hexokinase as well as glucose transport—both of which had been suggested to play a role in the Pasteur effect—as essential components of this regulatory phenomenon in HeLa cells. Second, it seemed likely that the aerobic regulation of glycogen breakdown was controlled by the availability of phosphate, in line with the competition mechanism discussed in the previous lecture.

Addition of both P_i and AMP to the cells markedly stimulated the endogenous formation of lactate. Measurements of phosphorylase activity in cell-free extracts of HeLa cells revealed an activity considerably lower than that of other glycolytic enzymes. In fact, lactate production from glycogen in the presence of AMP and P_i appeared to proceed at a rate limited by the phosphorylase activity itself.

HeLa cells grown in a medium that was allowed to become depleted of glucose (employed by most investigators for the growth of HeLa cells) contained at times so little phosphorylase activity that it could not be detected. Cells grown in a high glucose medium contained considerable phosphorylase activity, while the other glycolytic enzymes were not influenced by the glucose concentration.

Small variations in the glucose concentration in the medium at the end of the experiment were accompanied also by drastic differences in glycogen content. As can be seen from Table 17.I, at a final glucose concentration of 0.79 mM the glycogen content of the cells was very high, and phosphorylase as well as glycogen synthetase activity were high. At 0.22 mM glucose, the glycogen content was drastically decreased, phosphorylase a could not be measured with any accuracy, and a distinct drop in glycogen synthetase activity was observed.

Nirenberg reported that a relatively large group of tumors, including HeLa cells, contained neither glycogen nor phosphorylase activity.[332] Since in conventional cell cultures no attempts are made to maintain a high glucose level, the data

[332] M. W. Nirenberg, *BBA* **30,** 203 (1958).

in Table 17.I, indicate that the failure to detect glycogen and phosphorylase may have been due to glucose depletion during growth.

To explore the cause of the rapid enzyme changes, HeLa cells were grown under conditions that lead to a depletion of glycogen. The cells were then exposed to a high glucose concentration, either in a salt medium or in a complete growth

TABLE 17.I

EFFECT OF GLUCOSE CONCENTRATION IN MEDIUM ON HeLa CELLS

Residual glucose in medium at time of harvest	Glycogen[a]	Phosphorylase[b]		Glycogen synthetase[b]
		a	b	
0.79 mM	102	0.69	0.79	1.6
0.22 mM	3.8	0.01	0.12	0.6

[a] Values expressed as micromoles of glucose equivalents per 100 mg of cell protein.

[b] Values expressed as micromoles per minute per 100 mg of protein. Data represent average values of three experiments.

medium. In both cases, a sharp increase in glycogen content, as well as in phosphorylase activity, were observed within 1 hour. Other glycolytic enzymes, e.g., lactate dehydrogenase, remained unchanged. The reverse experiment was also carried out. "High glucose" cells were exposed to a buffered salt medium in the absence of glucose. Analysis after 12 hours revealed a striking loss in glycogen and phosphorylase activity but no change in lactate dehydrogenase activity.

These observations are not readily interpreted. As listed in Table 17.II, metabolic regulation may occur at the level of either enzyme synthesis or enzyme activity. Enzyme synthesis may be controlled by specific mechanisms of regulation, such as induction and repression, or by the availability of amino acids, or by the limitation of factors involved in protein synthesis in general, e.g., amino acid-activating enzymes. Enzyme activity may be influenced either directly, by alteration of the enzyme itself, or by control of the availability of substrates, cofactors, etc.

At first, the increase in phosphorylase and glycogen synthetase in response to the glucose content of the growth medium looked like another example of induction, well known to all of you from courses in bacterial physiology. There were, however, a few peculiarities. First, hexokinase, the enzyme

TABLE 17.II
METABOLIC REGULATIONS

Process	Regulatory factors
I. Enzyme Synthesis	
1. Induction	Substrates, substrate-analogs
2. Repression	End products of biosynthetic pathways
3. Kinetics	Availability of amino acids, activity of enzymes involved in protein synthesis, DNA, RNA, etc.
II. Enzyme Activity	
A. Enzyme protein-level	
1. Inhibition	Feedback inhibitors, "product inhibitors," etc.
2. Activation	Hormones, cofactors, ion antagonisms, etc.
3. Protection against inactivation	Substrates, cofactors
B. Substrate-level, cofactor-level, energy-level	
1. Kinetics of multi-enzyme systems	Availability of substrates, ATP, etc.
2. Competitions between multi-enzyme systems	Properties of enzyme profiles, etc.

which acts directly on glucose, was unchanged. The enzymes that were affected were those which react with derivatives of glucose (glycogen and UDPG) rather than with glucose itself. Such a relationship between inducer and induced enzyme does not exclude induction, since, quite frequently, the true substrate is by no means the best inducer. Furthermore, glucose itself may not be the inducer but may control the formation of intermediates that act as inducers. We could readily visualize that UDPG may act as inducer for the synthetase, and glucose 1-phosphate as inducer for phosphorylase. The intracellular concentration of both of these compounds may be a function of the concentration of glucose in the medium. However, a number of experimental observations did not seem to fit a mechanism of enzyme induction. First, the time course seemed too rapid for induction. Cells that have a generation time of 1 to 2 days would not be expected to synthesize considerable amounts of enzyme within 1 hour. Second, when an enzyme is induced, it is usually quite stable in the absence of inducer. In the case of phosphorylase, the activity was lost within a few hours after depletion of substrate. One could still propose that this is a special case of a very rapid induction of an enzyme which is also stabilized by the inducer. On the other hand, the experiments in a salt medium containing glucose but no exogenous nitrogen source suggested that no net protein synthesis was necessary. Moreover, experiments with an inhibitor of protein synthesis such as ethionine revealed no effect on the appearance of phosphorylase activity.

These experiments pointed to a site of regulation other than enzyme synthesis, and other possibilities were explored. Protection of enzymes by substrates against proteolysis or other modes of inactivation is a common phenomenon in cell-free systems. For example, hexokinase is protected by glucose against trypsin and against proteolytic enzymes in yeast extracts. The possibility that proteolytic inactivation may occur *in vivo* or during the preparation of cell-free extracts had to be considered. A striking example of this kind was observed in studies of slime molds.[333] Pronounced differences in enzyme patterns were traced to the presence of substrates which protected against proteolytic digestion during preparation of the extract. Extracts of HeLa cells were therefore prepared in the presence of glucose 1-phosphate or glycogen; however, the phosphorylase activity was not influenced by these precautions

Another explanation for the rapid changes observed in

[333] B. E. Wright, *Proc. Natl. Acad. Sci. U. S.* **46,** 798 (1960).

phosphorylase activity in HeLa cells is a regulatory effect on the activity at the enzyme level. Numerous examples of such allosteric effects have been quoted.[334] The essential feature is that the catalytic activity of an enzyme is affected by an induced conformational change of the protein. Among the most widely discussed phenomena of this kind are the activation of phosphorylase *b* by AMP and of glycogen synthetase by glucose 6-phosphate. A few other examples from a rapidly growing list are the dependency of glyceraldehyde-3-phosphate dehydrogenase on DPN for transphosphorylation, which I mentioned in earlier lectures; the effects of CTP and ATP on aspartate transcarbamylase; the product inhibition of hexokinase by glucose 6-phosphate; and the inhibition of phosphofructokinase by excess ATP.

With some of the compounds that produce an allosteric effect, an induced conformational change of the protein can readily be detected by physical measurements. In other cases, the conformational changes are not so readily measured, but can sometimes be demonstrated indirectly, e.g., by an altered susceptibility to proteolytic digestion, as mentioned in our discussion of glyceraldehyde-3-phosphate dehydrogenase.

In the case of phosphorylase from skeletal muscle, changes in physical properties and enzyme activity have been well documented. Phosphorylase *a*, with a molecular weight of 500,000, is converted to phosphorylase *b* (M.W. 250,000) by the action of a specific phosphoprotein phosphatase (PR-enzyme). Phosphorylase *b* is rephosphorylated by ATP in the presence of phosphorylase *b* kinase. The control mechanisms that govern the interconversions of the active and inactive phosphorylase are almost incredibly complicated. In the center of the problem is cyclic 3,5′-AMP.[335] This compound is synthesized in muscle from AMP and ATP under the influence of epinephrine. There is a specific and active diesterase that cleaves cyclic AMP. This enzyme is inhibited by

[334] J. Monod, J. P. Changeux, and F. Jacob, *J. Mol. Biol.* **6,** 306 (1963).
[335] T. W. Rall and E. W. Sutherland, *Cold Spring Harbor Symp. Quant. Biol.* **26,** 347 (1961).

methyl xanthine and by caffeine. In some other organs, the intracellular concentration of cyclic AMP is influenced by ACTH or serotonin rather than by epinephrine.

How does cyclic AMP act? Krebs *et al.* have shown[336] that under certain rigidly controlled conditions cyclic AMP activates phosphorylase *b* kinase in the presence of ATP, thus explaining the increase of phosphorylase *a* due to epinephrine administration. Curiously enough, Ca^{++} will activate the kinase without the aid of cyclic AMP. Furthermore, cyclic AMP appears to have more than one effect,[335] complicating the studies of its mode of action.

In HeLa cells, we found[331] that extracts from cells grown at low glucose concentrations caused a more rapid conversion of crystalline phosphorylase *a* from rabbit muscle to phosphorylase *b* than extracts from "high glucose" cells. This observation may explain the finding that there is a relatively high proportion of AMP-dependent phosphorylase activity in these cells. It does not explain, however, the diminution in total phosphorylase activity in these cells. Addition of phosphorylase *b* kinase and ATP to extracts from "low glucose" cells yielded a 3.5-fold activation with respect to total phosphorylase and a 20-fold activation with respect to AMP-independent enzyme, a pattern of activation that resembled the response of liver phosphorylase more than that of muscle phosphorylase.

In the light of these observations, I would like to summarize briefly the events that may occur in intact HeLa cells following deprivation of glucose. The most striking initial metabolic change is the precipitous drop in glycogen content. This is followed by the rapid disappearance of phosphorylase *a* activity, whereas the glycogen synthetase activity rarely drops to less than 30 or 40% of the activity in the controls. There are some indications that even this loss of activity may be due, at least partly, to a secondary phenomenon occurring during the extraction of the enzyme. When the cells are again exposed to glucose, both glycogen and phosphorylase activity reappear.

[336] E. G. Krebs, D. J. Graves, and E. H. Fischer, *JBC* **234**, 2867 (1959).

These observations may be explained as follows. When more glucose is available for phosphorylation, higher intracellular levels of glucose 6-phosphate, UDPG, and ATP are maintained. With the aid of glycogen synthetase, glycogen is being synthesized and deposited. The increased ATP level, however, results also in an activation of phosphorylase by the previously outlined mechanisms, giving rise to glycogen breakdown. Finally, a balance between glycogen synthesis and breakdown is reached which is dependent on the relative activity of glycogen synthetase and phosphorylase as well as on the availability of ATP, UDPG, and P_i. We have discussed earlier the particularly central role of P_i as a regulator of glycolysis and glycogenolysis. In favor of this formulation is the experimental finding[331] that the intracellular concentration of ATP in "low glucose" cells (0.24 mM) was below the K_m value for phosphorylase b kinase, whereas the ATP concentration in "high glucose" cells (1.6 mM) was several times as high. Since ATP is also involved in the biosynthesis of cyclic 3,5'-AMP and in the activation of the kinase, its steady-state concentration and availability must play a key role in the maintenance of a metabolic balance in glycogen metabolism and of the glycogen level in the cell.

This formulation does not, however, fully explain our observation with "low glucose" and "high glucose" cells. Even after full activation of "low glucose" cells with ATP and phosphorylase kinase, the phosphorylase levels reached were only 60 to 70% of those in the "high glucose" cells. It is conceivable that after dephosphorylation by phosphatase, phosphorylase becomes more susceptible to further degradation, e.g., by proteolysis, and that substrates and cofactors protect against this inactivation. Glucose 1-phosphate has been shown to protect phosphorylase against attack by trypsin.

We are left with the impression that the deposition of glycogen and the phosphorylase activity in HeLa cells is under the direct control of energy metabolism and the availability of ATP. When ATP becomes available, glycogen is deposited. At the same time, phosphorylase is activated.

When the ATP concentration falls and inorganic phosphate rises, glycogenolysis sets in and the deposited source of energy is utilized.

RATE-LIMITING FACTORS IN LEUKOCYTES AND BRAIN

Chicken leukocytes, the next cell population that we studied,[337] catalyzed an oxygen uptake similar to that of ascites cells, but glycolysis was only about one-third as rapid. The difference in the relative activity of these multi-enzyme systems may account for the pronounced Pasteur effect observed in leukocytes. A comparison of the enzyme profiles (Table 16.II) revealed that the level of two enzymes, glyceraldehyde-3-phosphate dehydrogenase and phosphoglycerate kinase, was considerably lower in the leukocytes than in the tumor cells. Pyruvate kinase and lactate dehydrogenase were also somewhat lower, but all other enzymes of glycolysis were about the same, and phosphofructokinase was actually considerably higher. Characteristically, the four enzymes with lower activity are those which compete in the hydrogen and phosphate cycles. Thus, the enzyme profile of the leukocytes is consistent with the ineffectiveness of the glycolytic system as a competitor of oxidative phosphorylation under aerobic conditions, and with the presence of a pronounced Pasteur effect.

A comparison between the uptake of glucose by intact leukocytes and the production of lactate revealed that a considerable portion of the glucose that disappeared could not be accounted for either as lactate or as CO_2. A calculation showed that the missing fraction was the same aerobically and anaerobically, and, therefore, was not affected by the Pasteur effect. This finding is reminiscent of the observations with yeast cells reported by Stickland,[338] who observed that

[337] E. Racker, R. Wu, and J. B. Alpers, *in* "Amino Acids, Proteins and Cancer Biochemistry" (J. T. Edsall, ed.), p. 175. Academic Press, New York, 1960.
[338] L. H. Stickland, *B.J* **64**, 503 (1956).

the conversion of glucose to glycogen did not exhibit a Pasteur effect. In fact, glycogen production was greater aerobically. We shall discuss later two experimental observations that have a bearing on this point. One is the lack of anaerobic glycogen synthesis in rat muscle, and the other is the greater aerobic synthesis of UDPG in ascites cells.

Direct studies with leukocytes on the effect of extracellular P_i and AMP were hampered by the inability of these compounds to permeate the cell. This experimental difficulty was also encountered with yeast cells and many others. Addition of either of these two compounds, even at a high concentration, had little or no effect. The rate of phosphate transport in leukocytes (Table 16.V) was quite inadequate to take care of the need for phosphate during aerobic glycolysis, not to speak of anaerobic glycolysis, which was several times as rapid.

Table 16.I reveals a profile of glycolytic enzymes in brain that is distinct from the others thus far investigated. Hexokinase and phosphofructokinase were very active. Phosphoglycerate kinase, pyruvate kinase, and lactate dehydrogenase were found to be variable, but in all instances they were high. The most outstanding feature was the low glyceraldehyde-3-phosphate dehydrogenase activity in comparison to hexokinase and phosphofructokinase. Brain homogenates fortified with cofactors fermented glucose very rapidly, and, even in brain slices, anaerobic glycolysis compared favorably with that in tumors. It appears, therefore, that the high glyceraldehyde-3-phosphate dehydrogenase in tumors is not required for a high glycolytic rate, but represents a feature permitting an effective competition with oxidative phosphorylation. To obtain a more quantitative evaluation of this relationship, the activity of glyceraldehyde-3-phosphate dehydrogenase, which represents the potential esterification of phosphate by glycolysis, was divided by the rate of P_i esterification due to oxidative phosphorylation. The latter value was calculated from the oxygen uptake, assuming a P:O ratio of 3. Mitochondria from ascites tumors have P:O ratios with various substrates similar to those of normal cells.

As shown in Table 16.I, the ratio between the two P_i esterification rates varied greatly with different tissues. The percent Pasteur effect, calculated from the values of glycolysis listed in Table 16.I, showed an inverse relationship to the ratio. The highest ratio was observed with HeLa cells, which have no Pasteur effect; the lowest ratio with brain, which has a very high Pasteur effect. Comparison of the ADP phosphorylation capacity of these tissues revealed a similar relationship. We shall return to the significance of this phenomenon later.

RATE-LIMITING FACTORS IN MUSCLE

I should like to turn now to some experimental work on the energy metabolism of intact muscle that was recently carried out in our laboratory.[219,339] Most of the work was done with the soleus muscle of the rat. This choice was based on observations by Dr. P. W. Robbins that in this muscle the addition of insulin stimulates about 10-fold the incorporation of C^{14}-glucose into glycogen. We were attracted by the magnitude and reproducibility of the stimulation of glycogen synthesis, particularly since total lactate production was hardly influenced by insulin. It almost looked as if there were a dichotomy of glucose utilization, with insulin acting preferentially on the glycogen pathway.

This simple view of the situation was quickly shattered by further investigations. We learned that the magnitude of the insulin stimulation was due to a rather deceptive process of metabolic amplification and did not signify stimulation of a specific step in the pathway of glycogen synthesis. The production of lactate from glucose was obscured by a somewhat variable contribution due to endogenous fermentation. The first step, therefore, was to devise a procedure by which the relative contribution of glycogen and glucose breakdown to the lactic acid pool could be evaluated. This was accomplished with C^{14}-labeled glucose, as in a typical experiment

[339] M. K. Gould and E. Racker, *Bull. Res. Council Israel* **11A**, 302 (1963).

shown in Table 17.III. It can be seen that insulin stimulated not only the incorporation of C^{14}-glucose into glycogen but also the conversion to lactate. Since insulin slightly suppressed glycogenolysis, the total lactate formation remained essentially unaltered. The differential effect of insulin on glucose metabolism thus disappeared, although the effect on glycogen formation, when calculated in absolute values, was still somewhat greater than the effect on lactate formation.

TABLE 17.III

EFFECT OF INSULIN AND DINITROPHENOL ON
RAT SOLEUS MUSCLE[a]

		Lactate production		
Additions	C^{14}-glycogen (as glucose)	From glucose	From glycogen	Total
None	0.073 (12)	0.3 (11)	0.7	1.0
Insulin (0.1 U/ml)	0.747 (5)	0.6 (6)	0.5	1.1
Dinitrophenol (0.5 mM)	0.003 (3)	0.6 (5)	4.2	4.8
Insulin + DNP	0.004 (1)	0.6 (1)	—	—

[a] All values expressed as micromoles per 100 mg of wet weight per hour. Figures in parentheses represent the number of muscles analyzed.

Such a preferential effect, however, can be readily understood in terms of two pathways competing for common intermediates. If the steady-state concentration of this intermediate is close to saturation for one pathway but well below optimal for the second, an increase in the concentration is likely to have a more profound effect on the second pathway. We believe that such a metabolic amplification is responsible for the more striking effects of insulin on the glycogen pathway in the soleus muscle, although secondary effects, e.g., activation of the glycogen pathway due to higher ATP concentrations, may also be contributory.

In the course of these studies, it was noted that there was hardly any incorporation of C^{14}-glucose into glycogen under anaerobic conditions or in the presence of dinitrophenol, as shown in Table 17.III. This uncoupler stimulated aerobic lactate formation from glycogen sixfold, from glucose two-fold. Under the conditions of these experiments, dinitrophenol has two major effects: It uncouples oxidative phosphorylation, and it stimulates mitochondrial ATPase, resulting in increased intracellular P_i, which favors a rapid glycogenolysis. In order to avoid the complication of multiple pathways of ATP generation, an analysis of the energy metabolism of soleus muscle was carried out under anaerobic conditions. As shown in Table 17.IV, the production of lactate from C^{14}-

TABLE 17.IV

EFFECT ON GLYCOLYSIS OF ACTIVATORS AND INHIBITORS OF ATPASE

Additions	Lactate production[a]		
	From C^{14}-glucose	From glycogen	Total
None	1.7 (8)	3.6	5.3
Sodium azide (5 mM)	0.9 (4)	—	—
Dinitrophenol (0.5 mM)	0.5 (5)	4.9	5.4
CCP (3 μM)	0.4 (2)	4.5	4.9
CCP (30 μM)	0.2 (2)	4.5	4.7
Sodium azide + DNP	1.8 (4)	—	—
Sodium azide + CCP (3 μM)	1.7 (1)	—	—
Sodium azide + CCP (30 μM)	1.8 (1)	—	—

[a] All values expressed as micromoles per 100 mg of wet weight per hour. No values were obtained for lactate from glycogen in the presence of sodium azide because of interference with the chemical determination. Figures in parentheses represent the number of muscles analyzed.

glucose was strongly inhibited by activators of mitochondrial ATPase, such as dinitrophenol or carbonyl cyanide *m*-chlorophenyl hydrazone (CCP). Lactate formation from glycogen was very high anaerobically and was slightly stimulated by dinitrophenol or by CCP. Sodium azide, a potent inhibitor of mitochondrial ATPase, also depressed lactate formation from glucose. However, when the inhibitor and stimulator of ATPase were appropriately balanced against each other, the rate of production of lactate from glucose was fully restored to its original value (Table 17.IV). These findings indicated that the mitochondrial ATPase can participate in glycolysis in intact cells in a manner quite analogous to that in reconstructed systems (Lecture 15). I should like to mention, in passing, that an inhibition of anaerobic glycolysis by dinitrophenol was also observed in rat diaphragm, but that in ascites tumor cells and in frog muscle dinitrophenol causes a stimulation of glycolysis, presumably because ATPase is rate-limiting. These differences emphasize again the need for analysis of each tissue as a metabolic individual, and the danger of generalizing even from studies of one muscle to another.

Current theories of the mode of action of insulin center on its effect on glucose transport. We analyzed the effect of glucose concentration on glycogen synthesis in soleus muscle and observed a continuous increase of C^{14}-glucose incorporation into glycogen when the glucose in the medium was raised from 10 mM to 150 mM. A pronounced stimulation by insulin was observed even at 150 mM glucose, which greatly exceeds the concentration required to saturate hexokinase. In view of this pronounced restriction of glucose entrance even at high glucose concentration, we examined the level of intracellular glucose under a variety of conditions that affect energy metabolism. There was little or no accumulation of glucose in the cells aerobically or anaerobically, with or without insulin. However, in the presence of either dinitrophenol or azide, glucose accumulated.[219] It thus appears that in the absence of these compounds, glucose entrance is rate-limiting for glucose utilization, whereas in their presence phosphorylation of glucose becomes rate-limiting. These findings point to the role of oxidative phosphorylation, which is affected by the uncouplers, in the utilization of glucose.

The mechanism of glucose transport and the role of energy in this process are still not understood. Randle and Smith[340] proposed that energy is needed to maintain a barrier against glucose entrance, since anoxia or dinitrophenol greatly increased sugar transport. However, a theory exactly opposite to that of Randle and Smith appears to fit as well, namely, that ATP is actually needed for the transport of glucose, but

[340] P. J. Randle and G. H. Smith, *BJ* **70**, 501 (1958).

that glycolytic rather than mitochondrial ATP participates in the process. Dinitrophenol is visualized, in such a theory, to act by stimulating glycogenolysis, thereby increasing the availability of ATP at the site of transport. If transport of glucose should be dependent on energy, as previously proposed, the availability of ATP for transport and phosphorylation of glucose emerges as a common denominator and as a possible rate-limiting factor for both processes. Insulin may either increase the actual level of available ATP at the site of transport, or alter the structures involved in these processes in a manner which permits a more efficient utilization of whatever energy source is available. Thus, it may influence the process of transport as well as the phosphorylation of glucose.

LECTURE 18

INDUCED CHANGES IN ENERGY METABOLISM

Many of the views which have been advanced are highly speculative, and some no doubt will prove erroneous; but I have in every case given the reasons which have led me to one view rather than to another. . . . False facts are highly injurious to the progress of science, for they often endure long; but false views, if supported by some evidence, do little harm, for everyone takes a salutory pleasure in proving their falseness; and when this is done, one path toward error is closed and the road to truth is often at the same time opened.

—Charles Darwin

In the previous lectures, we have analyzed the rate-limiting steps in carbohydrate metabolism of various cells and some of the metabolic factors which govern them. I should like to discuss now the possibility of inducing changes in the rate-limiting factors. In ascites tumor cells, the level of intracellular P_i appears to be rate-limiting in glycolysis. Since about 50% of the total energy in ascites tumor cells is derived from glycolysis, it seemed of interest to influence the metabolic pattern in such a manner that the relative contributions of energy from this source are altered. We therefore searched for chemical compounds that would either raise or lower the intracellular concentration of P_i, or change the rate-limiting step by specifically impairing the activity of an individual enzyme of glycolysis.

I shall discuss experiments[294] with various compounds listed in Table 18.I, that (1) reduce the Pasteur effect, either by stimulating aerobic glycolysis or by decreasing anaerobic glycolysis, and (2) increase the Pasteur effect by specifically inhibiting aerobic glycolysis.

241

1. The uncoupler of oxidative phosphorylation, dinitro-phenol, raises the intracellular P_i concentration and accelerates both aerobic and anaerobic glycolysis. Whereas acceleration of aerobic glycolysis is readily explained as due to the elimination of competition with aerobic phosphorylation, the

TABLE 18.I

COMPOUNDS DECREASING AND INCREASING THE PASTEUR EFFECT

Compounds Decreasing the Pasteur Effect

1. Relative increase of aerobic glycolysis
   (a) Imidazole
   (b) Inorganic phosphate
   (c) Dinitrophenol and other uncouplers
2. Relative decrease of anaerobic glycolysis
   (a) N-ethylmaleimide
   (b) Iodoacetate

Compounds Increasing the Pasteur Effect

1. Ferricyanide and other electron carriers
2. Pyrimidine and purine nucleotides

---

increase in anaerobic glycolysis suggests that dinitrophenol acts by stimulating mitochondrial ATPase. It seems, therefore, that the regeneration of P_i and ADP from ATP is rate-limiting in anaerobic as well as in aerobic glycolysis. Since the stimulation by dinitrophenol is greater aerobically than anaerobically, an inhibition of the Pasteur effect is observed.

A compound that acts like dinitrophenol in some ways, and yet differently, is imidazole. In Table 18.II, the effects of high P_i, dinitrophenol, and imidazole are summarized. High P_i (50 mM), high imidazole (40 mM), or dinitrophenol stimulated both aerobic and anaerobic lactate production in ascites tumor cells. It appears, however, that these agents act, in part, independently of each other, as indicated by their almost additive effects when present in various combinations. In the presence of all three compounds, the rate of glycolysis—more than 400 μmoles of lactate per milliliter of packed cells—approached the maximum values obtained with extracts fortified with coenzymes. It is difficult to explain the independent mode of action of these agents. There are some indications that ADP may become rate-limiting at high P_i concentrations, which might explain the added stimulation by dinitrophenol, through activation of mitochondrial ATPase. The mode of action of imidazole, however, is quite obscure. An effect of imidazole on mitochondrial ATPase from ascites tumors, similar to the effect of dinitrophenol,

TABLE 18.II

EFFECT OF IMIDAZOLE, DINITROPHENOL, AND P_i ON
LACTATE PRODUCTION IN ASCITES TUMOR CELLS

Additions	Micromoles of lactate formed	
	Air	Nitrogen
None	80	189
Imidazole (40 mM)	154	280
Dinitrophenol (0.1 mM)	195	252
P_i (50 mM)	175	260
P_i + DNP	273	388
P_i + imidazole	204	380
P_i + DNP + imidazole	365	444

could not be detected; nor was a soluble ATPase from these cells stimulated by imidazole. Since relatively large amounts of imidazole were required to stimulate glycolysis, the possibility of a simple buffering effect was considered. This possibility was ruled out by experiments in which the lactic acid formed was neutralized at short intervals by addition of calculated amounts of alkali. In searching for other mechanisms of imidazole action, a partial uncoupling of oxidative phosphorylation catalyzed by tumor mitochondria was observed. The P:O ratio with various intermediates of the Krebs cycle was lowered by the presence of imidazole. Most pronounced were the effects with succinate as substrate, suggesting the possible localization of the effect between cytochrome *b* and oxygen. These observations are interesting because under identical conditions imidazole seemed to have no effect on the P:O ratio of liver mitochondria. In any case,

the effects of imidazole on oxidative phosphorylation were not
sufficient to explain the stimulation of glycolysis, particularly
in the presence of dinitrophenol. The only clue to its mode
of action was an increase in protein leakage from cells suspended in imidazole, which indicated alterations in permeability and in the intracellular rigidity of compartmentation.

N-ethylmaleimide (NEM) diminished the Pasteur effect
by inhibiting anaerobic and stimulating aerobic glycolysis. At
concentrations of 0.4 to 0.45 mM NEM, a negative Pasteur
effect was occasionally observed; the anaerobic glycolysis was
slower than the aerobic. You may remember from the experiments with reconstructed systems that a negative Pasteur
effect was observed when the rate of glycolytic ATP formation was too low to cope with the ATPase activity, and
mitochondrial ATP contributed to glucose phosphorylation.

Experiments with iodoacetate strikingly illustrate the fact
that a very precarious balance exists between phosphorylating and dephosphorylating processes within the cell. When
glycolysis was inhibited by about 40 to 50%, very drastic
changes occurred in the intracellular level of adenine nucleotides. I have mentioned before that the loss of nucleotides
was due to a deamination and dephosphorylation of AMP,
leading to an excretion of inosine. This phenomenon occurred
only in the presence of both glucose and a glycolytic inhibitor
such as iodoacetate or oxamate, since it required a conversion
of ATP to AMP (by hexokinase and adenylate kinase) as well
as a block in the regeneration of ATP. Sodium fluoride was
much less effective than iodoacetate, because in addition to
its effect on enolase, it inhibited both phosphatase and
adenylate deaminase.

2. About 30 years ago Mendel reported that ferricyanide
specifically inhibits the aerobic glycolysis of Jensen sarcoma,
thus increasing the Pasteur effect. Since no work had appeared since 1937 on this rather interesting observation, we
explored the effect of ferricyanide on Ehrlich ascites tumor
cells.[294] While these studies were in progress, a paper appeared
by Birkenhäger,[341] who had recently resumed, in Mendel's

[341] J. C. Birkenhäger, *BBA* **40,** 182 (1960).

laboratory, an analysis of the phenomenon. He reported two observations which were of special interest to us. One was that Ehrlich ascites tumors were resistant to ferricyanide inhibition, whereas many other tumors were as susceptible as those reported by Mendel. His other finding was that crystalline aldolase from rabbit muscle, as well as aldolase activity in crude tissue homogenates, were strongly inhibited by ferricyanide. He proposed aldolase as the site of ferricyanide inhibition of aerobic glycolysis in tumors. Meanwhile, we had observed that ferricyanide strongly inhibited aerobic glycolysis in Ehrlich ascites tumors, provided that the cells were incubated with the inhibitor before glucose was added. We confirmed Birkenhäger's observations on the effect of ferricyanide on soluble aldolase, but several observations convinced us that in the intact cell aldolase was not the site of ferricyanide inhibition. I want to describe some of these experiments here, because they illustrate how misleading it may be to extrapolate from observations with cell-free extracts to events in intact cells.

At 10 mM ferricyanide, lactic acid production in ascites tumor cells was inhibited aerobically by more than 70%, but anaerobically by only 15%, increasing the Pasteur effect from about 50 to 80%. Glucose uptake was also inhibited, but not so markedly, thus leaving unaccounted for a considerable amount of glucose that had disappeared. When cells that had been exposed to ferricyanide were washed free of excess ferricyanide and reexamined, they were still inhibited aerobically but not anaerobically. If glycolysis was measured in the presence of 30 mM P$_i$ instead of 4 mM, the inhibition due to ferricyanide dropped from 70 to 30%. These results were not compatible with the localization of ferricyanide inhibition at the aldolase site. Moreover, direct chemical determination of ferro- and ferricyanide revealed intracellular concentrations below 1 mM, which in our hands did not inhibit aldolase or glycolysis in tumor homogenates.

Since ferricyanide stimulated the oxidation of glucose via the pentose-phosphate cycle by serving as electron acceptor for TPNH, other electron acceptors were examined.[294]

Menadione, which had no effect on aldolase activity, inhibited aerobic glycolysis, though somewhat less effectively than ferricyanide. Phenazine methosulfate, a most effective electron carrier, inhibited lactate production, but actually stimulated the uptake of glucose. In this case, the diminished lactate production was probably due to a simple competition between glycolysis and the pentose-phosphate cycle, as observed in reconstructed systems. It is apparent that the mode of action of ferricyanide is more complex than that of other electron carriers, since it inhibits glucose uptake and is partly counteracted by P_i. Studies of the carbon balance suggest that ferricyanide also shifts the aerobic glycolysis of the tumor cell in favor of alternative pathways. Dr. Wu is still pursuing this problem and is attempting to elucidate the fate of the missing carbons.

We turn now to the discussion of another group of compounds that specifically inhibit aerobic glycolysis. Woods[341a] observed that uridine inhibits aerobic glycolysis of ascites cells in a phosphate-free medium. This was confirmed in our laboratory.[294] As shown in Table 18.III, several pyrimidine

TABLE 18.III

EFFECTS OF NUCLEOSIDES ON GLYCOLYSIS IN ASCITES TUMOR CELLS

| | Micromoles of lactate formed | | | |
| | From glucose | | From nucleosides | |
Nucleosides added	Air	Nitrogen	Air	Nitrogen
None	138	315	—	—
Uridine (2 mM)	46	310	12	28
Cytidine (4 mM)	46	310	3.2	5.4
Guanosine (4 mM)	68	312	—	26
Inosine (4 mM)	68	315	—	24
Uridine + guanosine	27	—	—	34

and purine nucleosides markedly inhibited aerobic lactic acid production and had no effect on anaerobic glycolysis. Thus a

[341a] M. Woods, Personal communication (1960).

Pasteur effect was produced which was as large as that of most normal cells. In the presence of uridine or 5-fluorouridine, the most effective of the compounds tested, there was a marked decrease in the concentration of intracellular P_i. Data on the fate of tritium-labeled uridine added to ascites cells are shown in Table 18.IV. The intracellular concentrations of UDPG and UTP which were formed from tritium-labeled uridine accounted for about 3.5 μmoles of esterified P_i, corresponding quite closely to the decrease of P_i from 6.0 to 3.1 mM. Uracil, which was formed from uridine by nucleoside phosphorylase in the course of P_i esterification, was found mainly outside the cells.

The formation of uridine nucleotides was compared under aerobic and anaerobic conditions, with and without glucose, in order to find a clue as to why the pyrimidines specifically affect aerobic glycolysis. Under anaerobic conditions in the absence of glucose, hardly any uridine nucleotides were formed. This was not due to a complete lack of ATP formation, since lactate formation from uridine itself was quite appreciable. In the presence of glucose, the levels of uridine nucleotides were anaerobically less than half of their aerobic levels, whereas glycolysis was 4 times as rapid anaerobically. Aerobically, the uridine nucleotides were almost as high without glucose as with it. These findings indicated that the phosphorylation of uridine was more effective with ATP formed by oxidative phosphorylation than with ATP formed by glycolysis.

The effect of several other nucleosides is shown in Table 18.III. Cytidine inhibited like uridine, although somewhat higher concentrations were required. The major nucleotide that accumulated was CTP, and almost 3 times as much was formed in the presence of glucose aerobically as was formed anaerobically.

Both cytidine and uridine appeared to inhibit glycolysis by serving as a trap for the P_i in the ascites cell. Since it has been shown[342,343] that the same enzyme phosphorylates cytidine,

342 P. Reichard and O. Sköld, *BBA* **28**, 376 (1958).
343 O. Sköld, *JBC* **235**, 3273 (1960).

TABLE 18.IV

FATE OF TRITIATED URIDINE IN ASCITES TUMOR CELLS[a]

Tritiated uridine added (μmoles)	Lactate produced	Intra-cellular P_i	Uracil produced	Nucleotides					
				UMP	UDPG	UDP	UTP	Total
0	58	6.0	—					
12	26	3.1	6.4	0.12	0.67	0.06	0.74	1.6

[a] Results expressed as micromoles per 140 mg of protein.

uridine, and fluorouridine, it was not surprising to find no additive inhibitory effect when the pyrimidines were added together. Inosine or guanosine at 4 mM produced less inhibition than the pyrimidine nucleosides, but further depressed lactate production in the presence of uridine. As can be seen from Table 18.III, guanosine and inosine were metabolized by ascites cells to lactic acid. This process involves the phosphorolytic cleavage of the nucleoside by nucleoside phosphorylase. In contrast to the metabolic fate of the pyrimidine nucleosides, only small amounts of guanosine and inosine were converted to the nucleotides. Thus the inhibitory effect of the purine nucleosides is probably also due to trapping of P$_i$, through the accumulation of phosphorylated intermediates of the pentose-phosphate cycle.

The fact that it is possible to inhibit aerobic glycolysis in ascites tumor cells almost completely by the addition of a mixture of pyrimidine and purine nucleosides should have a bearing on our concept of what is representative of the carbohydrate metabolism of the normal and of the tumor cell, and I should like to discuss this controversial subject. As most of you know, 40 years ago Warburg proposed, and he has maintained ever since,[344] that the transformation of a normal to a cancer cell is the result of an injury to the respiratory machinery. As a consequence of this lesion, a fermenting cell emerges with a low Pasteur effect and with the properties of autonomous growth. This hypothesis seems untenable in view of the fact that many tumors have a relatively high content of respiratory enzymes and an over-all respiration rate within the range of normal tissues. On the other hand, high lactic acid production by tumors both *in vitro* and *in vivo* is a well-established experimental fact. During 40 years of numerous reports confirming this phenomenon, occasional exceptions have been described: tumors which produce only small amounts of lactic acid. These observations with tumors that were growing very slowly appear to underline rather than negate the relationship between malignancy and lactic acid

[344] O. H. Warburg, "New Methods of Cell Physiology," p. 627. Wiley (Interscience), New York, 1962.

production. But at the same time they help to challenge Warburg's concept that there is a causal relationship between glycolysis and tumor formation.

Whatever the primary change may be, it is apparent that tumor cells lack an important control mechanism of energy metabolism. In normal cells most of the energy is produced in the mitochondria. Glycolysis contributes little; in brain, for example, less than 3%. In ascites tumor cells, about 40% of the ATP is produced by aerobic glycolysis, in other tumors, even more. This shift in energy metabolism, which leads to the production of intracellular acids, may have profound secondary effects on tumor metabolism. We know that small changes in pH may have pronounced effects on individual enzymes or on multi-enzyme systems. It would be surprising if a change in intracellular pH did not seriously affect the physiology of the cell. A high aerobic glycolysis may indeed be an essential feature for rapid growth or for the capacity to infiltrate normal tissues. The experimental observations on the Pasteur effect, particularly the alterations achieved by the addition of nucleosides, may stimulate attempts to explore the role of acid production in the growth and spread of tumors *in vivo*.

It has become apparent from the preceding discussion that the glycolytic energy metabolism of ascites tumor cells is controlled by the steady-state concentration of P_i, but we have not dealt with the question of what reactions contribute to the intracellular P_i and ADP pools. I mentioned previously that all ATP-utilizing reactions, such as ion transport, biosynthetic reactions, and muscular contractions, contribute to the "cellular ATPase activity in the broadest sense." In the resting tumor cells, these reactions are probably insufficient to keep pace with the rapid glycolysis. Moreover, there are two experimental observations which suggest that mitochondrial ATPase might participate in the process of glycolysis. One is the stimulation of anaerobic glycolysis by dinitrophenol, pointing to mitochondrial ATPase as a potential participant in glycolysis. The second is that even carefully prepared mitochondria exhibit ATPase activity provided that a regenerating system of ATP is used which removes the inhibitory ADP.[290]

I should mention that the concept of mitochondrial ATPase as a participant in glycolysis is not universally accepted. Dr. Lipmann has expressed the view that "ATPase is something which we have constructed and which does not exist."[345] What Dr. Lipmann means, of course, is that the cell does not hydrolyze ATP for fun and that all apparent ATPase activities are an expression of a functional activity which utilizes ATP. Dr. Lipmann may be correct, but perhaps not entirely so. Adenosine triphosphate is certainly not hydrolyzed by cells for fun, but it may be hydrolyzed for regulatory purposes. For example, the problem of temperature regulation in animals as well as in plants is yet to be examined at the basic metabolic level. Furthermore, the Krebs cycle not only functions in energy metabolism but also participates in other reactions, such as the synthesis of glutamate and porphyrins. It seems unlikely that these important reactions are rigidly linked to phosphorylation processes without any safety valves. Finally, I should like to mention that there is increasing evidence that some energy-requiring processes preferentially use glycolytic ATP. A mechanism for releasing this energy which is restrained by the Pasteur effect is therefore likely to exist. In an earlier lecture, I discussed the fact that natural uncouplers, such as long-chain fatty acids, can be released in either free or bound form from mitochondria or microsomes.[220] These uncouplers are also activators of mitochondrial ATPase. If they elicit ATPase *in vivo*, and if P_i is rate-limiting, they should stimulate glycolysis. Thus "hotter" and less efficient energy-generating machinery would be brought into play. At the same time, respiratory control would be eliminated, allowing for a free passage of intermediates through the Krebs cycle.

It is very likely, however, that under physiological conditions the major contributions to the P_i and ADP pools are derived from useful work processes. The physical proximity

[345] F. Lipmann, *CIBA Found. Symp., Regulation of Cell Metabolism, 1958* p. 229 (1959).

of the protein-synthesizing reticulum containing ribosomes to the mitochondria is probably a morphological expression of this important functional relationship.

In Lecture 15, I described a reconstructed system of glycolysis which was controlled by competition with mitochondria for the available P_i supply. This system exhibited a Pasteur effect in regard to lactate production, but it utilized glucose at an undiminished rate until the P_i pool was exhausted and trapped as fructose-1,6-diphosphate. I pointed out that this was not representative of the Pasteur effect in intact cells. In these reconstruction experiments, we had used yeast hexokinase which was pure but not inhibited by glucose 6-phosphate. In contrast to the yeast enzyme, the mammalian enzyme is crude but inhibited by glucose 6-phosphate. Although a possible role for this phenomenon of glucose 6-phosphate inhibition in the Pasteur effect was visualized many years ago,[322] it was realized that this inhibition by itself was insufficient to control glucose utilization. When the inhibition of phosphofructokinase by ATP and its release by P_i were described,[304,346] and when glucose metabolism in numerous tissues was reported blocked at the level of fructose 6-phosphate,[347] the possibility of sequential control mechanisms was considered. In collaboration with Dr. K. Uyeda, another attempt was made to reconstruct the Pasteur effect, this time with a purified preparation of hexokinase from ascites tumor cells.[306] While these experiments were in progress, an effect of P_i on the inhibition of hexokinase by glucose 6-phosphate was described.[305] This observation, together with the effect of P_i on phosphofructokinase,[304] suggested the possibility of a coordinated stimulation by P_i on three key enzymes of glycolysis, namely, hexokinase, phosphofructokinase, and glyceraldehyde-3-phosphate dehydrogenase, which have been shown to be rate-limiting in crude tissue extracts.[313] In recent experiments with reconstructed systems with mammalian

---

[346] H. A. Lardy and R. E. Parks, Jr., *in* "Enzymes: Units of Biological Structure and Function" (O. H. Gaebler, ed.), p. 584. Academic Press, New York, 1956.

[347] R. Wu, *BBRC* **14**, 79 (1963).

hexokinase and appropriate amounts of phosphofructokinase and glyceraldehyde-3-phosphate dehydrogenase, a characteristic Pasteur effect on both lactate and glucose utilization was obtained.[306]

I should now like to summarize briefly how we visualize the operation of control mechanisms of energy metabolism in intact cells.

The most basic regulatory feature is the tight coupling of the oxidation steps to phosphorylation. This applies to glycolysis as well as to oxidative phosphorylation in mitochondria: Oxidation takes place only when ATP is utilized and P_i and ADP become available. Energy is produced only when it is needed.

This control mechanism suffices for mitochondria, but in the case of glucose utilization the first step, catalyzed by hexokinase, is dependent on ATP rather than on P_i or ADP. Additional control mechanisms are therefore required. They can operate at the level of P_i and glucose transport, or at the level of hexokinase and phosphofructokinase activity. In many cells, P_i transport is dependent on glucose, and glucose transport is influenced by the energy metabolism (cf. Lecture 17). Glucose utilization is controlled by the level of glucose 6-phosphate; fructose 6-phosphate utilization is controlled by ATP. Both controls are in turn regulated by the steady-state concentration of P_i, which at high concentrations releases the inhibitory effects of both glucose 6-phosphate and ATP. Furthermore, P_i is required for glycogenolysis and also controls the oxidation of glucose 6-phosphate via the pentose-phosphate cycle.

In view of the critical role of P_i in the regulation of energy metabolism, it is not surprising to find that cells have learned to put up barriers against the free entrance of phosphate and thereby conserve their energy supplies. We conclude that the control by phosphate is the most essential feature in the regulation of energy metabolism. It is indeed surprising how little we know about the key aspects of this control: the nature of the cellular barrier against phosphate entrance, and the mechanism of its transport with the expenditure of energy.

INDEX